Topophobia

Topophobia

A Phenomenology of Anxiety

DYLAN TRIGG

Bloomsbury Academic
An imprint of Bloomsbury Publishing Plc

B L O O M S B U R Y
LONDON · OXFORD · NEW YORK · NEW DELHI · SYDNEY

Bloomsbury Academic

An imprint of Bloomsbury Publishing Plc

50 Bedford Square	1385 Broadway
London	New York
WC1B 3DP	NY 10018
UK	USA

www.bloomsbury.com

BLOOMSBURY and the Diana logo are trademarks of Bloomsbury Publishing Plc

First published 2017

© Dylan Trigg, 2017

Dylan Trigg has asserted his right under the Copyright,
Designs and Patents Act, 1988, to be identified as Author of this work.

British Library Cataloguing-in-Publication Data
A catalogue record for this book is available from the British Library.

ISBN: HB: 978-1-4742-8322-9
PB: 978-1-4742-8323-6
ePDF: 978-1-4742-8321-2
ePub: 978-1-4742-8324-3

Library of Congress Cataloging-in-Publication Data
A catalogue record for this book is available from the Library of Congress.

Typeset by Integra Software Services Pvt. Ltd.
Printed and bound in India

For Audrey

[My patient] believed he had recently seen a work on agoraphobia in a bookshop window and was now looking through all the publishers' catalogues in order to get a copy. I was then able to explain to him why his efforts were bound to be fruitless. The work on agoraphobia existed only in his phantasy, as an unconscious intention: he meant to write it himself.

FREUD, *THE PSYCHOPATHOLOGY OF EVERYDAY LIFE*

CONTENTS

LIST OF ILLUSTRATIONS

All photos by the author.

ACKNOWLEDGEMENTS

Writing a book on the experience of anxiety and agoraphobia is a paradoxical task in many senses, especially when the experience is one's own. Notwithstanding the question of *why* one would undergo such a project, the very question of *how* such a book is possible remains an even greater enigma. Throughout this paradoxical aim, from its inception to its eventual completion, the development of this book has been shaped thanks to the generosity, patience and understanding of many people. Above all, this book owes its existence to the friendship and intellectual camaraderie of Dorothée Legrand. This book is rooted in discussions started at the Centre de Recherche en Epistémologie Appliquée before moving to the École Normale Supérieure, and resurfacing time and again at Le Sully and Le Coude Fou. My gratitude in sharing this book with you is equal only to the appreciation I have for our friendship.

The experiences outlined and discussed in this book take place in Paris, principally between January 2011 and October 2011. Despite this localization, much of the book was written in Memphis, Tennessee, several years later. My thanks to colleagues at the University of Memphis, who, true to the spirit of Southern hospitality, have made my arrival in Memphis a warm and gratifying one. In particular, my thanks to Shaun Gallagher, Kas Saghafi, Verena Erlenbusch, Luvell Anderson, Mary Beth Mader, Andrew Daily, Tom Nenon, Somogy Varga and Connie Diffee. Thanks also to everyone at Cafe Keough, Memphis for providing a space to think, work, and drink in. In the midst of completing this book, Pleshette DeArmitt, Chair and Associate Professor of Philosophy at the University of Memphis, died suddenly. The philosophical community is a lesser place in the absence of her intellectual generosity and warm-hearted presence, and I will miss her greatly. Additional thanks to colleagues from the University College Dublin, especially to Dermot Moran, Joseph Cohen, Tim Mooney, Helen Kenny and Margaret Brady.

The research of this book has been supported from several funding bodies and institutions. I herein gratefully acknowledge the support of the Centre National de la Recherche Scientifique/ VolkswagenStiftung for a fellowship at the Centre de Recherche en Epistémologie Appliquée (École Polytechnique) and Husserl Archives (École Normale Supérieure) (2011–2013); The Wellcome Trust for a visiting research position at Husserl Archives (École Normale Supérieure (2013); The Irish Research Council for a fellowship at University College Dublin (2012–2014); and, principally, Marie Curie Actions (FP7-PEOPLE-2013-IOF 624968) for a fellowship at the University of Memphis and University College Dublin (2014–2017). My gratitude to all of these funding bodies for their support.

In addition, my sincere thanks to those colleagues who, with warmth and intellectual generosity, invited me to present some of the ideas detailed in this book in seminars, lectures and workshops in both Europe and the United States. Thanks above all to Bryan Norwood, Liam Heneghan, Melissa Pokorny, Annika Schlitte, Kevin Aho, Bruce Janz, Martin Nitsche, Anneke Smelik, László Munteán, Dianna Niebylski, Jeremy Northup, Justin Pearl, Tom Sparrow, Alina Popa, Irinia Gheorghe, Florin Flueras and Gretchen Schiller. Thanks also to Luna Dolezal and Kirsten Jacobson for their invaluable comments on aspects of this manuscript. My thanks, as ever, to my family for their love and support.

Let me also thank the speakers invited to several conferences and workshops organized by myself and colleagues over the last few years. For the 'Understanding the Body We Can Never Know' workshop, which took place in Paris in October 2012, organized by Dorothée Legrand, Line Ryberg Ingerslev and myself, my thanks to: Pierre Henri Castel, Natalie Depraz, Thomas Fuchs, Kirsten Jacobson, Anneleen Masschelein, Helena de Preester and Manos Tsakiris. For the 'Is there a phenomeology of unconsciousness?' conference, which took place in Dublin in February 2014, organized by Dorothée Legrand and myself, my thanks to: Joseph Cohen, Nataile Depraz, Dieter Lohmar, Tim Mooney, Dermot Moran, Alexander Schnell and Emmanuel de Saint Aubert. Finally, for the 'Phenomeology and Embodiment of Anxiety' workshop, which took place in Memphis in March 2015, organized by Shaun Gallagher and myself, my thanks to: Drew Leder, Dorothée Legrand and Louis Sass.

At Bloomsbury, my thanks to Liza Thompson and Frankie Mace, who have graciously and warmly supported this project from the outset to its completion. My thanks also to Carrie Kania for her encouragement on this book.

It remains only to thank my wife, Audrey Petit-Trigg, '*pour ta tendresse, ta beauté, ton intelligence, pour tes jeux de mots, et pour ton amour*'. Your patient and loving presence, etched in this book in both a figurative and literal sense, is everything to me. I dedicate this book to you with love and appreciation.

Parts of Chapter 3 were previously published in *Continental Philosophy Review* as 'The Body of the Other: Intercorporeality and the Phenomenology of Agoraphobia' (Volume 46: Issue 3, 413–429 (2013) and in *Body/Self/Other: Phenomenology of Social Encounters* (New York: SUNY Press) (2016) as 'Agoraphobia, Sartre, and the Spatiality of the Other's Look.' My thanks to the editors for their permission to publish these extracts.

Dylan Trigg, Memphis, Tennessee

PREFACE

A Vast Empty Place

The appearance of the Dirschauer Bridge, where the curve had a wide span, was an uncomfortable experience; during the times he had to cross it, a great feeling of anxiety overcame him, combined with the fear that he could become insane and would jump over the bridge during such a condition.

(CARL FRIEDRICH OTTO WESTPHAL, *DIE AGORAPHOBIE*)

The Pont Marie

13 March 2011. You are standing beside the Pont Marie, a small bridge positioned just off the Rue des Nonnains-d'Hyères. The bridge arches gently over the Seine before disappearing into the crowds on the Île Saint-Louis. Out of view, the Pont Marie will continue until it merges with the Pont de la Tournelle, before resuming its journey on the Left Bank, at which point Paris will cease to be accessible to you. At the entrance of the bridge, you will re-enact a series of attempts at crossing the structure, each time finding yourself unable to master the unfamiliar terrain that divides you from the rest of the city. Faced with the prospect of navigating the bridge, your body emits a series of sensations and movements, which, despite being familiar to you, still mark the possibility of a trauma yet to be written into your flesh.

Having broken free from the tip of the bridge, a dozen or so people pass you by. Disorientated, you stand ground, waiting for the glare of the sun to withdraw into the shadowline. Other people come and go in this process. Some move beyond the bridge back into the Marais while others proceed onwards towards the bustle of the Left Bank. A handful of people stop in the middle of the Pont Marie, pausing in the twilight. For you, no such freedom is available. You remain at the arch of the structure, impatient with your inability to journey beyond the adjoining Quai des Célestins and onto the bridge itself. Part of this ritual, as you will admit to yourself, is not without a certain love and fascination. As much an experience of anxiety, the ritual of the bridge crossing is also a form of infatuation. In your inability to cross the bridge, you are also overwhelmed with a fixation on the bridge, and without this fixation, your sense of self would come undone.

Where to place yourself in this dizzying world? Two options present themselves. The first option is to align yourself in relation to the road, which carries with it the risk of being overwhelmed by the passing traffic, much of which consists of cyclists and the occasional bus, though very few cars. The alternative is to cling onto the small wall, which defends you from the river below. The wall is continuous with the road, forming a barrier against the depths, and at first glance, strikes you as the favourable option. As you position yourself towards the edge of the bridge, holding the wall with one hand and supporting your balance with the other, you look down to the river below. The waters flow evenly and gently, interrupted only by the passing of tourist boats, who proudly proclaim how the Pont Marie has entered the mythology of the Parisian landscape as the 'lover's bridge'.

But in the romance there is also anxiety. In the midst of your attempt at getting placed on the bridge, an opposing desire to jump into the river below emerges. To descend into the Seine would mean desensitizing yourself to your problematic relation to bridges by way of affirming the anxiety that engenders the phobia in the first place. Having survived the fall, you would resurface on the riverbanks a different person. Thereafter, the bridge would lose its power to determine where you can and cannot move in this world. But before you can find it within yourself to make the leap, you gain sight of the image of your body drenched and humiliated on the banks below, and thus abandon the project. For the decisive minutes that follow, this middle ground between earth and water will become your home in the world. On it, you will attempt to

FIGURE P.1 *Pont Marie, Paris.*

transform not only your own body, but also the bridge, which, until now, has shaped your body just as your body has shaped the bridge.

One foot follows the other. Those feet make small steps, but nevertheless proceed in the right direction. Methodically, you divide the bridge into smaller chunks of space, each of which you contend with on its own terms. Thus, the opening of this expedition begins by reaching the first lamppost. Hereafter, the central point of the bridge marks the next waypoint on your voyage. As the middle draws near, your experience of space undergoes a transformation. Whereas you had previously been the centre of your own experience, now, space is encircling you. The distance between you and the Quai des Célestins, from where you began, seems to have extended not only in space, but also in time. The duration that has passed between now and then is lost in an abyss that neither belongs to the bridge nor to you, but to some other world between inner and outer space.

Meanwhile, the very materiality of the bridge, its surrounding roads, together with the water that runs beneath it, has lost its reassuring familiarity and now become impregnated with a strange texture. No matter how hard you grip onto the lamppost, that same texture remains alien. Looking into the distance, towards the adjoining Pont Sully, which connects to the Île Saint-Louis on the eastern side, the perspective becomes marked by a flat dimensionality, as though it were a theatrical backdrop lacking all depth and for this reason, unreal. Likewise, the apartments off the Rue Le Regrattier, which you have often admired from afar, now sway in the wind, as if made of cardboard.

Against this dizzying world, your body cramps and recoils. Your posture stoops like a man who, having prematurely aged, has either lost his way in a forest at night or has otherwise been exposed to a sudden trauma. In an attempt to recover balance, you cling to any available surface. As you lose your grip on things, you simultaneously become lost on the bridge itself, lost in a world of no discernible dangers. Your body jolts violently; each of your

FIGURE P.2 *Rue Le Regrattier, Paris.*

limbs is now beginning to lose its coherence, becoming a mass of extension with nothing other than their proximity to one another in common. As for your central nervous system more broadly, at any given moment, you are prepared for death. Were you to suddenly lose consciousness – which, for some fortuitous reason, has never happened in the past – you will need to find the softest patch of concrete to fall upon, lest your head falls on the ground beneath. In the absence of a patch of grass, you cling harder to the lamppost, which has now become your home by proxy.

This precipice that you have encountered in the middle of the Pont Marie serves to modify your relation with other people. Several people have paused to collect their thoughts just beside where you are standing. In the midst of your collision of space and time – a crisis that you are encountering in an invisible depth accessible only in your anxiety – the others are unwelcome visitors, who serve as external observers of your internal drama. With their obtrusive gaze, they enflame your anxiety by breathing new life into it. In return, you experience them through a scornful eye, which you hope will be felt by each of them in turn. Moments after, they move on of their own accord, unconcerned with your crisis.

As the sun withdraws behind clouds, you find shelter in the darkness, and surge towards the Île Saint-Louis, which until now has resembled a distant island, as much a mythical entity as it is an actual reality. Freeing yourself from the lamppost, which has proven itself to be central in your attempt at getting placed in the world, you stride forcefully to the other side of the bridge. With your heart palpating frantically, you veer right and find shelter in a doorway on the Quai de Bourbon.

Your first time on the Île Saint-Louis carries with it a sense of the uncanny. Looking back across the river, you see the Right Bank, from the Hôtel de Ville to Sully Morland in all its splendour. It is massive, much wider than you previously imagined, in fact. The contours of the landscape range from steep inclines to apartment blocks, each of which is punctuated by metro stations. Having never seen this vista from the perspective of the Quai de Bourbon, except for when passing in a taxi one night, you become attuned to the sense of awe the astronauts on board the Apollo 17 must have had when seeing the Earth in its totality for the first time. Indeed, as with the astronauts who allowed us to gain a sense on our own place in the cosmos, you too take a photo, not

FIGURE P.3 *Quai de Bourbon, Paris.*

only to record this moment, but also to attest to the fact you were here, standing in a doorway in 7 Quai de Bourbon, despite your phobia of crossing bridges.

The bridge gathers

Intuitively, we take bridges as objects that encourage movement and connection. Indeed, the very term 'bridging' has come to signify an agreement, in which two or more parties come to a covenant through (and on) the mediating structure of a bridge. The bridge provides common ground, a public space, whereupon one transgresses one's own boundaries in order to meet the boundaries of the other person. The bridge is an exemplary space of neutrality, from which sheer possibility is forged and then extended to surrounding space. In Heidegger's famous terms, the bridge *gathers*

(Heidegger 1977, 330). Heidegger refers to the way the bridge is not simply a passive space that connects one place to another, as if the bridge were the background in this movement. Beyond this, the bridge articulates the meaning of places that cross over or pass under it. For Heidegger, the bridge is emblematic of this act of place-making. If it were not for the bridge, the land and river surrounding the immediate space would be sealed off from one another, and, in some circumstances, made uninhabitable. Across vast ravines, and over rivers wider than the Seine, life becomes possible thanks in part to the bridge rendering boundaries, not a series of limits, but 'something [that from which] begins its essential unfolding' (332).

If the bridge has the unique power to build relations between places and people, then it is precisely for those reasons the bridge also serves to cut those place and people into parts. Just as a bridge can soften, if not sometimes erase the boundaries between places, so it can simultaneously render those boundaries more pronounced. From the perspective of a subject suffering from spatial anxieties and phobias – the subject under question in this book – a bridge can become illustrative of an existence that is both circumscribed and constrained. For such a subject, the bridge does not enter the horizon of experience as a boundary, from which life begins, but instead as a fundamental limit, against which life ends. Indeed, beyond the bridge, any such life remains speculative, seen from afar but never experienced in the flesh.

But how does a bridge, which is ordinarily an object of unification and harmony, become an anxious space? To gain a sense of the multifaceted complexity involved in such questions, let us return to the bridge from a phenomenological perspective. We can observe several relations. The first relation is with the bridge itself. The bridge is a material thing in the world. It has a reality – let us assume – that is not dependent on the perception of an observer. The bridge, in its structural and material integrity, persists both spatially and temporally. Thanks to this persistence, a relation with the bridge is possible in the first instance. At which point does anxiety enter the bridge? Does the bridge emit an anxious quality in and of itself or is anxiety carried to the bridge? That the experience involves several environmental factors that extend beyond the bridge suggests that the onset of anxiety involves neither the subject nor the bridge in isolation, but instead takes place in their very pairing, thus constituting a general 'mood' of anxiety. As the sun moves beyond the clouds, the bridge reveals itself in a different way. Now, space becomes more welcoming. This unfolding of the bridge as a more inviting place involves the subject, the bridge, and the surrounding world coming together as a whole. To ask, then, would another person be as troubled by the rays of the sun as is the case for the anxious person is to underplay the relational structure involved in such an experience. The issue, after all, is not one of locating the 'cause' of how the bridge becomes a site of anxiety – as though the anxiety were 'in the head' of the subject – but instead, of attending to the specificity of this relation as it comes into existence, a relation which privileges neither subject nor object, but the exchange between them.

In this rapport between the bridge and its dweller, we face a complex and dynamic involvement, which centres at all times on the role of the body. In our illustration, the body is less the foundation of an integrated experience, and more a site of alienation and uncanniness. Throughout, the body becomes an object of suspicion, in which each of its sensations is experienced as a potential betrayal against the self. Note also that this disturbed relation to the body not only unhinges the coherence of the self, but also folds back upon the world, with the anxious body coexisting alongside an anxious world.

With the body, another relation unfolds: to that of place. Where to place oneself on the bridge? The answer is not obvious, but instead involves a relational dynamic, which entails both calculating potential dangers in abstraction and finding one's footing intuitively. Far from uniform, the relation between the body and place is thematically altered depending on where we are positioned. Added to this question of getting placed, the structure of space is also modified in accordance with the experience of anxiety. As we see, spatiality loses its form as a unified whole, and instead is reduced to a series of fragmented parts. Thematically, this disturbed sense of orientation and distance means that the world loses its familiar constancy, and now assumes the quality of being partly unreal. Body, space, self. To this tripartite group, we must now add the relation between the body and others. In our illustration, other people are not inconspicuously set in the background, but are instead accented in their obstructiveness. They assume a special role, not only in preventing movement, but also in amplifying the experience of anxiety itself, an experience that would be wholly different were the bridge devoid of other people.

A final relation emerges in this account: between the subject and their own anxiety. Far from a wish to eliminate anxiety, as though it were simply an inconvenience to an otherwise 'normal' life, throughout this expedition there remains a strong attachment to anxiety, such that the affect would even be increased by jumping into the Seine – a movement that is stalled only when confronted with the possibility of anxiety being replaced by humiliation. This compressed outline reveals the complexity at stake in the present book. At least five distinctive relations can be identified: between the mood of the subject and the world; between body and the self; between spatiality and the body; between the body and others; and between anxiety and subjectivity. The task of this book is to investigate these themes under the rubric of what we call *topophobia*.

Topophobia and agoraphobia

The usage of the term 'topophobia', as it will be used, refers to a broad set of spatial phobias such as agoraphobia, claustrophobia and, not least, gephyrophobia (fear of bridges). The advantage of using the term 'topophobia', however, is that the concept remains ambiguous enough to include an entire spectrum of relations a person might have with place, including both the anxiety of being exposed (agoraphobia) and enclosed (claustrophobia), being in the darkness (lygophobia) or in the light (photophobia), and both of falling (vertigo) and of rising (acrophobia). Our concern, then, is not solely with the connection between urban space and home, as would classically tend to be the case for agoraphobia. Rather, our concern is with the disordering of space more broadly, be it in the city square, on a plane at night or in a forest at dawn.

The seeds for the use of the term 'topophobia' were planted in my previous book, *The Memory of Place* (Trigg 2012). In that book, the term is employed to describe a form of 'spatiotemporal homesickness' (194). In this context, topophobia refers to the way in which the boundary line demarcating one place from another loses its porousness and becomes fixed. This fixing of boundaries serves not only to define but also to restrict the character of place. Such an approach to place would be evident in the case of nostalgia, where an effort is made at fixing a certain place in both space and time, thus sealing it off from the surrounding world in an attempt at fabricating a specious sense of 'home'. Against the threat of difference, the nostalgic subject and, as we will see later, the phobic subject rely on a series of strategies to ensure the outside, in its otherness, never encroaches upon the inside, in its intimacy. Indeed, the relation between the nostalgic and the phobic subject are rooted in a joint disordering of home, where 'home' denotes not only a relation to space, but also to one's own body. This is especially true in the case of agoraphobia, and indeed, it is around the theme of agoraphobia that our study encircles.

The relation between topophobia and agoraphobia is a relation of generality and specificity. If topophobia refers to a generalized disordering of spatiality (and thus embodiment), then agoraphobia marks a particular instance of this disordering in terms of focusing on public space as a space of fear, thus the etymological heritage of 'agora' returns us to the ancient marketplace or gathering space in Greece. Yet the structure of agoraphobia reveals a more complex mode of experience than a localized fear of space alone, and if the condition can be framed as an anxiety disorder concerning public space, then it is such only in relation to an adjoining attachment to home. Throughout its rich history, the agoraphobic condition has developed into various spatial phobias, including 'la peur des espaces', 'horreur du vide', 'platzschwindel' (square dizziness) and, finally, agoraphobia (cf. Marks 1987). The Greek heritage of the term 'agoraphobia' – 'phobia' extending from the mythical figure Phobos – only gains a medical sense in the late nineteenth century, along with a series of other disorders that have since become part of the medical lexicon, not least anorexia and claustrophobia (cf. Trotter 2004; Vidler 2000). Writing a few years after the conception of agoraphobia, the French psychiatrist Henri Legrand du Saulle provides us with an accurate and still relevant description of the main symptomatology involved in agoraphobia:

> This anxious state, which mostly consists of an exaggerated and absurd feeling of fear faced with emptiness, usually goes with a sense of weakness in the legs, a passing circulation hyperactivity, mild pins and needles, a growing sensation of numbness, coldness, heat waves, cold sweats, shaking, impulses to cry, irrational apprehensions, hypochondriac concerns, muffled laments, and a general state of truly painful turmoil, with diverse alterations

of facial coloration and physiognomic expressions...The intelligence remains sane and moral freedom is entirely intact. (Legrand du Saulle 1878, 7–8)

In terms of precipitating factors, the clinical literature on agoraphobia confirms Legrand du Saulle's analysis in finding a specific triggering event, such as the sudden onset of illness or the loss of a parent, as either bringing about the onset of agoraphobia or otherwise solidifying its incipient role in the structure of the subject (cf. Marks 1987, 330). Prior to Legrand du Saulle, the term 'agoraphobia' was coined in 1871 by the German psychiatrist Carl Friedrich Otto Westphal (Knapp 1988). Westphal identifies a series of themes still applicable to the experience of agoraphobia:

> [T]he less an open space is interrupted by objects, the easier it is for the [agoraphobia] to appear; but also the passing of long fronts, now and then through unknown or empty streets, or in the highest level even a short walk through a familiar environment, has the same effect. The condition can be lessened or forced to disappear through an escort, especially while engaging in conversation; at the sight of a vehicle going the same direction, or seeing an open door in one of the houses located on abandoned streets, and so forth. (Knapp 1988, 74)

As we see, homogeneous space – space perceived as having no horizon – becomes especially problematic as it leaves the agoraphobic subject 'stranded' in a void, without any means of escape. Westphal locates two rejoinders to the subject's anxiety: the role of what will become the 'trusted other' and the function of a 'prop', be it a moving vehicle or, archetypically, an umbrella. Indeed, already in this preliminary account, we see that an 'open door' is the bearer of a symbolic meaning that fuses the experience of space with the importance placed on other people. As Westphal goes on to say, the transformation of others and objects cannot be reduced to 'a common feeling of dizziness', but instead points more specifically to an anxiety, which is to be distinguished from mere vertigo (74). As to the prognosis, Westphal's patients appear to have benefited from the then prevalent forms of treatment, such as spending time in a water spa, complemented with a 'few glasses of strong wine' (40).

The development of agoraphobia after Westphal follows two broad developmental trajectories. In the first case, agoraphobia is presented as a disorder in space. According to this line of thought, what instils anxiety in the subject is a fault in urban design, which agoraphobic patients would be especially sensitive towards. Emblematic of this view, the Austrian architect and city planner Camillo Sitte, writing only twenty years after Westphal's invention of agoraphobia, localized agoraphobia [*platzscheu*] to the act of 'walk[ing] across a vast empty place', thus rendering the condition a peculiarly urban one:

> Agoraphobia is a very new and modern ailment. One naturally feels very cozy in small, old plazas…On our modern gigantic plazas, with their yawning emptiness and oppressive ennui, the inhabitant of snug old towns suffer attacks of this fashionable agoraphobia. (cited in Collins 2006, 183)

Observing how plazas can have a 'pernicious influence on their surrounding structures', Sitte reduces the agoraphobe to a passive agent, overwhelmed by a landscape in which the subject's own psychological disposition plays a minor role. Indeed, of key interest to Sitte is not the psychodynamics of the agoraphobe's world view, but the very presence of the agoraphobic subject as a symptomatic manifestation of a fault in modern urban design, the implication being that agoraphobia is ultimately a concern of aesthetics rather than psychiatry (cf. Carter 2002). Sitte's anti-modernist aesthetic is consistent with the medical literature of the late nineteenth and early twentieth centuries. In each case, agoraphobia gains its quality as anxiety inducing in response to changes in the environment, be it as a vertical movement of building space upwards or as a horizontal movement of accelerating modes of transport. The diagnosis of agoraphobia as an environmental problem is not solely the province of urban theorists and architects, but is also evident in philosophers. Writing in 1890, William James makes a series of striking observations on a condition 'which has been described of late years by the rather absurd name of *agoraphobia*':

> The patient is seized with palpitation and terror at the sight of any open place or broad street which he has to cross alone. He trembles, his knees bend, he may even faint at the idea. Where

he has sufficient self-command he sometimes accomplishes the object by keeping safe under the lee of a vehicle going across, or joining himself to a knot of other people. But usually he slinks round the sides of the square, hugging the houses as closely as he can. This emotion has no utility in a civilized man but when we notice the chronic agoraphobia of our domestic cats, and see the tenacious way in which many wild animals, especially rodents, cling to cover, and only venture on a dash across the open as a desperate measure even then making for every stone or bunch of weeds which may give a momentary shelter when we see this we are strongly tempted to ask whether such an odd kind of fear in us be not due to the accidental resurrection, through disease, of a sort of instinct which may in some of our ancestors have had a permanent and on the whole a useful part to play? (James 1950, 421–422)

James proceeds beyond the level of critique offered by Sitte in compounding a disorder in space with a disorder in the very idea of the human. Now, the agoraphobic subject is presented not simply as an aesthete, overly sensitized to his or her surroundings, but quite the opposite: as an uncivilized being, who finds him or herself in the company of feral animals, and seemingly in danger of regressing back to a primitive state of development. Such a disparaging account of the agoraphobe is not out of place in the earlier characterization of the condition as a 'sickness', be it of urban spatiality (Sitte), or of will due in some cases to an 'excess of wine and venery', or, in the case of Freud, of sexuality (Neale 1898, 1322).

Writing only a few years after Legrand du Salle, Freud comes to the topic of agoraphobia in his 1895 paper 'Obsessions and Phobias' (Freud 2001a). Freud's references to agoraphobia in the corpus of his work are infrequent though significant, not least because the psychoanalyst was himself prone to bouts of agoraphobia (cf. Jones 1974). As Freud sees it, obsessions and phobias constitute 'separate neuroses' (Freud 2001a, 74). Their difference is primarily in their affective structure. Where phobias are concerned, the enduring emotional state is anxiety. In obsessions, the affective dimension is subject to flux, just as the idea itself that the patient is obsessed with can also change. To demonstrate the dynamic nature of obsessional neurosis, Freud provides several illustrations of seemingly incongruent fixations, such as a woman compelled to count floorboards in an anxious state, another woman in the grip of an obsession with her breathing and yet another woman obsessed with collecting stray pieces of paper (77–78). In each case, Freud provides a 'reinstatement' explaining the motivation behind these acts. The strength of such obsessions comes about, so Freud suggests, as a defence against an 'incompatible idea', which would threaten the ego more radically than that of an obsessive disorder, chiefly, of course, in the form of a repressed sexual desire. Far from a loss of control, what connects obsessions with phobias is their role in concealing an anxiety greater than that experienced in the moment. Consider a scene from *The Interpretation of Dreams*:

> Let us suppose that a neurotic patient is unable to cross the street alone – a condition which we rightly regard as a 'symptom'. If we remove this symptom by compelling him to carry out the act of which he believes himself incapable, the consequence will be an attack of anxiety; and indeed the occurrence of an anxiety-attack in the street is often the precipitating cause of the onset of an agoraphobia. We see, therefore, that the symptom has been constructed in order to avoid an outbreak of anxiety; the phobia is erected like a frontier fortification against the anxiety. (Freud 2010, 546)

Instead of being an expression of anxiety, and that alone, the symptom serves to keep anxiety in its place. As tension accumulates, the avoidance of anxiety-inducing situations intensifies, until the patient's movements become inhibited by a series of rituals and obsessions, all of which strive to frame anxiety as an intentional object of experience. As we will see later, the phobic object serves to divide the world into zones of familiarity and unfamiliarity, safety and danger. What this means is that anxiety's object is not identifiable with anxiety itself. Indeed, the construction of the object of anxiety is generated by a need to manage an anxiety greater than that of the object. To see how this plays out experientially, let us envision how agoraphobia comes into existence.

A subject prone to anxiety leaves her home and suffers from a sudden sense of being ill-at-ease. Dizziness, nausea, migraine or a feeling of faintness follows, leading the subject to feel weakened and unable to control herself. Soon after, her body feels as though it is on the verge of giving way, possessed by an invisible agency that has no correlating object. If the subject is caught in a transitional or interstitial space – it need not be a bridge, but may be an elevator, a queue or a hallway – then an urge to flee or cling to the nearest surface will emerge. Alongside clinging to the walls and floors, the anxious subject is overwhelmed with the urge not simply to flee, but also to hide. Columns, alleyways, corners and imposing trees with overhanging branches all serve to conceal the subject's anxiety from the surrounding world. Once in proximity to a reliable object – a second home, so to speak – the anxiety dissipates rapidly and the subject regains control of her body, albeit a body that is now fatigued. Despite recovering from the episode, the subject is likely haunted by the extent of the transformation. Indeed, the power of this haunting is so great and leaves such a visceral imprint on the subject's sense of bodily self that she will now adjust her existence in the world, so as to avoid endangering herself to the same ordeal in the future.

Isaac Marks describes what happens next: 'Once she cannot get off an express train, as soon as anxiety starts she will restrict herself to local trains; when these, too, become the setting for anxiety she retreats to buses, then to walking, then to going only a few yards from home, until finally she becomes unable to proceed beyond the front gate without a companion' (Marks 1987, 336). The zone of safety for the agoraphobe becomes increasingly more circumscribed as the anxiety assumes a more pervasive role in the subject's world. From anxiety, then, we move to avoidance, and then to phobia itself. The invention of phobia within the subject's life splits the world into parts, placing a sanction on places and situations that have a tendency to destroy the subject's sense of control. In avoiding anxiety-inducing situations and places through a series of elaborate rituals and practices, the phobic subject retains the illusion of having a control over the world and her bodily response to the world. If the illusion involves an element of superstition and blind faith, then such practices merely testify to the precarious structure upon which the agoraphobe stands.

***

As we will see in this book, psychoanalysis brings to light in an especially effective way the dynamic structures that give rise to phobia anxiety. One way the method does this is through attending to unconscious dimensions, which empirical psychology traditionally overlooks. Thus, the avoidance response inherent in agoraphobia is not simply a Pavlovian response to discomfort, which can be explained in terms of conscious perceptions and beliefs about perceptible danger. More than this, the ritual of avoiding certain places and situations takes place, for the most part, on an unconscious level, and precisely for this reason, is felt experientially as a shock to the subject. How to explain the avoidance of a bridge, or a queue, or even a hallway? The subject himself or herself is unable to rationally account for his or her response, other than discerning a sense of danger in spite of the fact that no danger is empirically visible. But agoraphobia, as with any phobic disorder, does not take its meaning from structures alone, and nor can agoraphobia be understood in terms of an intrapsychic conflict. What tends to be underplayed in the psychoanalytical perspective, to say nothing of cognitive behavioural models, is the bodily dimension of anxiety, not least in terms of the body in its relation to unconsciousness. Because of this neglect of corporeal existence, the world in which the agoraphobe inhabits – including its spatio-temporal-intersubjective aspects – is often presented as a static backdrop, against which intrapsychic conflicts are played out. Thus, in the case of the Freudian analysis, space gains a phobic quality only insofar as it is an expression of unconscious content. What such an analysis does not attend to is the co-constitution of spatiality and subjectivity as being in a dialogical relationship. The understanding of spatiality as being a static backdrop is even more pronounced in the earlier studies of agoraphobia, where the agoraphobe is presented as a passive agent responding to the environment around him or her. In what follows, we aim to put the body, in all its complexity, back in place.

A phenomenological perspective

To speak of the experience of topophobia in the sense of a relation with the world requires a clarification of terms. For Merleau-Ponty, the term 'world' conveys an overarching significance. In particular, 'world' points towards the circularity between body, subjectivity and others. This notion of a circular relation between these three aspects is phenomenologically exemplary insofar as it relies on the idea of the world as a dynamic and fluid totality rather than a fixed milieu. Throughout Merleau-Ponty's thinking, from the early works to the late conception of flesh, world and the body mark two sides of the same plane of existence. Indeed, both world and body gain their defining characters through being paired with one another, and to this extent cannot be considered in isolation from each other, as he has it, 'far from my body being for me merely a fragment of space, there would be for me no such thing as space if I did not have a body' (Merleau-Ponty 2012, 104).

Because of this reversibility between body and world – again, a theme that is consistent throughout Merleau-Ponty's work – the experience of one's own body is at the same time a perception of the world. Likewise, the perception of the world can only be understood within the context of the perceiving body. It is for these reasons, that Merleau-Ponty will write the following words in *Phenomenology of Perception*: 'The body is our general means of having a world' (147). This action is possible thanks to the fact that the body is primordially rooted in the spatial world. Spatiality, considered from an objective side, is the condition of there being a bodily experience of space in the first place. For Merleau-Ponty, therefore, it makes no sense to speak of objective space without reference to the body, leading him to remark 'to be a body is to be tied to a certain world, and our body is not primarily in space, but is rather of space' (149).

What, then, is spatiality? On the one hand, space is a homogeneous extension of matter that can be analysed in geometrical and topological terms. It is a grid of references, uniform in its objective properties, and thus able to be viewed from an isotropic perspective. Of course, this is not how we actually experience space. Our experience tells us that space is not homogeneous, but rather defined by a multiplicity of affective and sensorial components, all of which sculpt the felt texture and shape of any given place. A mood shapes our experience of the world, binding us with things in a meaningful and singular fashion (Heidegger 1996; Trigg 2013b). One human being loses another and the person left behind experiences the world in a new way. Laden with a heavy atmosphere, the world becomes cast in an equivalent light. Familiar streets and roads that once assumed a background presence are now accented by what they lack. Those same streets protrude more pointedly into the person's experience of the world, losing their character as being a horizon onto other places and instead marking a distance from the world one once knew. Likewise the home, formerly a place of sanctuary, now becomes enshrouded by the presence of those who no longer inhabit it. In this place, the body of the survivor experiences the home not as a centre of life, but as a memorial to that which has passed beyond the living.

Let us also consider the misfortune of being broken into. The intrusion is not contained to the house itself, but instead disperses an atmosphere of insecurity throughout the broader region. Insecurity is carried through the body, such that the transgression of the house extends into an entire experience of both spatiality and other people. Suspicion and mistrust enter the person's world, as other people become marked with a sense of insidious threat. As for the home itself, it becomes a locus of insecurity and danger that was previously absent prior to the intrusion. Whereas the pre-broken home – and thus pre-broken world – was a place of privacy, now, it feels watched, as though it could at any time be broken again. The body that occupies this home is no longer rested in the world but instead exists in a state of tension.

Finally, the body becomes damaged. A limb is broken and now the body must find its way through the world in an impeded manner. Patterns of daily life that were never a problem, now present themselves as formidable challenges, which must be approached both cautiously and slowly. The stairs leading to the home lose their inviting quality and now become a hindrance separating the broken person's body from his or her home. Broader patterns of navigation must now be reconsidered so as to accommodate the broken limb in its readjustment to the world. Moreover, the readjustment returns to the identity of the person. Having taken it for granted that the person's identity was constituted by the usage of four limbs, now this identity must undergo a process of reconfiguration. Both body and world share in this joint adjustment, with each co-partaking of a broken body and world.

These examples give us three ways in which the body–world relation is modified in accordance with a multiplicity of factors. In the first example, the bodily experience of the world undergoes a shift in meaning in accordance with a mood of mourning and loss. In the second case, the broken house extends its reach to a feeling of insecurity that permeates the body and the world. And in the final case, the focus moves to the body itself as the fundamental bearer of

a particular world, which, at all times, hinges on the body's ability
to move through the world. In each situation, it is not the case that
there is a world outside of the body, which is then animated by
the body's involvement. The world is not constituted by the bodily
subject in a causal way, but instead defines itself in a dialogical
relationship with the body.

A phenomenology of anxiety

In the current book, the mood we are concerned with is anxiety.
Phenomenology's relation to anxiety is an intellectually rich, if not
wholly intoxicating, one. One of the reasons for this intellectual
intoxication is due to the venerated status of anxiety not only
within phenomenology but also within philosophy itself. How is
it that anxiety has become the philosophical mood *par excellence*?
There are at least two reasons: a conceptual reason and, what might
be called, a transformative reason.

In the first case, while moods such as fear, love and boredom have
all assumed an importance within the history of philosophy, there
can be no doubt that anxiety occupies an especially pivotal place.
If we follow this question through a Heideggerian route, we find
that anxiety presents itself as an 'original mood', original because
anxiety confronts us with the fact that 'they are beings – and not
nothing' (Heidegger 1977, 105). This appeal to the contingency of
being provides anxiety with its ontological structure, going so far
as to reveal 'being as a whole' (102). How does anxiety do this?
Heidegger's argument is that in anxiety, the pregiven meaning of
things in their everyday context slips away, including that of our
own selves. In this slippage of things, the subject 'hovers' above and
beyond their personal existence, revealing the 'pure Da-sein' that
dwells beneath this personalized being (103). The result is that we
feel 'ill-at-home' in the world, as the world reveals itself to be the
site of an irreducible and original strangeness (111). All of which
is to distinguish anxiety from other affects, not least fear. If fear is
thought of as being 'fear in the face of something…in particular',
then anxiety, inversely, is thought of as lacking a determinate object
of concern (102). We might think of this distinction in another way.
If fear concerns itself with a particular object, then this implies
that fear has a localizable quality to it, which the fearful subject

can develop a relation to. Anxiety, on the other hand, lacks this localized dimension, and thus assumes an omnipresent hold on the subject, such that the structure of the subject itself is put into doubt. It is precisely this relation between the structure of the subject and its possible dissolution that is peculiar to anxiety.

As to the second reason why anxiety has assumed the importance it has, as an original mood anxiety is not a value neutral affect, but instead imbued with a *transformative* structure. What this means is that anxiety – in some capacity – instigates a fundamental insight into the nature and structure of the subject. Quite obviously, we can think of Kierkegaard's account of anxiety as having an educative value, so much so that he will even go so far as to speak of anxiety as a 'school' (Kierkegaard 1981, 156). Let us also think here of Heidegger's reflections on the value of anxiety as having the capacity to individualize the subject such that an authentic relation towards being-towards-death is possible. These reflections, which no doubt constitute some of the richest passages in *Being and Time*, are interwoven with the conceptual structure of anxiety. As the everyday presentation of the world slips away from us, so the world is revealed to us in an uncanny way. Stripped of its familiar attributes, our taken-for-granted relation to the world is momentarily ruptured by the advent of anxiety, leaving us with a sense of being ill-at-home in the world (Heidegger 1996). In anxiety, it is not just that things intrude upon us, but that the 'world has the character of complete insignificance' (174). What is uncanny in this movement is not simply that meaning is proven to be contingent, but that not-being-at-home 'becomes phenomenally visible' as a mode of fleeing from anxiety (176). We can think of this act of uncanniness becoming visible in terms of becoming aware of the role we as individuals play in being complicit with the production of a meaning. Gaining a self-reflexive awareness of how meaning is produced brings about a moment of anxiety in knowing at the same time how precarious that meaning is. For these reasons, anxiety is not one mood among many, but is instead a 'fundamental kind of attunement belonging to the essential constitution of Da-sein' (177). Yet Heidegger does not leave us stranded in anxiety. The crevice between being and world establishes the possibility of other ways of being-in-the-world afforded by a movement of separation between self and other. Anxiety thus carries with it a realization of other possibilities in the world, and without the confrontation with anxiety, Dasein's eventual appropriation of its own existence remains impossible. In Heideggerian phenomenology, anxiety tends to be treated as an opportunity for what Levinas terms a space of 'supreme vitality' (Levinas 2005, 70). The alliance between anxiety and freedom presupposes not only a value to anxiety, but also a fundamental nature. The nature of anxiety, as it is presented in Heidegger, Kierkegaard and to some extent Sartre, attests to the transformative function of anxiety, a function that is not simply prescribed as an ethical framework, but instead takes root in the conceptual status of anxiety itself. From a critical – that is, Levinasian – perspective, the task becomes one of rupturing the narrative of anxiety, and, more specifically, of attending to the way anxiety assumes a voice to what is ostensibly an enigmatic if not mute experience. Levinas provides an outline of the problem we face:

> And when one writes a book on anxiety, one writes it for someone, one goes through all the steps that separate the draft from the publication, and one sometimes behaves like a merchant of anxiety. (60)

Levinas identifies a risk problematic to any philosophical treatment of anxiety. The risk has two aspects. On the one hand, to write about anxiety means reproducing the experience of it, and so modifying it. In becoming a 'merchant of anxiety', the mood is tied to the page on which it is written, however loosely. More than this, the writing of anxiety also reveals a performative dimension, in that anxiety is written before the face of another person. Yet if the writing of anxiety is a confrontation with the other for whom one writes, then it is also a dialogue with oneself. In each case, a phenomenology of anxiety, such as it is practised in this book, proceeds to move around the edges of anxiety, encircling it, returning to it, discarding it. There is necessarily an element of repetition at work, as a phenomenological study of anxiety requires returning to the same scene from different angles. The anxiety itself shifts, articulating itself primarily through the body, then in our relation with others, before then manifesting itself through the spatiality of the home. Each of these articulations does not claim to exhaust the meaning or definition of anxiety. Rather, the phenomenology in question attempts to outline the singularity of a given experience.

Despite this shifting movement of anxiety, the experience outlined in this book can be characterized in a precise way and attached to a specific form of bodily existence. The form is characterized by the felt transformation of the body from a locus of meaning, ownership and unity to an impersonal site of alienation and anonymity. In what follows, we will see that this transformation is both expressive of anxiety and the object of anxiety. Moreover, at stake in this movement is not only a transformation of the body, but also of our relation to spatiality and intersubjectivity. Thus, when confronted with the anxious quality of the home or of the gaze of another person, our concern remains with a fundamental change in our experience of a personalized and familiar world to an impersonal and unfamiliar world.

Why, then, should we take the impersonal aspect of the body as being related to the experience of anxiety? As I will suggest, it is with the lived experience of the body in its anonymity and impersonality that the boundary line between self and the non-self is put into question. In speaking of an impersonal level of existence, we mean that aspect of existence that serves to destabilize, threaten and dissolve the image we have of who we are. We are taking the theme of impersonal existence, therefore, not as an innocuous structure of subjectivity, but as a presence that menaces the very image of selfhood. This formulation of impersonal existence, which will be unfolded in dialogue with Levinas and Merleau-Ponty, is specific to the experience of phobic anxiety. However, the anxiety intertwined with bodily life is present for both phobic and non-phobic subjects and can be formulated as a question: Where does the body *as my own* begin and end? The extent to which this question will provoke anxiety is contingent on several factors. For some people, the boundaries between self and other(ness) are porous if not elastic, such that gradients of ambiguity and uncertainty are experienced without any considerable peril to the integrity of selfhood. For them, a sense of self is a malleable construct. For other people, especially anxious subjects, the 'gap' between one's sense of self and what lies outside of this sense is rigidly construed, such that there is an intolerance of uncertainty. This intolerance is especially striking in the case of the anxious person's relation to their body. In the gap where the body comes to the edge of its personalized existence, a space is created from where the body's otherness comes to the foreground. The issue does not concern how my body is distributed or extended through space, such that I still retain possession of that extended materiality. Rather, we are concerned with the point at which the ongoing renewal of the body as my own – that is, my set of memories, values, dreams, phantasies and fears – is no longer capable of supporting those personalized values, and thus reveals itself in its resistance to accommodate selfhood. This resistance may take shape in the gaze of another person, or it may be felt in specific buildings, or on certain bridges. In each case, what prompts and sustains anxiety is an unknowable and unknown dimension of the body, which is revealed, not as an accident disclosed by a sickly perception, but as the very constitution of corporeal existence.

The anxiety we are concerned with in this book is remote from an entire range of related phenomena, not least a generalized anxiety, which spreads itself through the world in a non-specific fashion. Nor is the anxiety at stake, one that can be localized as a 'given' of the everyday that each human being invariably has to contend with, such as economic insecurity, loneliness or the indeterminacy of freedom. Although this book hinges upon aspects of existential phenomenology, our orientation departs from a humanism, in which anxiety becomes sublimated as a mode of reintegration for the subject. Primarily, our concern is neither with the 'value' of anxiety nor with its 'management'; less even the function of anxiety in the individual's 'self-realization' (cf. Goldstein 1966; May 1977). Any such conversion of anxiety as an opportunity to be mastered for the subject is an anxiety conceived retroactively, and guided at all times by a predefined value. In all this, we do not deny the possibility of anxiety as having a value. Indeed, two of the fundamental aims of this book are to contribute to the understanding of anxiety as it is lived and to identify the specificity of what is at stake when we feel anxious. If our analysis serves as a source of insight for sufferers of anxiety, then our aim will have been achieved. However, to elaborate on the relation between anxiety and value is the task of a different project, and a project that can only begin once we have an understanding of how the body is shaped by anxiety and likewise how anxiety is shaped by the body.

Our phenomenology disembarks from a Heideggerian approach in identifying anxiety, not as a mood of existence reducible to human subjectivity in its appeal to self-realization, but as the site of an irreducible anonymity that outstrips subjectivity. For this reason, Heidegger does not assume a central figure in what follows. Despite this distancing from Heideggerian phenomenology, throughout this book, we rely extensively on the lived experience of the body. Indeed, the recurring motif we will encounter is that of experiencing one's body as uncanny or alien. To this extent, our foray into anxiety does not consist simply in mining insights in collaboration with Merleau-Ponty. We wish, instead, to develop a new understanding of anxiety. This understanding has its basis in a series of concepts outlined in my previous books – especially 'un-place', the 'phantom zone', together with the 'unhuman body', and 'unhuman phenomenology' – all of which accent the uncanny aspects of experience, whereupon the lived experience of the body in its everyday habitat becomes the vehicle for an anonymous body at the fringe of personal perception (Trigg 2012, 2013a, 2014a). The precise structure of the experience of anxiety extends beyond descriptive phenomenology and requires a careful look not only at what appears for consciousness, but also at what refuses to appear. As such, we will require both a conceptual and experiential analysis of the movements of the body as considered phenomenologically and non-phenomenologically.

The case studies

A brief word of explanation is needed on the methodology of this book. The 'case studies' analysed in this book, those experiences of anxiety and phobia from where our interpretations and conceptual insights are drawn, have their roots in my own experience. Such experiences are affixed to a time and a place, a circumscribed zone of experience from where this book draws both its reserves and its strengths. For this reason, the gender pronoun employed most frequently (though not exclusively) in this book is masculine. That *Topophobia* is based upon my own experiences of phobic anxiety does not mean that this book is limited to those experiences. Indeed, these personal experiences are in turn described and interpreted alongside historical case studies, both as a means to deepen our understanding of the experience in question and also to broaden our understanding of anxiety as involving diverse and complex patterns of behaviour. Above and beyond (or more accurately, beneath and prior) the cultural and social dimensions shaping the experience of spatial phobias, this book implicitly maintains that a series of

invariant structures defines such experiences. In particular, we hold
that phobias such as agoraphobia adhere to a general principle.
The principle underlying such experiences can be characterized as
*a boundary disorder framed by the transformation of one's own
bodily experience of the world, in its subjective and intersubjective
dimensions, such that the perception of the world becomes almost
anonymous and formless.* We understand this almost anonymous
and formless presence to be anxiety.

Given that any such phenomenological study of anxiety or
agoraphobia depends in large upon the sources being presented –
be they historical or contemporary – the question emerges of how
a phenomenology of topophobia will proceed without succumbing
to mere anecdotal description. In fact, the question is something
of a misnomer. If phenomenology begins with the descriptive level
of thematic content, then it is not obvious that it should remain
at that level. Phenomenology is a critical method of inquiry,
meaning that it is distinct from the introspective examination of
one's psychological contents. Thus, for an applied phenomenology
to proceed – whether it is a phenomenology of agoraphobia or
a phenomenology of spaceflight – a balance between the careful
description of experience and the subsequent critical interpretation
of that experience must each play a role.

Our concern, then, is with what we can broadly call a hermeneutics
of the body. What this means is that our understanding of the body
is not exhausted by a descriptive account of the lived experience
of the world. The body exceeds such descriptions, belying another
surface not always available to phenomenology. Despite this
limit, we begin with the body, and it is to the body that we must
always return. The body we find in *Topophobia* is one marked
by a series of sensations or symptoms that require interpreting.
The body speaks, though what it is saying is not always clear.
Faced with an object of phobia, devoid of all objective dangers,
the body comes to a standstill. Something intervenes, an invisible
presence. In this gap between the experience of the world and the
world as it presents itself in objective terms, the role of a corporeal
hermeneutics assumes a central place. To the extent that the current
book involves a descriptive account of bodily experience alongside
a critical interpretation of that experience, the method used in
Topophobia remains the same as of that in my previous books, *The
Thing* (2014), *The Memory of Place* (2012) and, to a lesser extent,

The Aesthetics of Decay (2006). In each case, phenomenology is employed to capture the specificity of a particular experience. This approach does not proclaim to exhaust the topic in question – indeed, the phenomenology outlined in this book is necessarily limited given the labyrinthine scope of anxiety. Our aim, in fact, is narrowly construed to the anxiety tied up with one's experience of the body as impersonal. Although central – necessary even – to the experience of anxiety, the account of anxiety as told in this book is mediated throughout from the perspective of the body.

Therefore, while I consult historical instances of anxiety and phobia, the main focus of this work is on the phenomenology of spatial phobias, as they are lived. What this means is that we take seriously the value of lived experience as a point of departure for understanding the nature of subjectivity, intersubjectivity and spatiality. The mention here of beginning with lived experience serves to underline the importance of experience within the phenomenological method, but at the same time avoids drawing a line between phenomenology's movement beyond conscious experience and towards unconsciousness. This focus on both conscious and unconscious aspects of experience does not imply that a social or cultural background is irrelevant, nor is it to suggest that issues of politics and gender are secondary to an understanding of anxiety. Much important work has already been written on this background specifically in relation to agoraphobia, debates which are worth pursuing (Callard 2006; Davidson 2003; Jacobson 2011). Likewise, given our focus on the experiential dimension, our analysis does not take its guidance from third-person studies, indexical definitions, less even statistical evidence detailing the prevalence of anxiety disorders, as one would find in the medical literature. For all these reasons, we do not engage in recent debates concerning the classification of anxiety within the DSM (*Diagnostic and Statistical Manual*). Important though these debates are, they occupy another set of concerns, which can be pursued elsewhere (Decker 2013; Horwitz 2013; Phillips and Paris 2013).

In spite of my preceding admission that this work draws and folds back upon my own experience of spatial phobias, I have chosen to describe a series of agoraphobic and anxious encounters not in the first-person narrative but in the second-person. My reasons are twofold. First, on a structural level, the use of second-person is employed to accent the dis-possessed structure of the phobic experience, an experience in which 'I' am not fully present to myself but instead dispersed through my body and through the landscape that surrounds the body. Where am 'I' when anxious? This question, in fact, will become the hinge around which *Topophobia* revolves. It is for this reason that the 'I' is used in a provisional sense, an indexical placeholder, which we will return to time and again. This surrounding ambiguity concerning the place of the subject is especially true given that the descriptions used are, in effect, memories, which, if shaping my experience of the world, nevertheless do not impede upon that experience.

In the light of this uncertainty over the place of the anxious self, I address myself to myself. Here, I am a stranger undergoing an experience that I identify as being me, and yet fail to integrate fully within an existential framework. Who, then, is the 'you', the reader or myself? Between self and other, the 'you' appears as another subject outside of each category, an impersonal subject who is in possession of a certain type of experience, at once addressing the self while also speaking beyond the self. This 'I' that devolves into the 'you' finds a special place in the phenomenology of anxiety, a phenomenology that cannot remain content with speaking with the centrality and certainty of the first-person voice, but instead must contend with multiple voices speaking through the body. Such a self – my own self – is being gazed upon by myself, a self that must be interpreted and interrogated before it can be understood, so far as understanding is possible.

To speak, then, of certain factual details – Paris beneath a grey sky, the number 87 bus crowded with passengers – means having to contend with a set of experiences, which exceed the limits of pure description. If phenomenology retains its pledge to return to the things themselves, then in the case of an experience where the subject occupies an ambiguous place, an indirect route must be mined. A phenomenology of anxiety is an atypical phenomenology in that it demands not only a fidelity to the experience in question but also a vigilance over not reducing such experiences to a coherent narrative, in which the subject looks on from afar. In this respect, the use of second-person is less the means by which I can remove myself from the scene of anxiety, and more the means to get closer to it.

Alongside this structural consideration of the role of the anxious subject, a thematic issue also plays a part in this second-person narrative. At all times, it is a question of attempting to do justice to a certain type of experience that cannot be captured by factual data alone. If phenomenology as a method concerns the attempt at outlining, not only the salient structural features of an experience, but also its thematic content, then there is a question of how this can be achieved with language. If we take the example of crossing a bridge, there would be any number of ways to describe this experience. One could cite the objective features of the act in terms of presenting first-person testimonial 'evidence', which is how much of the contemporary literature on anxiety and agoraphobia is narrated. What tends to follow is a clinical study of patient reports that is divested of its dynamism and restricted to the level of factual existence. This is not to underplay or dismiss the legitimacy of these reports, but simply to address the possibility that where a phenomenology of phobia is concerned, a particular attention to language is required in order to convey both the structural and affective aspects of anxiety beyond a factual level.

The peculiarity of a condition such as agoraphobia is that it resists empirical evidence. We are, to be sure, in the realm of a specific kind of strangeness, as though in a dream. This strange dimension of phobic anxiety is captured in the intersecting of the everyday and the extraordinary. The inability to cross a bridge does not derive from empirical danger, but of a danger that has *spooked* the subject. It is a danger that has no place on the bridge, but instead draws back upon the subject. The subject sees or otherwise senses something out-of-joint on the bridge, yet he himself cannot find the source of the disorder. The anxiety on the bridge seems to fall through the body, and thereby elude understanding. To articulate the nature of this encounter, it is necessary for language to give voice to the strangeness inherent in anxiety. Phenomenology is an attempt to discover such a language, a language that is able to both attend to the phenomena on a descriptive level but also to push that description to a threshold, in which phenomenology itself comes to its own limit.

* * *

Topophobia begins by considering the relationship between topophobia and topophilia through the figure of the home. Historically, phenomenology has tended to centralize the home as a privileged place for human dwelling. The same is true of agoraphobes. We begin on a theoretical level by exploring the ambivalence of home in the works of Levinas and Bachelard, taking as our example the sickness of the home as unveiled by the night. There, we will find that the philic attachment to place belies a phobic repulsion towards other places. This dialectic between the home and the non-home reappears in the case of phobic subjects, who operate between the poles of agoraphobia and claustrophobia, between a fixation on place as the centre of unity and the experience of place as the centre of disintegration.

If our first chapter is concerned with the conceptual status of home as a privileged place for phobic subjects, then in the second chapter we give flesh to this status through considering the body. Consistent with our overarching theme of homeliness and unhomeliness, we take the phobic body to be an articulation of the uncanny body. As understood in this context, uncanniness refers to a tension in bodily existence involving two aspects. On the one hand, we have a sense of the body as something irreducibly *mine*. Yet at the same time, the materiality of the body is not reducible to my lived experience of being a self. Instead, who I am is implicated by a set of automatic and anonymous functions, which operate irrespective of who I am as a person. In the course of our investigation, we will frame this body both in Merleau-Pontyan terms of anonymous corporeality and in Sartrean terms of nauseating sliminess.

A phobic subject does not exist only within the interiority of his or her body. This body is also constituted by its relation with others. Chapter 3 focuses on the role of others within the world of the phobic subject. We begin with a question: How is our experience of the world affected by our experience of others? We will see that intersubjectivity is essentially an issue of intercorporeality, and that our relation with others defines our thematic and affective experience of the world. Far from a formal connection with others, the corporeal basis of intersubjectivity means that our lived experience of the world is mediated via our bodily relations with others. We will explore these issues through the experience of travelling on a bus in Paris. What this illustration will reveal is that our relation with others is not causally linked, as though there were a body, then a world, and then a subject that provided a thematic and affective context to that experience. Instead, body, other and world will be shown as intertwined in a single unity that cannot be considered apart.

In the fourth chapter we return again to a central topic of *Topophobia*: home. Building on the analysis in the first chapter, we will consider the function of the home, not only as a discrete entity, but also as a presence that structures the agoraphobe's experience of spatiality more broadly. This exploration involves both an analysis of the structure of spatiality alongside a specific consideration of the home as a centre. We shall pursue this aim through several illustrations, each of which is united by the sentiment of being lost in place. In fact, we will discover that the home involves two sub-centres: an ontological centre and a world centre. As inseparable and co-constitutive, these centres enable us to understand how certain features in the agoraphobe's world gain their quality as anxiety inducing through involving an interplay between unfamiliarity and unreality.

Our final chapter marks a departure from what is broadly a phenomenological analysis through considering from a psychoanalytical perspective the role of the body image as a means of placing anxiety. To this end, we will turn to both Lacan and Merleau-Ponty's analysis of the mirror stage, as well as recent research on the phenomenology of body image. What we will see is that through providing a specular image of oneself, the mirror stage outlines the transformation of the fragmented body to the illusion of unity. In this turn towards psychoanalysis, we will be in a position to question the place of anxiety itself. Does anxiety derive from a conflict within the subject, or does the subject itself derive from anxiety? With each possible answer, we end up with an entirely different account of both subjectivity and anxiety.

CHAPTER ONE

The Home at Night

The home is a place where things can go wrong.

(DAVID LYNCH)

Something in the night

You are home. Over an expanse of time, the place has become part of you, part of your bodily habits and memories, such that you experience the world in and through the lens of your home, which you return to time and again when the day draws to an end. More than this, you try to carry the home with you, as a presence that accompanies you in an otherwise uncertain world. Together, you and the home co-inhabit the same world, such that you both share a joint understanding of each other's intimate existence: just as the home bears witness to your unguarded moments in this world, so you have become a witness in the home's own evolution. In turn, the home in its specificity as a place in the world has integrated itself into your perceptual horizon. Your knowledge of the precise topography of the home extends not simply to its corners, crevices and nooks, but also to obscure details in the wallpaper and floorboards, which perhaps are only accessible to you in your incisive knowledge of the place. For you, the creaking of floorboards is not a backdrop to a life that takes place above, but is instead a rhythm that has become part of your pace in the world. Within these recesses, sounds and strange patterns in the wallpaper, traces of your memories are lodged. You are able to sketch an entire world in the movement from the hallway to the kitchen, and within the kitchen, you find an atlas of memories held in place.

You turn to the window. The window of your home affords you a glimpse of an alien world. For you, the frame to the outside world serves less to connect you with that world and more to fortify your distance from it. In and through the window you observe another world taking place. If there is a rapport between you and this world, then it is only a visual one, vulnerable at all times to alienation and anxiety. You know your place in the cosmos. It centres at all times on the intersection between your home and the existence that takes place outside of that space. Dare you move beyond the home to find yourself in the world of contingency and chance, then almost immediately you are overwhelmed with regret. For you know that unlike the outside, your home maintains your presence in the world, securing you within a boundary line, which you have no reason to transgress.

One night, you awake before the dawn. Much to your surprise, you are in the darkness, only now the sensuous quality of the dark

FIGURE 1.1 *Rue Saint Paul, Paris.*

differs from that of the evening. In the liminal hours between the dawn and the night, between sleepfulness and wakefulness, the stillness of this darkness unnerves you. Your body is inert, but your eyes are wide open and affixed upon the ceiling above your bed. In the shadows, you sketch the outline of the room around you. There, you find that much of what is familiar to you – the stray pattern in the wall that resembles a forest, the silhouette of the door and the sound of the home creaking in the darkness – but these same features now assume an unfamiliar impression. Now, those aspects become unnerving in their silence, as though they no longer reciprocated your presence, but instead gazed on, with a mute indifference to your awakening.

Your home has revealed another face, less discernible to you than when you are fully conscious, and now impregnated with an alien quality. Indifferent to your awakening, the voice of the home undergoes a transformation. Whereas the creaking of the home in the day expresses a solidarity with your presence, now those same sounds serve to dismantle your existence. From a depth in the wall, a crack can be heard, which, far from marking a reassuring reminder of the home's fortitude in the elements, now sounds as though the bones of the place were breaking.

You are anxious. But when you attempt to localize this anxiety, your thinking reaches an impasse. All that you are left with is the vague and horrifying sense that your home is now drifting away from you, leaving you stranded in an anonymous and silent world indifferent not only to your situation in the present, but also to the memories and histories etched within the home. Such is your disquiet, that for once you are struck not with a radical attachment to the home as a sanctuary in an otherwise hostile world, but instead a recognition that this same place is the centre of hostility. Instead of succumbing to an urge to stay, you are now resisting the impulse to flee, as if you had seen a ghost and wanted nothing more but to free yourself of the place, which you shared with the dead. Your agoraphobia becomes enmeshed in claustrophobia, each spatial disorder freely borrowing from each other in the midst of this sleepless dawn. Having lost the depth of intimacy, which you were under the impression of having co-created over time, the home appears as a flat dimension, almost reducible to an exterior alone, with no fixed perspective upon which to survey the space. The home retains its material place in the world – you can still touch, taste

FIGURE 1.2 *Rue Saint Paul, Paris.*

and smell it – but this materiality has become homogeneous and possessed with a coldness, as if seen from the outside. You are not an innocuous bystander in the transformation of the home, but instead are part of the dissolution and alienation. Just as the home becomes displaced from its moorings, so your body, in its discordance with the fragmenting home, is now situated in a depersonalized and derealized zone. As with the home, which is no longer possessable as your own, the same is true of your body. The thing lies motionless, unable to rid itself of the phantom night through resuming the act of sleep. In each case, the home and the body – the two pillars of stability – reject the narrative you have assigned to them through habit and memory. Something in the night has intervened in this narrative, unveiling the contingency of your bodily relation to the home, and revealing, in the dead of the night, the anonymous infrastructure of the home before the dawn.

Homesickness

The history of the home within the phenomenological tradition is distinguished. Taking its strengths from experiences of intimacy and unity, phenomenology has proceeded to draw us within ourselves, finding therein an entire world that is comprised from the primal sanctuary of the home. Such a love of place – truly, a *topophilia* – remains one of the method's greatest strength. Yet this partial focus is also phenomenology's most acute limit. Overlooked in this phenomenology of intimate spatiality are those places that dislodge and disrupt our being-in-the-world, such that even – *especially* – in the case of homelessness, what we tend to find is an anxiety that resolves itself through the restorative and primordial function of the always present home.

In all this intimacy, the presence of the outside is left suspended, with the phenomenologist's love of place countered by an uneasy if not anxious relation to places outside the remit of the home. The problem is not a novel one. Already in 1967, Foucault had diagnosed the problem phenomenology faces when confronted with its own limits; namely, a disquiet in the face of otherness, be it in the form(lessness) of the outside or in the amorphousness of interstitial space (Foucault 1986). By way of example, Foucault considers here the 'monumental work' of Bachelard (23). What Foucault finds in Bachelard is a treatment of place as being 'thoroughly imbued with quantities and perhaps thoroughly fantasmatic as well' (23). This is the space interwoven with our affective existence, full of the rich complexity of any given human subject. Yet if these places constitute beacons of stability in our lives, then they do so by implicitly privileging certain types of spatiality. Foucault counters the phenomenological tendency towards intimate and internal space by positioning us in the in-between, as he writes:

> The space in which we live, which draws us out of ourselves, in which the erosion of our lives, our time and our history occurs, the space that claws and gnaws at us, is also, in itself, a heterogeneous space. In other words, we do not live in a kind of void, inside of which we could place individuals and things. We do not live inside a void that could be coloured with diverse shades of light, we live inside a set of relations that delineates sites which are irreducible to one another and absolutely not superimposable on one another. (23)

Writing a few years after Foucault, Levinas indirectly responds to the challenge to breach the interiority of intimate space by criticizing phenomenology's tendency to reduce the Other to what he terms, the 'imperialism of the same' (Levinas 1969, 39). What he means by this is that phenomenology accommodates otherness only within the remit of a subjectivity that has already formulated a concept of the Other, as he writes, 'It is other with an alterity constitutive of the very content of the other', whereas to be genuinely other, the Other must be the 'Stranger who disturbs the being at home with oneself [*le chez soi*]' (39). How can we call upon the stranger who disturbs being-at-home without converting that stranger to an extension of our homeliness? The question concerns a blind spot in our vision. To contend with this blindness it is not a question of moving beyond the home, but of precisely remaining within it, and seeking in its familiar surroundings the stranger who lurks within habitual space. To find the stranger who disturbs the being-at-home is to turn as much to the home as it is to turn to our own selves.

Alongside phenomenologists, another set of people privilege the home as the centre of subjectivity: agoraphobes. Only, in distinction to phenomenologists, agoraphobic people recognize the home not only as a site of intimacy, but also as the centre of fragmentation.

In this respect, they give voice to the homesickness at the heart of phenomenology's topophilia. To grasp a sense of the importance of the home for the agoraphobe, let us consult the following passage from Carl Westphal. Of a patient named 'Mr. P', he writes as follows:

> During an attempt to cross an open space the fear begins as soon as the houses of a street leading to an open area increases their distance from him. Suddenly, a feeling of uneasiness occurs in his heart region as if one were terrified … A feeling of insecurity appears, as if he were no longer walking secure, and he perceives the cobble stones melting together … Sometimes he begins to increase his speed to reach the other side faster. He compares the feeling of crossing the place to that of a swimmer, who swims through a canal into an open lake and is afraid that he will not be able to cross it. The condition improves by merely approaching houses again. Once he has crossed the place he feels as in a dream. (Knapp 1988, 70)

We will encounter Mr P in following chapters. Let us register that already in Westphal's description of agoraphobia, the critical issue is not the objective features of space – large, small, circular, flat, etc. – but the relational distance to home. As Westphal's patient leaves the confines of his zone of safety, so his body opens up to a different way of being. Now, movement is stifled with the very materiality of the world suffering from a lack of reality. Into this abyssal unreality, space becomes problematic, not because of its geometrical properties, as such, but because certain aspects of the environment serve to divide the home from the non-home. As the analogy with swimming across an open lake makes clear, to venture into the outside world carries with it a risk not only of failing to get to the other side but also of never again returning to the home. Crossing the square – the archetypal agoraphobic motif – the danger is not of the square itself, nor even of the public eyes that descend upon the agoraphobe. While all of these things contribute to the agoraphobe's concern, what is principally at stake here is the loss of home.

This relationship between anxiety and the loss of home is evident in that a deviation from the fixed locality of the home carries with it a 'feeling of insecurity', such that the materiality of the world is put into question. What is peculiar about the agoraphobe's relationship to home is that his or her home is identified with a specific locale or site in the material world. The home is not a construct that is carried in the lived experience of the body, nor is it a more generalized way of being-in-the-world. Rather, home, for the agoraphobe, is grounded in the sensibility of the material place. Of this fixed locality, Yi-Fu Tuan writes as follows:

> With agoraphobia a more or less stable world does exist, and that is the home; so long as they stay within that charmed circle they feel competent – only beyond it is the frightening public space, the agora. One symptom of this affliction is the fear of crossing any large and open space. The sufferer feels dizzy, as though his body, like the space stretching before it, were about to lose its center and limits…the agoraphobic's greatest fear is the loss of control. (Tuan 1979, 204)

In turn, this highly pressured attachment to the locality of the home – be it an apartment or a broader neighbourhood – establishes a divisive boundary line between the reality of the home and the disembodied unreality of the non-home. It is against the backdrop of this tension that key experiences such as 'the cobble stones melting together' become instructive. The consequence of this highly pressured attachment to the home is that home itself assumes an anxious presence in the experience of the agoraphobic patient. Of one patient named Meg, the following report is made:

> Two needlepoint plaques adorned the entryway: 'Home is where the heart is.' 'The home of a friend is never far away.' These sentiments cast the home as a safe haven. Yet paradoxically, while at home Meg spends much of her time ruminating over past experiences of panic and imagining similar experiences in other hypothetical situations. Home is not a safe haven, after all. It does not protect her from being engulfed by reconstructions of past events that channel rising tides of panic into the present. Home is a place where distressing emotions from past times and places creep up on, invade, and overwhelm Meg's experience. As John Milton writes in *Paradise Lost*, 'The mind is its own place, and in itself can make a heav'n of hell, a hell of heav'n.' Home is a paradise lost in that it cannot provide

refuge from the mind and the scenarios it (re)creates. (Capps and Ochs 1995, 4)

The illustration highlights the problematic relationship the agoraphobe has to home in two ways. First, the home is shown to have a troubled relationship with the outside world, such that the outside is opposed to the home. Second, the home is proven to be not a reliable and objective 'friend' that one can turn to at the end of a hard day, but instead a mirror of one's subjective contents that is constructed in the light of the agoraphobe's anxiety. As the line from Milton indicates, what forms the experience of a place is ultimately one's own mind (or body) rather than the material conditions governing those places.

These illustrations reveal something common to agoraphobes and non-agoraphobes alike: far from a mere container, spatiality is dynamically constructed and constituted at all times by our affective relation with it. More than a backdrop against which life takes place, home is the very ground upon which life begins. As both the holder of memories and also the expression of those memories, the home installs itself within the life of the dweller, just as the dweller installs him or herself within the life of the home. Accordingly, in the absence of the home, or in the face of its collapse, what is lost is not simply the materiality of the home, but an entire world that springs forth from the home. To undertake a phenomenology of the home – and by implication, to understand the nature of topophobia – we need to understand how the home gains its homely quality and in turn risks losing that quality.

A twilight zone

To dwell, to be at home. What phenomenology alerts us to is the contingency of these relations. To be at home does not simply mean implanting oneself within the concrete spatiality of a unit, or otherwise comporting one's body in a particular way to a set of rooms. To dwell requires more than this and, indeed, occurs in a more primordial way than that of simply inhabiting a space. Levinas writes, 'Dwelling is the very mode of *maintaining oneself*...as the body that, on the earth exterior to it, holds *itself* up and *can*' (Levinas 1969, 37). In other words, to inhabit the world and make sense of it means already being in a site upon which to stand and apprehend the world in a pre-reflective way: 'Everything is here, everything belongs to me; everything is caught up in advance with the primordial occupying of a site, everything is com-prehended' (37–38). This sense of being-at-home is thus a sense that derives from a certain relation to the world, in which the world is available to me as a constantly unfolding possibility, and a possibility to be possessed. If the world resists us, as it will do, then this resistance only gives us space to assert and redefine our relation to the world.

In the midst of this confidence, a Stranger appears, 'over him I have no *power*' (39). What the Stranger brings into the site of dwelling is an absolute resistance to comprehension. The otherness of the Other does not lie simply in a distance between myself and the Other. Rather, there is a necessary strangeness within the Stranger, given that to have an understanding of the Other in their totality would mean fusing with the Other, reducing their otherness to a product of my existence. But the Stranger who is not in my site, who is not my world, defies my expectations, strips my memories of their value, and disarms my grasp on time and space. That I have no power of the Stranger means precisely this: that I am unable to mould the Stranger to my anticipations of how the world ought to conform to the narcissism of my selfhood.

The home that emerges in the twilight zone between the night and the day – *L'heure entre chien et loup* – reveals a materialization of the non-possessable strangeness that is ordinarily masked in our being-at-home in the world. Already we sense how a germ of strangeness infects the home during certain moments, such as when we become defamiliarized from the materiality of the place. What happens is that the home becomes impregnated with an unhomely quality. Losing form, the home drifts away from us, destabilizing and disorienting our place in the world. What remains is something that cannot be reintegrated into the home.

On a phenomenological level, there can be no doubt of the importance revealed in the act of waking up and finding one's familiar surroundings enshrouded in an atmosphere of strangeness. In the moments prior to full consciousness, in which the sleeper has not yet fully awoken, this interstitial state closes in on the very genesis of things assuming the meaning they do, and, in turn, losing that meaning. Indeed, in this micro-phenomenology, we are faced with the co-joining of different worlds colliding within the same body, one part seized from the trust placed in the world that allows us to sleep, the other part disrupted by the alienation that is unveiled through awakening. More than a partial glimpse of something transient and trivial, this collision of waking and sleeping states captures the trace of an elemental existence that is ostensibly veiled in the confidence we assign to the world. Levinas guides us through this journey into sleep and place, writing that:

A place is not an indifferent 'somewhere', but a base, a condition. Of course, we ordinarily understand our localization as that of a body situated just anywhere. That is because the positive relationship with a place which we maintain in sleep is masked by our relations with things. Then only the concrete determinations of the surroundings, of the setting, and the ties of habit and of history give an individual character to a place which has become our home [*le chez-soi*], our home town, our homeland, the world…Sleep reestablishes a relationship with a place qua base. In lying down, in curling up in a corner to sleep, we abandon ourselves to a place; qua base it becomes our refuge. Then all our work of being consists in resting. Sleep is like entering into contact with the protective forces of a place; to seek after sleep is to gropingly seek after that contact. Where one wakes up one finds oneself shut up in one's immobility like an egg in its shell. This surrender to a base which also offers refuge constitutes sleep, in which a being, without being destroyed is suspended. (Levinas 2001, 66–67)

Levinas begins with place, not as a set of geometrically defined positions, but as the locus of existence. To sleep in place is to entrust place as the site of an irreducible intimacy. One cannot, therefore, 'decide' to sleep, as if it were a formal matter. Giving oneself over to sleep is not an act that takes place in abstraction, but instead is rooted in the primordial liaison between the body and place. This 'reestablishment' of our relationship with place emerges as a reunion with a place that has already become a sanctuary for us, not as a newly discovered site in the world, but as part of a surrounding world, which we ourselves derive from and return to. As Levinas has it, upon sleeping, our movement is one of returning, and our expectation consists of reappearing in the same place. By contrast, the perversion of sleep consists not only in its disruption and deferral but also in the fact of stranding us into another place. This damaged awakening breaks continuity with both the place of the sleeper and also the intimacy at the centre of sleeping. In place of the closed nest, the awakening positions us in a space of exposure, indeed at the very edge where place recedes into anonymity. Merleau-Ponty writes:

> The night is not an object in front of me; rather, it envelops me, it penetrates me through all my senses, it suffocates my memories, and it all but effaces my personal identity. I am no longer withdrawn into my observation post in order to see the profiles of objects flowing by in the distance. The night is without profiles ... Even cries, or a distant light, only populate it vaguely; it becomes entirely animated; it is a pure depth without planes, without surfaces, and without any distance from it to me. (Merleau-Ponty 2012, 296)

Merleau-Ponty uncovers the anxiety at the heart of the night. The anxiety concerns not simply an absence of light, as if the night occluded vision, and that alone. Rather, the night, in its omnipotent embrace, cocoons me in an all-encompassing totality. Through penetrating my flesh, the night becomes me, as I become the night, effectively annihilating my personal identity through rupturing all spaces of perspective, and thus forcing a collusion between the remains of identity and the night, which now subsumes that trace into its zone of darkness. This collapse of identity gains special prominence in the home at night. What is revealed in this darkness, paradoxically, is the transparency of the home as a formless space, no longer conditioned by the memories and values ascribed to it retroactively. Merleau-Ponty writes, 'The anxiety of neurotics at night comes from the fact that the night makes us sense our contingency, that free and inexhaustible movement by which we attempt to anchor ourselves and to transcend ourselves in things, without there being any guarantee of always finding them' (296). We are at the centre of the insomniac's nightmare, and the nightmare is materialized in and through the home. In revealing itself for what it is – no longer a centre of being, but an indiscriminate zone of space propped up through the work of memory and imagination – the home reveals our role as being complicit in its construction. The contingency of the home is, thus, stipulated on a certain affective relation, which is displaced through anxiety, and which, in turn, renders the home the site of its own betrayal.

The menace of space

Our exploration of the shadowy side of the home and its relation to a broader topophobia will be greatly rewarded by retaining our relation with Levinas. What Levinas will enable us to do is to place the site of the home in relation to an elemental existence. Indeed, Levinas is an astute reader of the spatiality of shadows, and he proceeds beyond Merleau-Ponty in describing the night not simply in phenomenological terms as the recession of light and the loss of visibility, but as the site of an anonymous being, which can also occur in the midst of daylight (Levinas 2001, 52). This separation of the night from its phenomenal status underscores the role of the night as a disordering of our relation to the world. Marked as much by horror as by anxiety, the disordering of light brings us to the anonymous *there is*, which underpins all things without ever being fully reclaimed by things. Against this horrific anonymity, the home assumes a central place in Levinas, forging the conditions for both a philic and a phobic relation to place.

For Levinas, the privileged status of the home is not simply due to sheltering one from the 'inclemencies of the weather', or any other utilitarian justification (Levinas 1969, 152). Rather, the home's place is vouchsafed through its role as being constitutive of human existence. The home, as Levinas sees it, is that which allows for the dweller to re-collect themselves, and it is only 'from this recollection [that] the building takes on the signification of being a dwelling' (152–154). Recollection is Levinas's term for the way a dwelling affords a subject space to suspend their 'immediate reactions [to] the world…in view of a greater attention to oneself, one's possibilities, and the situation' (154). What emerges from this act of recollection is a 'gentleness that spreads over the face of things', and thus shapes the world into a familiar and intimate form (154–155). Such an intimacy is not a relation one occupies with the home as a physical space, and that alone. Rather, the gentle intimacy that recollection produces is taken up as being an '*intimacy with someone*' (155). The house of Levinas, so to speak, remains an open place, forever exposed and receptive to the welcome of the Stranger who constitutes the very essence of dwelling, as Levinas puts it: 'To dwell is not the simple fact of the anonymous reality of being cast into existence as a stone one casts behind oneself; it is a recollection, a coming to oneself, a retreat home with oneself as in a land of refuge, which answers to a hospitality, an expectancy, a human welcome' (156). The warmth of this retreat is not reducible to a 'turbid mystery of the animal and feline presence', which Baudelaire would like to evoke, but instead marks a 'new relations with the elements' (156).

With his mention of elements, we are in a position to understand the unrivalled importance of the home. Levinas's reference to the elements is not a reference to the tangible elements found in the surrounding world. Instead, the term carries with it a metaphysical horror that can be envisioned as the 'absolute emptiness that one can imagine before creation – there is' (Levinas 1985, 48). This idea of the *il y a* (the there is) reappears time and again in his thinking, but becomes increasingly less visible from the time of *Totality and Infinity* onwards, though no less important. What Levinas means when he writes of the *il y a* is an oppressive, impersonal and 'horrible thing', which strips me off my personality and reduces both the world and the body to a mute and formless thing. It can be described in abstract terms, but also in the concrete situation as that of insomnia, or otherwise putting an 'empty shell close to the ear, as if the emptiness were full, as if the silence were a noise', or even in the following way: 'A night in a hotel room where, behind the partition, "it does not stop stirring"' (48–50).

Let us pause to consider the atmosphere of a motel room in contradistinction to the embrace of the home. We are situated between places. This no where spatiality is the home of an anonymous unit, used by voyagers passing from one place to another, who stop only to rest such that they can proceed to the next point. It is a space divested of all personal attributes, appealing to both everyone and no-one at once. The furnishings, such as they are, have been stripped of all their history, and now they emerge as bland units of matter in and around which the fundaments of existence occur. The shower to wash in and bed to sleep strive only to perform their duties in the most minimal sense. The room is presented in its brute facticity as a zone of raw space to be recreated and reimagined by each guest who passes through its doors. Yet this noble aim fails, and far from being a space of creative potential, the impersonality of the room is both stifling and depressing. Levinas is with us in the motel and asks that we place our ear to the wall, such that 'one does not know what they are doing next door' (50). But the sounds can be heard as anonymous murmurs of another life. If there is life going on elsewhere, then it is nameless and without form. Between places, the room is also between different states, at no point fixing itself within relation to the broader world. Despite its minuscule size, the room is a space of disorientation, structured by a series of interchangeable surfaces, each of which strip the guest of his or her sense of belonging to the world. In the motel, we are far from home. In this outpost, the intimacy and interiority of the home has been lost, and we have been assaulted by the horror of the *il y a*. Yet if the room expresses the *il y a*, then it is not strictly reducible to it: 'It is never attached to an *object that is*, and because of this I call it anonymous', Levinas writes (2005, 48). The anonymity of the *il y a* precludes it from being firmly lodged in place. Resisting a 'personal form', it makes no sense to speak of inside and out, subject and object, given that such a distinction would presuppose a beginning and an end to the *il y a* (Levinas 2001, 52).

As to the night, it is the exemplary experience of the there is, 'if the term experience were not inapplicable to a situation which involves the total exclusion of light' (52). Thus, the night positions itself in an interstitial and ambiguous spatiality, at once given to experience while at the same time withdrawing from it. The primordial anxiety of the night is absolute. Thanks to its power to deform things, the night enters the home as an invader of presence, not as pure negation that would destroy everything in its wake, but as a 'universal absence [which] is in turn a presence, an absolutely unavoidable presence' (52). In the face(lessness) of this nocturnal silence, the subject is pacified and desubjectified before a silence, which, if interwoven with the materiality of the home, is nevertheless infinite. As such, the night induces anxiety in its capacity to disguise itself in things, and in turn, to make those things ambassadors of an impersonal enigma. Moreover, the I does not remain as a bystander to this dissolution of form, but is precisely ensnared in and through the night: 'What we call the I is itself submerged by the night, invaded, depersonalized, stifled by it' (53). With the *il y a*, the egological relation to the world is ruptured by an otherness, which, if having a face, is a face that refuses to be tied down: 'There is a nocturnal space, but it is no longer an empty space…Darkness fills it like a content; it is full, but full of the nothingness of everything' (53). Into this 'heavy atmosphere belonging to no one', the night testifies to something outside of itself, to that which cannot be contained by darkness, even if it is only in and through darkness that the *il y a* can speak (53). And then the I disappears, and what remains is that stubborn and elemental residue, which is there all along in the daytime, but only now revealed in its specificity as the horrific 'menace of space' (55).

Against this elemental horror, the home – in radical contradistinction to the motel room in which we hear anonymous rumblings through thin walls – provides both a concrete and a metaphysical sanctuary to rupture the 'plenum of the element' (Levinas 1969, 156). In this retreat where I return to myself, 'set back from the anonymity of the earth', I am separated from the elements insofar as the home adjourns and delays the elements, preserving their presence at the door to the home (156). This distancing is taken up in an experiential fashion in the specificity of a home that assumes a gaze upon the world; thus Levinas writes, 'The ambiguity of distance, both removal and connection, is lifted by the window that makes possible a look that dominates, a look of him who escapes looks, the look that contemplates' (156). This poetics of the window is foreshadowed in Bachelard, who also employs the screen as a means of forging distance:

> We are at home, hidden, and looking *outside*. In a house in the countryside, a window is an open eye, a gaze over the plain, at the distant sky, and – in a profoundly philosophical sense – at the *exterior* world. To those who dream not at but *behind* their window, behind a little window, behind the attic skylight, the house gives a sense of an *exterior* whose difference from the interior increases as the interiority and Universe is made explicit by the impressions of a hidden being who sees the window framed by a window. (Bachelard 2011, 84)

For Levinas and Bachelard, the window is a framing device. Through it, the world is filtered by way of an invisible gaze not only upon the world but also *against* the world. There is, then, an asymmetry in the home, in which the dweller has the freedom to leave the elements as they are, or otherwise transform 'nature into a world' through the work of labour (Levinas 1969, 157). As understood by Levinas, the home is diffused throughout with the presence of a warm humanity, in which the 'the primordial function of the home' as separating the dweller from the elements, leads to nothing less

FIGURE 1.3 *Quai des Celestins, Paris.*

than the birth of the world itself (157). This birth is transformative: with it, the elements are fixed in both place and time, conferring an almost aesthetic quality upon what is otherwise formless and terrible.

The enormous space

Levinas presents to the reader a vision of the home as a sanctuary, defending the dweller against the anonymity of the elements, which threatens to destabilize if not destroy our enjoyment of things. More than a material unit to fend off the cold, the home has a transformative capacity to tame the anonymity of elemental existence. Without the home, the subject would lose their separation as a subject, and thus become part of the anonymous infrastructure of elemental existence, dissolving the singularity of selfhood. In the phobic subject, we are confronted with an amplification of the insecurity inherent in the Levinasian dweller. As we will see, time and again, the phobic subject's being-in-the-world carries with it the trauma of being separated from home, where home signifies, with Levinas, not simply a geometrical unit, but the very source of stability and protection. We shall give voice to the experience of travelling beyond the home in further chapters. There, we will see how the landscape of the phobic subject is defined at all times by the felt distance from home. For now, let us remain within the home, attending to its ambivalent role as both a source of freedom and servitude.

As restorative in character, the home provides the grounds of the subject's existence, and it is precisely this grounding that is instable in agoraphobic subjects. This concern over the delineation and protection of boundaries is not novel to phobic subjects, but remains intact as an invariant feature of subjective existence. In the case of phobic subjects – especially agoraphobes – the insecurity assumes a heightened sensibility, rendering the porousness and contingency of boundaries visible. Against this background, particular spatial configurations bring to light a primordial anxiety concerning the very place of the subject. Yi-Fu Tuan provides us with a concrete illustration of the need for spatial ordering amongst certain subjects:

At the Ittleson Center [for disturbed children], the open land surrounding the building is partitioned to advance purposive activities. Fences are erected to define small areas, each of which has a clearly assigned function: this is a bicycle area, that is a garden area. Interior space, too, is carefully delineated according to function and purpose … The children need to draw closed, safe circles around themselves; the open circle, the boundless area, and any space with ambiguous edges provoke anxiety rather than pleasurable excitement. (Tuan 1979, 203–204)

Into this uncertain world, the home emerges as a closed circle, edged off from an otherwise infinite abyss. Intolerant of the dizzying anonymity of a world outside of the home, the agoraphobe withdraws from this open circle, seeking in the home a landscape that is immunized to contingency. An amplified vision of the 'boundless area' that elicits anxiety can be found in the literary imagination of J. G. Ballard's short story 'The Enormous Space' (Ballard 2002).

We find in this story the fruition of the agoraphobe's attachment to home as a retreat from the world, whereupon the home becomes the site where the 'latent birth of the world is produced' (Levinas 1969, 157). The premise of the story is simple, and the philosophical value we find in Ballard's writings, as ever, derives not from the narrative, but from his acute and penetrating study of the intertwinement and disturbances between inner and outer space. A divorced man, Mr Ballantyne, decides one day to not go to work. Instead, he will retreat back into his home in an innocuous suburb in London, where he will undergo an experiment:

> I would never again step through the front door. I would accept the air and light, and the electric power and water that continued to flow through the meters. But otherwise I would depend on the outside world for nothing. I would eat only whatever food I could find within the house. After that I would rely on time and space to sustain me. (Ballard 2002, 698)

What follows is a careful study of the gradual transformation and eventual disintegration of the rapport between Ballantyne and his home.

Our 'Crusoe' begins by calculating his rations, burning the traces of his past, which 'come to life briefly in the flame, and then write themselves into the dust', and rediscovering his home, which now assumes an increasingly more airy atmosphere (700–701). At first glance, the alliance between Ballard's solitary dweller and his home appears reinforced and renewed, with both now enjoying a greater freedom than was previously available during his contact with the outside world. Indeed, this rediscovery of the home is phrased at first as a moment of privileged access to a world that is otherwise concealed by habit and the dead weight of a sedimented past, 'as in those few precious moments when one returns from holiday and sees one's home in its true light' (705). Far from becoming constricted, this shared space opens itself up, such that, in the words of Ballantyne, 'when I wake in the morning I almost feel myself on some Swiss mountain-top, with half the sky below me' (701).

The dizzying view afforded in the newly discovered home coincides with a rectification of his values, the house now reduced to its fundamental structure devoid of its temporal legacy as a home of the past: 'I am free at last to think only of the essential elements of existence – the visual continuum around me, and the play of air and light. The house begins to resemble an advanced mathematical surface, a three-dimensional chessboard. The pieces have yet to be placed, but I feel them forming in my mind' (701). After a month of this topophilia, a change occurs. Now, instead of forming a union, the home begins to depart from the topological structure previously inscribed in Ballantyne's body and mind. Rooms seem to appear from nowhere, and another past, different from his own, seeps in through the floors and walls: 'These quiet streets were built on the site of the old Croydon aerodrome, and it is almost as if the perspectives of the former grass runways have returned to haunt these neat suburban lawns and the minds of those who tend them' (703). In addition to the home's new growth, perspective becomes displaced, and the very geometry of the home assumes an increasingly distorted set of angles:

> I have strayed into an unfamiliar area of the room, somewhere between Margaret's bathroom and the fitted cupboards. The remainder of the room sheers away from me, the walls pushed back by the light…Another door leads to a wide and silent corridor, clearly unentered for years. There is no staircase, but far away there are entrances to other rooms, filled with the sort of light that glows from X-ray viewing screens…The house is revealing itself to me in the most subtle way…The true dimensions of this house may be exhilarating to perceive, but from now on I will sleep downstairs. Time and space are not necessarily on my side. (705)

Ballard's sober description captures the moments in which our phobic dweller loses grip on the home, as its closely guarded set of rules slowly disband, invoking at once Levinas but also Lyotard in *The Inhuman*: 'Domesticity is over, and probably it never existed, except as a dream of the old child awakening and destroying it on awakening' (Lyotard 1992, 201). From a manageable yet rarefied set of contours, the home now slides irreversibly into the anonymous state of existence it was originally intended to defend its dweller against. As this mutation unfolds, the shift from an agoraphobic topophilia – a love of the home as an emblem of human warmth – towards a claustrophobic topophobia – a repulsion of the home as a beacon of inhuman alterity – begins. The Pascalian void of outer space is seized by the home, which, in its subtle expansion, reveals itself as being on the inside. Now, the home is no longer marked as the retreat, and in order to counter this eternal expansion, microcosmic space must be invented in the midst of spatial uncertainty. Thus, Ballantyne makes a decision: 'The house enlarges itself around me. The invasion of light which revealed its true dimensions has now reached the ground floor. To keep my bearings I have been forced to retreat into the kitchen, where I have moved my mattress and blankets. Now and then I venture into the hall and search the looming perspectives' (Ballard 2002, 707).

We are at the final stages of domestic existence, where agoraphobia and claustrophobia are no longer distinct conditions, but instead mutually edifying responses to an elemental and anonymous being, which renders even the most prosaic of objects indistinct zones of materiality: 'The cooker, refrigerator and dishwasher have become anonymous objects ...' (707). In 'the almost planetary vastness

FIGURE 1.4 *Rue Oberkampf, Paris.*

of this house', Ballard's suburban explorer succumbs to collapse, having murdered a colleague and cannibalized the TV repairman. In the end, Ballantyne's body, as with the assemblage of anonymous objects that surround him, loses all referential meaning, and becomes part of the fabric of the real: 'The perspective lines flow from me, enlarging the interior of the compartment. Soon I will lie beside her, in a palace of ice that will crystallise around us, finding at last the still centre of the world which came to claim me' (707–709).

* * *

Ballard's story is a parable of the agoraphobe. In the grotesque scenario of the agoraphobe regressing back to a primitive form, we cannot help but be reminded of William James and his envisioning of agoraphobia as having no place in a 'civilized man' but instead belonging to the domain of feral animals and other such primitive forms of life (James 1950). We are also reminded of Freud's incisive comments on the function of the phobic object to master and conceal an anxiety greater than that of what is presented before one's eyes. In the case of Ballantyne, we have an exemplary illustration of the attempt to contain anxiety. Ballantyne's retreat from the world consists of a refusal to contend with the uncertainty of a world that resists conforming to the egocentric perspective of a self incapable of negotiating with alterity. Thus, the home enters existence as a response to the problem of anxiety. Yet, the successful retreat into the home as a response to the problem of the outside is tenable only insofar as the home operates under the logic of what Ballard terms elsewhere, a 'benevolent psychopathology' (Ballard 1991, 138). As the home betrays this benevolence, so its protective form dissolves, and anxiety reappears in another guise. It is a movement we will be confronted with time and again, a movement of both concealment and evasion peculiar to the relation between anxiety and its object.

'A hurricane in Paris'

In both Levinas and Ballard, we bear witness to the home's refusal to be fully mastered and possessed, at once revealing itself to be a site of love and horror. Alongside Ballard's hyperreal vision, Levinas accents the ambivalence running throughout the home. If the home makes room for the dweller to re-collect themselves, and in doing so, forge a spatiality that both suspends and defers the 'uncertain future of the element', then it does so through sealing itself off from things in order to create a world within itself, as Levinas has it: 'Proceeding from the dwelling, possession, accomplished by the quasi-miraculous grasp of a thing in the night, in the *apeiron* of prime matter, discovers a world' (Levinas 1969, 163). This birth of a world takes place as an act of mastery and possession, such that even within the night, we remain open to the world as graspable. To grasp the elements in their impersonality, we must, as Levinas says, 'run up against the very strangeness of the earth' (142). The ambivalence of the Levinasian home is thus not a question of it revealing several faces, but rather of it refusing to face us at all. Without interval and without origin, the *il y a* has no side against which and through which we might approach it. Lacking face, the element conceals itself from within, yet deposits itself nevertheless as a trace of 'the fathomless obscurity of matter', including that of the home itself (159).

We turn now from images of anonymity and obscurity to that of warmth and clarity. We assume this turn through Bachelard. Our reason for turning to Bachelard – a turn we will make on several occasions – is to give specificity to the felt experience of the home. In fact, despite Bachelard's ostensible occupation with felicitous spatiality, we will see that ultimately he is closer to Levinas than may be obvious. Bachelard's text, *The Poetics of Space*, is critical given that, for him, the bodily basis of the home is as important as the homely basis of the body (Bachelard 1994). This idea is crystallized in the main thesis of the book: 'All really inhabited space bears the essence of the notion of home' (5). Far from the body as a passive receiver of the external world, Bachelard's formula implies a reversibility between home and body. If all inhabited space bears the essence of home, then this is because home is created in the dynamic spark between inhabited and bodily space. It is for this reason that Bachelard cites the proverb 'We bring our *lares* with us' approvingly (5). That we bring our lares with us rather than leaving them behind means that ontological security is grounded in the centrality of the home, a precarious relation exemplified in the case of agoraphobia. Despite this ontological confidence, Bachelard is especially sensitive to the precariousness of the home, and also to its role in both the unification of the subject as well the fragmentation of the subject on an experiential level. Thus, this movement from Levinas to Bachelard is a movement towards specificity and thematization; it is, in other words, a movement that returns us to the concrete place of the home in its philic and phobic aspects.

Bachelard begins with Levinas, in asking, what is the home? If Levinas situates the home in relation to elemental and non-elemental being, then for Bachelard, the situation is no less mythical. For him, the importance of the home is guaranteed through its role as mediator between memory and imagination, and to this extent is 'a real cosmos in every sense of the word' (4). Once inhabited, the home gains its power through fortifying itself as the locus of memory and imagination. Indeed, it is thanks to the home that memory and imagination are able to work together in their 'mutual deepening' (5). The home, as such, is a place of monumentalization, and it allows us in no uncertain terms to 'live fixations of happiness ... by reliving memories of protection' (6). As with the Levinasian recollection, this place of dreaming serves to restore and renew the dweller back to their original unity. Even more than this, the house, as the primary home, is what 'thrusts aside contingencies', and without this seal of protection, human being 'would be a dispersed being' (7). In a rejoinder to Heidegger, Bachelard writes, 'before he is "cast into the world" ... man is laid in the cradle of the house' (7). For this reason, the Bachelardian home is described in terms of possessing 'maternal features' – a 'bosom' – and the site of an original existence that both contains and compresses time (7). This primordial dwelling is not simply the realm of one's own personal existence. Rather, it gestures towards a 'pre-human' or 'immemorial' plane of existence from where personal existence emerges (10).

Here, Bachelard joins Levinas in resisting the localization of home by rendering it an ontological concept. The continuity of the subject is guaranteed thanks to the fact that each of the homes he or she inhabits bears witness to a more abstract home that is enacted in these subsequent dwellings. All of this is thanks to the fact that the home reanimates and recollects what was already present – the literally unforgettable home that is manifest as, in Bachelard's terms, 'the embodiment of dreams' (15). To approach this dream, Bachelard conceives a methodology, which he terms 'topoanalysis', allowing us to study 'the sites of our intimate lives' (8). If successful, topoanalysis would allow us to see beyond our perception of space and time as a series of discrete points in order to recognize that beneath this abstraction spatiality compresses time. This recognition is restorative: through it, our relation to place is renewed thanks to our heightened attention to the power of place as rendering memories 'motionless' (9). Against this backdrop, Bachelard emerges as a thinker of peaceful nights, for whom the home is the emblematic shell, into which we retreat without resistance. Indeed, if sleep provides us with a trace of the elemental horror in Levinas, then in Bachelard it offers us quite the opposite. He writes, 'And when we reach the very end of the labyrinths of sleep, when we attain to the regions of deep slumber, we may perhaps experience a type of repose that is pre-human; pre-human, in this case, approaching the immemorial' (10).

In his earlier work, *Earth and Reveries of Repose*, Bachelard gestures towards several of the themes that will become central in his later work. Already in his earlier thinking, the home at night assumes a pivotal place in his thought. Describing the home as a protection *'against the night'*, Bachelard invokes the twilight home as a softly lit beacon of intimacy in the midst of cosmic space (Bachelard 2011, 82). In opposition to the endless black, the 'nocturnal life' of the home stations itself between worlds, fending itself against that 'huge beast that is everywhere, like some universal threat' (83). Here, Bachelard rages against the sphere of cosmic darkness in favour of a night that is available to the home, and 'for our night to be human, it has to be against the inhuman night' (84). His language of the home being *against* the world, *against* the night, *against* the outside is a testament to his genuine topophilia, a love that borders on an equally volatile anxiety.

This intimate sanctuary, which inside of itself reveals a series of nests and nooks, requires a certain type of relation to the outside world in order for it to function, as such. As we join Bachelard in his Paris apartment, we find a discontent with the 'big city' and its 'superimposed boxes' (Bachelard 1994, 26). What Bachelard finds especially disturbing about the Parisian apartment is the lack of roots, which is compounded by the jarring assemblage of space built upon space, crammed into a unit, which deprives the dweller not only of the 'heroism of stair climbing', but perhaps more importantly, its fundamental lack of 'cosmicity' (27). Bachelard's critique centres on the synthetic nature of urban space. Lacking roots, the home in the city is unable to grow, and thus at no point does the home exist in an edifying relation with the elements, Bachelard laments how 'our houses are no longer aware of the storms of the outside universe...A hurricane in Paris has not the same personal offensiveness toward the dreamer that it has towards the hermit's house' (27). Confronted with insomnia on the Place Maubert, Bachelard's response is to invoke 'metaphors of the ocean' (28). Rendering the chaotic movements of Paris an oceanic lullaby, proceeding even to transform the hum of cars to the sound of distant thunder, Bachelard is finally able to sleep: 'My bed is a small boat lost at sea; that sudden whistling is the wind in the sails' (28).

Far from drifting away from our phobic preoccupations, we are instead gliding closer and closer to the core of anxiety. The reason for this is that Bachelard reveals to us the captive power of the home as a sanctuary in an otherwise hostile world. Like Ballard's home dweller, Bachelard's sensibility is to retreat and draw the curtains

FIGURE 1.5 *Place Maubert, Paris.*

on a world, which can never compare to that of the interior of the home. Indeed, the very existence of the outside only gains its quality as real thanks to being offset by the warmth of the home. One need only think of Bachelard's evocation of the 'great dreamer of curtains', Baudelaire, who 'added "heavy draperies that hung down to the floor"... to protect the winter-grit house from the cold' (39). This ornate gesture serves not only to adorn the home in a thick veil, but also to mould and define the outside according to the needs of the home's interior. This reshaping of the outside through the lens of the home's interior finds its extension in Bachelard's account of the snow-covered home, against which the winter beyond the home becomes a 'non-house', marking the homogeneity of whiteness (40). As the outside world loses its definition, so the interior of the home gains an increased value as being sealed off. In this respect, Bachelard relies on a certain kind of relation between the house and the universe in order to privilege the former as centre of things, he writes in no uncertain terms: 'The house invites mankind to heroism to cosmic proportions. It is an instrument with which to confront the cosmos' (46).

Between claustrophobia and agoraphobia

Bachelard's voyage between domestic space and cosmic space is mirrored with the movement between inside and out. Towards the end of *The Poetics of Space*, Bachelard investigates the topic of inside and outside explicitly. There, he will engage with Henri Michaux's prose-poem *L'espace aux ombres*, finding within it evidence of the home's steadfast refusal to withstand the elements, but also an admission of the home's fundamental porousness:

> Space, but you cannot even conceive the horrible inside-outside that real space is.
>
> Certain (shades) especially, girding their loins one last time, make a desperate effort to 'exist as a single unity'. But they rue the day. I met one of them.
>
> Destroyed by punishment, it was reduced to a noise, a thunderous noise.
>
> An immense world still heard it, but it no longer existed, having become simply and solely a noise, which was to rumble

on for centuries longer, but was fated to die out *completely*, as though it had never existed. (216–217)

In his response to the poem, Bachelard uncovers a series of spatial anxieties situated at the intersection between inside and out. His first response to Michaux is to recognize that what is destroyed in the 'horrible inside-outside' is 'a spirit that has lost its "being-there"' (217). This de-spiritualization takes form in another kind of spatiality, 'a confused hum that *cannot be located*' (217). Space becomes not simply an echo of something that still resounds in the present, but a formless murmur, elemental, we might add. And now, in the space that is left over as a remnant, the thing becomes impregnated with the quality of being a 'sonorous echo from the vaults of hell' (217). This hellish place, no longer serving its function in keeping the elements at the door, instead serves to inadvertently invite those anonymous forces precisely to the heart of the home. Once this vault of hell enters the home world, there it 'is condemned to repeat the world of its evil intention, a world which, being imprinted in being, has overthrown being' (217). 'A part of us', Bachelard continues on this doomed note, 'is always in hell', always exposed, that is, to the boundless space that forms a swarming yet non-localizable point in and around the home.

Following the partial dissolution of inside and out, perspective is lost, and what is 'heard on the outside' may just as easily be situated on the inside (217). The rot sets in, 'being is slowly digesting its nothingness', and time, alongside space, is also dragged into this collapse of order (217). As space enters the throes of death, a final attempt is made at seeking primordial unity. As the attempt fails, the *genius loci* that originally gave birth to place is now 'the backwash of expiring being' (217). Throughout this hellish ordeal, what is painful is not the collapse of inside and out, as such. After all, as Bachelard reminds us, spatiality is dynamic, and inside and outside are 'always ready to be reversed' (218). The pain dwells not in their separation, but in their contact within the 'border-line surface between inside and outside' (218). In this ungrounded place, lucidity is disbanded: 'Intimate space loses its clarity, while exterior space loses its void, void being the raw material of possibility of being. We are banished from the realm of possibility' (218).

To withdraw, as Levinas and Bachelard urge, is no longer possible. Where, Bachelard asks, are we to live now that the home has become the haunt of hell? The fear has no face, and nor does it pertain to specific content, less even the incursion of memory returning from the grave and finding expression in the home of the living. Rather, we are in the sphere of the Levinasian *il y a* – a realm that takes being itself, in its nameless indifference, as the source of horror. Into this elemental existence, there is no place to find refuge, and as a result, 'the mind has lost its geometrical homeland and the spirit is drifting' (218).

Bachelard comes to the end of his reading of Michaux:

> I accept it as a phobia of inner space, as though hostile remoteness had already become oppressive in the tiny cell represented by inner space. With this poem, Henri Michaux has juxtaposed in us claustrophobia and agoraphobia; he has aggravated the line of demarcation between outside and inside. (220)

We are on the edge of intimacy. On this verge, agoraphobia and claustrophobia mark two mutually edifying ways of negotiating with the anonymity and alterity of space. This movement from inside to outside, from enclosure to exposure, delineates not a paring of opposites, but a union, in which both phobias operate within the same space. As if by accident, Bachelard discovers the 'dark entity' (in his own telling formulation) guarding the home from the 'horrible outside-inside', and in doing so, reveals the structure of the home as being defined by the juxtaposition between agoraphobia and claustrophobia. Here, Bachelard revolves around the vertiginous limit of the home, a limit in which both the excess of space and the absence of space hinge on the same anxiety, as Bachelard says by way of Jules Supervielle: '*Trop d'espace nous étouffe beaucoup plus que s'il n'y en avait pas assez*' ('Too much space smothers us much more than if there were not enough') (221).

The panic room

To end this reflection on the sickness of the home, let us return to the home at night. We see now that the act of waking up prematurely forges a bridge in which claustrophobia and agoraphobia not only meet, but also dissolve into a joint anxiety. In the peaceful sleep of the Bachelardian reverie, we take the home as a sanctum for the agoraphobe, a place of retreat into which boundaries are sealed and enclosure is contained. As the outside, in its elemental anonymity, presses down upon the agoraphobe, so the home becomes reinforced as the centre of stability. Rising up against the world, the home establishes a world within itself, indeed going so far as to reshape the world around its core, such that the movement and inhibition of the agoraphobe is guided at all times by the axis of the home. In all this, both Levinas and Bachelard reveal the overarching significance of the home as a mode of delimiting infinite space – and thus, infinite terror – into a domesticated and constricted nest.

The intermediary between claustrophobia and agoraphobia in spatial form can be expressed by the image of the home as a *panic room*. Not content with the home as a container, Bachelard and Levinas frame the home as a shelter inside of a shelter. For Bachelard, we can think here of his love of nooks, corners and nests. For Levinas, meanwhile, the space within a space is confirmed in the image of the dwelling giving birth to the world. This overlapping of enclosures upon one another takes spatial form in that of the panic room: a double of the home, the entrance of which is veiled to the outside, but yet from within, the dweller is able to survey the space outside of the panic room. This paranoiac spatiality is not a departure from the home, but instead its logical conclusion, so far as it fortifies the subject against the hostility of the outside world, but only at the expense of simultaneously imprisoning him or her.

In the direction of claustrophobia, then, this domestic container, idyllic and serene, reveals another dimension to its sickness, whereupon the urge is not to remain within it, but to flee. From where does this urge to flee emerge when waking up into a home that has been transformed from a locus of intimacy and tenderness to a site of alienation and anonymity? For that matter, how to read the walls of a home when they become impregnated with an oppressive dimension? Far from fortifying the subject against an anonymous world, which is to be avoided as much as possible, the home betrays the trust of the dweller, carrying within it the seed of its own alienation, the reaction to which is one of repulsion.

Under such circumstances, the home is thought of as being a hostile space, in some sense opposed to the existence of the dweller insomuch as the subject feels trapped in the home: that is, of the dweller not only becoming part of the wall, but actually being *buried* within the wall. Furthermore, the same dynamic is carried through the world more broadly, and, as we will see in subsequent chapters, the *idée fixe* of the phobic subject's anxiety is the transmutation of the world – including the world of the body and of others – from a fully realized, familiar and homely nexus of places to a partly derealized, unfamiliar and unhomely grid of points, each of which threatens to disintegrate the structure of the subject.

In the home at night, spatiality becomes deformed. This incursion of elemental existence breaks the idealism of the home and returns it to a fabric of the raw matter, depriving us of space in which we can freely move and breathe. In return, this loss of boundary destroys the distinction between subject and world, forcing both aspects – the dweller and his room – to inhabit the same anonymous cavity, without any line to separate them. The anxiety of being swallowed or otherwise destroyed by space appears in both agoraphobia and claustrophobia, with only their contours and accents changing. In each case, what is at stake is the elimination of the subject through a lack of differentiation between things, reducing those things to a 'plenum of the element', and in turn destroying all spaces of retreat (Levinas 1969, 156).

This movement between claustrophobia and agoraphobia is thus a movement not only of enclosure and exposure, of outer space to inner space, but also of inhalation and exhalation, of breathlessness and breathfulness. Indeed, the image we often find in the case of claustrophobia is that of being buried alive. From a psychoanalytical perspective, the anxiety returns us to the first home, that of the womb, thus Freud will write of phantasies of this place as 'contain[ing] an explanation of the remarkable dread that many people have of being buried alive... Moreover, the act of birth is the first experience of anxiety, and thus the source and prototype of the affect of anxiety' (Freud 2010, 377). The anxiety over being stuck in place is at once an anxiety of space as revealing to us something horrific and abject as it is how our bodies, in their porousness and contingency, respond to this image. The task we face now is to give voice to this bodily experience.

CHAPTER TWO

Under the Skin

It's nothing: I am the Thing.

(SARTRE, *NAUSEA*)

The supermarket

16 January 2011. It is a cold morning on Rue Saint-Antoine. For the last twenty minutes, you have been pacing up and down outside Franprix, a small supermarket. You are on the outside looking in, peering through the window, towards the back of the store. A strip of lights illuminates the place aggressively, saturating the environment in a homogeneous tone, depriving it of contours and shadows. You are hovering at the door, sensing the weight of the light as you verge towards the entrance before once more pulling away into the cold. Eventually, you make your way through the electric doors, walking beyond the gate, which automatically swings open upon your arrival but leaves no space to exit, and thus entraps you in the interior of the supermarket. You straddle the last remnants of the door, absorbing the proximity to the exit before beginning your long voyage in and through the many aisles, recesses and alcoves of the supermarket.

As soon as the view of the door is out of sight, the heaviness of the fluorescent light begins to infiltrate your body. At first, you sense it as a low level humming in your head, but before long the humming transforms into a thudding, which can then be visually observed as vibrations in the supermarket itself. A series of jagged lines distorts your perception of the fruit, causing the apples to obtrude and deform before reforming into the orthodox shape of an apple. Disoriented, you turn away. To survive this expedition, you have dissected the supermarket into different regions, just as you did on the bridge. These zones circumscribe where you can and cannot place yourself in the world. By the door, which is now out of view, you are able to hold ground, reassured at all times by your relation to the exit. But in the space, there is depth as well as light. The greater you stray from the exit, the greater your anxiety becomes. For you, the mission to the frozen goods will carry with it a great danger, such that you remain unsure if you will ever return the same person. In the recesses of this vast space, the distance to the exit feels immense, as if occupying another world, now inaccessible to you.

Your grip on the cart is tight. The prop serves to steady you in the world, supporting your whole body with its solidity. In the absence of this item, you would feel as though you were floating haphazardly from one point in space to another, without ever being the centre of things. Despite this slippage, your thinking is precise: at all times, you retain a vigilance over both the environment and your body. You keep a constant eye on the signs above the aisles, lest you risk getting lost in this labyrinth. Above all, you are concerned that the light might cause you to faint, leaving you inert on the floor, as other people trample upon your body. That this fate has yet to happen does nothing to dissuade you of a conviction that this place is fundamentally opposed to your existence. The aggression of the light is beginning to damage you. Your anxiety is tinged with hostility. Other people are now experienced as obstacles that must be conquered in order for you to get out of here alive.

Pausing, you try to retain control over the body. You are in the frozen aisle, situated at the very depth of the supermarket. Within this frosted world, you see your face reflected in a freezer door. Through the icy veneer, the face emerges as a dissolving set of images; your two eyes, now gaunt and hollow, burrow through the door, as if they had detached themselves from the surrounding region of flesh known as your face. That you continue to recognize your face as your own is nothing more than a formality. Experientially and existentially, your face has detached itself from the sense of being your own. In its place, a trace remains, which becomes increasingly unrecognizable the more you interrogate it. You turn to your hand.

FIGURE 2.1 *Franprix, Rue Saint-Antoine, Paris.*

It looks numb, distant, an artefact that no longer belongs to you. The hand is held above you, pointing towards a non-visible skyline. Is this the same hand that belongs to you in the home, where it assumes the familiar presence linking you not only to your body, but also to a personal history? In the supermarket, the body part assumes a pallid quality: no longer a hand but a memory of a hand that once belonged to you.

Several minutes have passed, and the urge to flee is intensifying. Alongside the alien hand, your legs have begun to tremble. The very ground beneath you feels as though it is slippery and unable to support your body. Alongside this movement of becoming ungrounded, the cart, previously a beacon of safety, is now losing form. Time is undergoing a series of violent palpitations, at once drawn and compressed, and you decide now is the chance to leave. Before you, several people are waiting to pay for their groceries. You contemplate abandoning everything. Against your instincts, you will see the ordeal through to its end. The four items in the trolley make their way through, a plastic bag is grabbed and the items are semi-packed. Blinded and rendered speechless by your anxiety, you force the credit card into the machine and wait for the code to be accepted while at all times keeping an eye on the exit. Once outside, you take a deep breath, look back into the foreign world from where you have come and shake your head in a state of disbelief.

Experiences of light

Any phenomenology that seeks to approach anxiety must contend in the first place with the central role of the body. As the most familiar and homely of things, the bearer of our sense of self, and the means in and through which our subjectivity assumes an expressive form, the body also reveals another side to it. If the body is 'one's own', then it is such only in a strange way, at all times leading a life of its own irrespective of how 'I' assume it as a personal dimension. From time to time, the body dissents from us, manifesting a series of rhythms and responses, none of which fully belongs to us. Anxiety reveals to us an especially striking way in which the body appears to take leave of its senses, responding to the world in a way that is often confounding and enigmatic. From where does the body's anxiety derive: from 'me' the personal subject, or, from another side of the body that senses a danger that I myself am not yet privy to? The very question suggests a dualism at the heart of the subject. If the body is cognizant of a world that I have yet to encounter despite being physically placed in that world, then can it be said that I am truly identifiable with my body? These questions and others will be of special concern to us. We will approach the role of the body from different levels, finding therein a series of increasingly complex issues, which challenge not only the scope of phenomenology, but also the notion of the self itself. Throughout, the body will appear for us as not only an expression of anxiety, but also anxiety's object.

The body's being is worldly. At all times, we are not simply situated in a place in an abstract or geometrical sense. Rather, our being is expressively spatial, taken up in the things around us, including supermarkets. A supermarket appears for us not only as a place where we purchase groceries, but as the site of a drama, which is both banal and significant at once. Everything within this space is mediated by something that exceeds it, an atmosphere that belongs to the supermarket itself but also pours into the surrounding world. Indeed, nothing in the supermarket is unaffected by the surrounding world, and we carry our anxieties as much into the supermarket as we do into our homes.

Take the light as an illustration. Consider the experience of exiting a dark room and opening the door upon a world of sunlight. As you pass through the thick door, the shard of light strikes your eyes violently, causing you to partially see only a few feet in front of you. You grimace and raise your hand to your brow. Rays of sunlight pierce through the cracks where your fingers meet. You move your head towards the darker earth, finding in the surface of the ground a respite from the sky above. Slowly but surely, your eyes reconfigure so as to see the world anew. Now, the sunlight seems to recede, integrating itself into the broader world, and allowing you to finally attain a clearer perspective of the street before you. We know from experiences as simple as exiting a dark room and entering the world of sunlight how our relation to light is dynamic and imbued with an affective value. Not only is light relationally defined in terms of where we have come from and where we are going to, but this dynamism carries with it a thematic quality as well, which is significant in its pervasiveness. If light can put us at ease in the world through the creation of corners, shadows and nooks to withdraw into it, then it can also render us ill-at-ease by exposing us to a lack of definition in the world, depriving the world of its homely attributes.

In the supermarket, our concern is with a certain type of light, characterized in part by harshness and homogeneity. For the anxious subject, the light is not an incidental background against which their distress takes root. Rather, the light itself becomes a defining object of their experience. The riddle of how light can induce the urge to flee leads us from an empirical question concerning light as an object in the world to the presentation of light as a certain way of ordering and interpreting the world. At first glance, we see that light is an objective feature of the supermarket – it has a reality independent of the subject. The light is there, illuminating the supermarket. The anxious subject is aware of the light, and long before he steps foot in the place, the light has already installed itself as a habit in the body. When entering the supermarket, a shift in attention occurs, such that the body, in its anticipatory anxiety, reflexively attunes itself to the light above. The subject feels impeded by the light, as though it exerted a physical pressure. Not only does light enter the body by way of the eyes, it also forms a surrounding force in and around the body, such that the experience of light transforms the whole of the body and not just the eyes that see the world.

From where does the anxiety derive: the light itself or the subject? Strikingly, this is not the first time this question has been asked. In fact, the relation between anxiety and lighting has been researched from several perspectives (cf. Hazell and Wilkins 1990; Marks 1987; Saul 2001; Watts and Wilkins 1989). By way of an example, in a paper concerning the relation between fluorescent lighting and agoraphobia, Hazell and Wilkins report that fluorescent lighting plays a key role in contributing to the anxiety of agoraphobic people (Hazell and Wilkins 1990, 591). Notably, the authors single out pulsations of light as being a prominent factor, in turn leading to headaches, eyestrain and a faster heart rate. Of their findings, the authors write, 'The results indicate that conventional pulsating fluorescent lighting produces a response in the nervous system which is not registered as a sensation of flicker but ultimately is responsible for a variety of bodily symptoms' (595). The idea, then, is that the body interprets the pulsations of the light as signals of anxiety, which are inextricably bound with the experience of frailty and danger common to the anxious subject, as they write the following: 'It is possible that some agoraphobia begins when symptoms associated with anxiety are elicited by supermarket lighting' (596). Limiting their study to a causal perspective, it is hardly surprising that the authors conclude that the onset of agoraphobia might be avoided by the invention of 'specially tinted glasses', which would be worn in the supermarket (596). To speak alongside Hazell and Wilkins, therefore, it makes no sense to think of anxiety as constituting a world. Rather, anxiety can be localized as a mis-interpretation of objective phenomena such as light pulsations.

We wish to move beyond the Hazell and Wilkins model of anxious experiences of light by addressing the relational dynamic involved in the supermarket. As we assume a phenomenological perspective on the experience, we see that, as with all instances of phobic anxiety, the mood is neither situated in the body nor in the world alone, but instead in the rapport between each of these aspects. Indeed, phenomenologically, the subjective experience of oneself being anxious is at the same time an experience of the world as inciting anxiety. The anxious experience of the light is not projected into the world by an anxious mind. Nor does the anxious subject 'imagine' or even 'hallucinate' the light as inducing symptoms. The experimental research on agoraphobia and light establishes that even in objective terms, the fluorescent lighting is a particular hazard for the anxious subject. But we do not require data of this kind to demonstrate that the light is real. That there is an anxious experience of the lighting testifies to the role of the body in establishing the mood of the world. The experience of the lighting in the supermarket is an experience of the world *as* an anxious place, taken from the centrality of the lived body. The lighting, to cite Merleau-Ponty, expresses 'the total life of the subject' (Merleau-Ponty 2012, 296). In other words, along with the body faced with the environment, the lighting coalesces into a specific experience, whereby the florescence of the beam is given its feel not through the objective pulsations being emitted, but through the expressive and synthesizing role of the body.

As we extend our discussion from light to the surroundings of the supermarket, we see how this relational dynamic is played out more broadly. Let us turn to the door. The door of the supermarket seals us from the world, enclosing us within the supermarket. The door is a border, not only between different spaces, but also between different bodily modes of being. As a border, the door delineates distinctive zones that exist both spatially and corporeally. Here, we can ask, how is it possible for the subject to transform himself so readily between exiting and entering the supermarket? In fact, it is precisely because the door is subjected to an over production of symbolic meaning that it establishes itself as the boundary between the familiar and unfamiliar, and between home and homesickness. Within this heightened framework, the gesture of the closing door gains an especially powerful motif of not only sealing the subject within the supermarket, but also of sealing him inside of his anxiety. Yet again, therefore, it is not a question of the door in and of itself engendering anxiety. But nor is the anxiety solely the projection of an anxious mind. In a multidimensional phenomenology, all aspects serve a mutually edifying role, shedding light upon the structure and content of anxiety from different shifts in perspective.

That our phenomenology is multidimensional does not, however, discount the fact it is centred at all times by the body. Thus, if anxiety is dispersed through the world, finding form in a diverse and heterogeneous way, then the same movement begins with the body as both the expression and object of anxiety. In speaking of the body as expressive we refer to the notion that our bodily existence cannot be considered in isolation from a surrounding world. Thus, to think of what can be termed a 'symptom' is also to think of that symptom in relation to one's own body, to the body of other people and to the spatiality in which those bodies are situated. To stop on a bridge, or respond anxiously to a specific kind of lighting is to express with one's body a certain *style* (to use a distinctly Merleau-Pontean term) of being. With these movements, the anxiety involved cannot be localized to the pairing of the person and the bridge, and that alone. Nor can we understand anxiety as something that happens to the objective body, a body to be understood solely in medical terms as a set of functions. Rather, this relation between a person and anxiety is taken up in a much wider and more complex dynamic, such that it involves life generally. To speak in this sense of the body's capacity for expression is simply to reinforce the relational structure of our being-in-the-world. As seen in this context, the manifestations of symptoms express in a singular form this lived and dynamic existence. In the spirit of Merleau-Ponty, Parnas and Gallagher refer to symptoms as 'certain wholes of interpenetrating existence … permeated by the patient's disposition and by biographical (and not just biological) detail' (Parnas and Gallagher 2015, 72). Such an account captures the nature of the symptom as a 'gestalt' involving a relational and intersubjective liaison with the world, which undermines any division between the symptom and the world existing separately (73). When we speak of the body as an expression of anxiety, then we refer to a communicative force that appears in our relation with architecture, with modes of transport, with other people and everything in between.

The other side of this bodily existence is the experience of the body as an object. What does it mean to experience one's body as impersonal and why does this experience induce anxiety? This is a complex question, which we will seek to untangle throughout this chapter. But let us stick with concrete phenomena in order to gain a sense of what is at stake. Already in two moments we have met with the body in its impersonality and foreignness: the bridge and the supermarket. In the inability to cross a bridge, the body appears for us as much an obstacle as the bridge itself does. This quality as being a hindrance is grounded in the apparent lack of rational sense as to why the body responds in the way it does before a bridge. In this departure from how I expect my body to conform to the world, it ceases to be experienced irreducibly as my own and is thereby manifest as a thing. The quality of the body as being impersonal is stipulated, then, on a self-alienation from the body when anxious. For this reason, the impersonality of the body is that which undermines the sense I have of who I am, and this sense assumes diverse forms. Note here the terminology of describing the body as impersonal. It is not that 'my' body is unable to cross a bridge; rather, the body seems to stop of its own accord, as though it were responding to something that I myself was unaware of. Of course, in describing corporeality in these terms, we are making an experiential claim about what it feels like to be anxious. This is different from a metaphysical claim about the nature of selfhood. At no point does the body in ontological terms cease to be me, as if it suddenly developed a different agency. Rather, I experience it as being impersonal, attached to an objectified quality and thus resisting my sense of self.

So, we have a sense of the body as expressive of anxiety as well as an appearance of the body as being 'thinglike'. In addition, in impeding my sense of self, the thinglike quality of the body is itself a source of anxiety, thus perpetuating the loop between expression and objectification. This rapport between expression and objectification is at work in spatial phobias, but it can also be thought of in terms of illness and ageing. When my body fails me, I experience the body as betraying the person I take myself to be. The limbs that ordinarily cohere together now appear disconnected, and this experience of fragmentation is also an experience of anxiety, insofar as anxiety takes place in the partial collapse of selfhood. Likewise, when I have a glimpse of myself as having aged, then I also experience the body as the site of a vulnerability, which, as it were, is trailing off without me. In such moments, the body becomes a thing to be observed and monitored. In the case of phobic anxiety itself, we have an especially clear sense of the affective dimension tied up with this quality. We have already encountered one such moment in the supermarket, as the body that pauses, looks at itself and finds that what is reflected back is alien or foreign. The parts of the body lose their overall coherence and now partially dissent from being 'one's own'. These and other experiences are by no means peculiar to anxious subjects, but are instead operational for all humans. With anxiety, however, these often-concealed dimensions are illuminated. Our concern in this chapter is with explicating these different dimensions of bodily anxiety, each of which is inseparable and interwoven into a totality.

The ambiguity of the body

To understand the specificity of the anxious body, we will be required to return to the beginning – to the body in its everyday situation in the world, long before it has been thematized as an alien presence. The motivation for turning to a conceptual analysis of the body is not only to address the central role embodiment plays in the structure of subjectivity, but to also consider in more specific terms how the body's impersonal existence marks a decisive aspect in the birth of anxiety. With Merleau-Ponty as our interlocutor, we begin this discovery by understanding that the body gains its structure, neither from its physical being nor from the ideas imposed upon it. Rather, the body, as Merleau-Ponty sees it, marks itself out as an 'organic thought', which is situated between the material and the mental (Merleau-Ponty 2012, 80). What this means is that to understand the body, it is not enough to approach it from a third person perspective, as if it could be understood in isolation from its environment. But nor can we understand the body from a purely abstract or intellectualist perspective. Rather, to understand the body, we need to move both within but also beyond our own experience, seeking at all times a prepersonal and primordial level, which allows us, as bodily subjects, to have a relationship with the world. Merleau-Ponty terms this 'pre-objective perspective' a 'being in the world' (81). With this phrase, synonymous with phenomenology itself, Merleau-Ponty is seeking a language to characterize our prereflective way of existing, which provides us with an experience of the world as having a 'particular consistency' that cannot be understood solely in abstract terms (82). Put another way, no matter how many changes our body undergoes, we are afforded at all times a certain integrity, which is independent of the contingencies of the body's physical modifications. Indeed, our relationship with the world persists in and through these modifications, even if those modifications entail losing a limb (82). What Merleau-Ponty finds in these manifold experiences is 'an I that continues to tend toward its world despite deficiencies or amputations' (83). This intimate and necessary bond between body and world coalesces through the expressivity of the body, as Merleau-Ponty writes:

> The body is the vehicle of being in the world, and for a living being, having a body means being united with a definite milieu, merging with certain projects, and being perpetually engaged therein... For if it true that I am conscious of my body through the world and if my body is the unperceived term at the centre of the world toward which every object turns its face, then it is true for the same reason that my body is the pivot of the world. (84)

Merleau-Ponty places the body in an interdependent relationship with the spatiality of the world, denying that each aspect can be understood in isolation. Just as the body constitutes the world, so the body is constituted by the world. In this twofold relation between body and world, both aspects are given structure and content though being intertwined with one another. To conceive of a phenomenology of lived space, as Merleau-Ponty will do, is to simultaneously contend with a phenomenology of the body. Thus when he reflects on his experience of Paris, Merleau-Ponty does not find a series of atomic points and objects located in space, but instead a 'flow of experiences that implicate and explicate each other' (293). As he makes clear, the structure of space and the structure of the body mirror one another in their pregiven fold:

> Paris is not a thousand-sided object or a collection of perceptions, nor for that matter the law of all of these perceptions. Just as a human being manifests the same essence in his hand gestures, his gait, and the sound of his voice, each explicit perception in my journey through Paris – the cafés, the faces, the poplars along the quays, the bends of the Seine – is cut out of the total being of Paris, and only serves to confirm a certain style or a certain sense of Paris. (294)

Body and space, far from being separable, are conjoined into the same 'primordial spatiality' (149). It is thanks to this primordial space that our experience of ourselves as both spatial and corporeal is unified as a relational whole. The identification of the 'same essence' in the hand of another person or in the bends of the Seine is possible because neither body nor world are inert chunks of materiality, but are instead involved in a living relation with one another. This interplay of the parts and the whole is thanks to a 'latent sense, diffused through the landscape or the town, that we uncover in a specific evidentness without having to define it' (294). We resist defining the sense because the affective essence cannot be reduced to a discernible object. Instead, body and world involve themselves in a mutually edifying relationship, whereby each shapes the other. Note how this intertwinement between body and space is rooted not in an abstracted concept of the world that takes place at the level of lived experience. Rather, the experience of bodily space as united finds its origins in the pre-personal body at work securing the unity of experience. This idea of another level of bodily life at work behind the scenes appears time and again in Merleau-Ponty's early work. In *Phenomenology of Perception*, it can be witnessed in the first instance with the idea of an 'intentional arc' (137). With this concept, Merleau-Ponty posits 'a more fundamental function…beneath intelligence and beneath perception' (137). The purpose of this function, he argues, is to:

> [P]roject around us our past, our future, our human milieu, our physical situation, our ideological situation, and our moral situation, or rather, that ensures that we are situated within all of these relationships. This intentional arc creates the unity of the senses, the unity of the senses with the intelligence, and the unity of sensibility and motricity. And this is what 'goes limp' in the disorder. (137)

The significance of the intentional arc is pervasive. Through it, personal existence is grounded in an overarching projection of space and time. At all times, the body prehends the world, mapping and layering the specific thematic and structural aspects of the surrounding environment in such a way so as to unify experience. In this respect, the intentional arc is the foundation upon which the temporality of the subject converges into a unified point, allowing us to be situated within a relationship to the world. The creation of space as being meaningful, value laden and expressive is dependent on a relationship between the body and world. Indeed, the world only has a meaning thanks to the fact that it is brought alive by the intentional arc of the body. And the same is true in reverse: without the world, the body would no longer have meaning.

The movement of the prepersonal body synthesizing the world into unity gives Merleau-Ponty's earlier conception of the body a certain kind of character. Beginning with the idea of the body as 'a work of art', Merleau-Ponty's philosophy of the body, as it is presented in *Phenomenology of Perception*, tends towards a philosophy of unity, in which the body and world seek to renew a reciprocal harmony. Such a unified relation, however, is exposed at all times to a process of disintegration that is not peculiar to traumatic instances of life, but is instead present as a subtheme of bodily life, as he writes, 'Now, if the world falls to pieces or is broken apart, this is because one's own body has ceased to be a knowing body and has ceased to envelop all of the objects in a single hold ...' (295). The unknowing body is precisely the body that has lost ground with the world, revealing its integral role in the infrastructure of the world itself. This precarious existence, in which the body must forever renew its relation to the world in order to restore harmony, belies another level of existence, which takes place irrespective of personal life. Such a level of bodily existence is not something that I give to the world as an attribute of my own life. Rather, the generalized and anonymous existence that takes place does so in some sense not only beneath me but also prior to my existence, as a prehistory that I renew in and through my lived experience.

To understand this, it is not necessary to invoke the level of traumatic experience suggested by the loss of a limb and the ensuing figuration of a phantom limb (82). Rather, we can think here of acts as simple as sensing an object or walking from one corner of a room to another corner. Who is it that walks from one corner to another? It is me, certainly, who takes up this task. But at the same time, another level of bodily existence is at work, directing me in the world long before I am aware of this directionality. To walk is not to calculate step-by-step how many feet I must take, nor does this operation occur 'at the level of thetic consciousness' (83). Rather, it is a movement of letting my feet take course. Those same limbs that enable me to get from one place to another belong to me insofar as I take possession of them, but they also belong to a natural world that both proceeds and outlasts me. At stake in the structure of the body, then, is a sedimented layer of knowledge that is outside of both cognitive awareness and a reflexive response to the world. Put another way, being able to walk (or, for that matter, developing a phantom limb) is not a mechanical procedure, but is instead an act imbued with an existential value, which is situated at all times in relation to a broader world.

We see, then, that the structure of the body is not reducible to thematic experience, but instead hinges at all times on another layer of intentionality that renders thematic experience possible in the first place. This level of existence generates an ambiguous depth in Merleau-Ponty's phenomenology of the body, ambiguous not only in the sense of being a particular kind of object, but also in the sense of never being entirely possessed by the subject, both temporally and spatially. Of this deep ambiguity, Merleau-Ponty writes, 'What allows us to center our existence is also what prevents us from centering it completely, and the anonymity of our body is inseparably both freedom and servitude' (87). As both free and servile at once, there is always something of our bodily existence that is anterior and unknowable to our experience. The unknowability of the body is not only structural but also experiential. If impersonal existence is thematically present, then it is only 'when I am in danger' (86). Beyond these fleeting moments, 'personal existence represses the organism' in order to return to itself *as* a self (86). Concerning this 'advent of the impersonal', Merleau-Ponty notes:

> A margin of *almost* impersonal existence thus appears around our personal existence, which, so to speak, is taken for granted, and to which I entrust the care of keeping me alive. Around the human world that each of us has fashioned, there appears a general world to which we must first belong in order to enclose ourselves within a particular milieu…my organism – as a pre-personal adhesion to the form of the of the world, as an anonymous and general existence – plays the role of an *innate complex* beneath the level of my personal life. (86)

Let us not underplay the striking quality of Merleau-Ponty's reflections. As a fusion of the personal and the impersonal, the body is that which I rely on without ever knowing what it is that I am placing my trust in. This blind trust renders the body a double-sided entity, at once revealing itself to me in that dimension of personal existence that situates me in lived time, but at the same time folding back upon an immemorial time that forms a trace in and around my existence without ever being identical with that existence. The double-sidedness of the body is neither causal nor linear. To be clear, the anonymous realm that haunts my existence is not a dormant sphere that is 'recouped' upon my arrival. Rather, the anonymous body inheres in an elemental way, as part of an immemorial dimension of bodily existence. We are subjected to our bodies in a quite literal way. Our bodies carve out a space for the 'I' to exist while establishing 'regions of silence', which belong to a different order of corporeal life (84). This independent bodily life mediates with the world prior to 'my' engagement with experience. Indeed, so far as it belongs to *all* bodies, then the anonymity of the prepersonal body does not belong to me, but instead underscores my personal life with a depersonalized foundation that is common to all bodies without ever rendering them the same. In a passage we shall return to, Merleau-Ponty writes:

> If I wanted to express perceptual experience with precision, I would have to say that *one* perceives in me, and not that I perceive. Every sensation includes a seed of dream or depersonalization, as we experience through this sort of stupor into which it puts us when we truly live at the level of sensation. (223)

To live truly at the level of sensation is to divest consciousness of its personal attributes, and thus enter into the dream state that characterizes the recognition of bodily sensation being both beyond possession (cf. 'I never have an absolute possession of myself by myself' [250]) and beyond knowledge (cf. 'I have no more awareness of being the true subject of my sensation than I do of my birth or my death…I cannot know my birth or my death' [223]). The 'one' who perceives in and through me is not strictly me, nor is it knowable by me: 'He who sees and touches is not exactly myself' (224). More than this, the 'one' is not only 'beneath' me, it also precedes and will survive me (224). Merleau-Ponty gives us an account of the body that is not only ambiguous in the sense that it is not one thing among many; it is also ambiguous in the sense that it is both *of the I* and concurrently *before the I*. The body is personal and prepersonal, particular and general, immemorial and contemporary at once.

Indeed, it is thanks to the fact the body is structured between the personal and impersonal, and between the human and the not-yet-human, that I am able to exist at all. As human subjects, we owe our lives to an anonymous level of existence, which remains latent and is never entirely incorporated into the realm of embodiment as cultured or gendered. Prior to these vital distinctions, another operation is at work, not as a substratum of personal existence, which can then be retrieved in and through experience, but as an alterity that prevents human beings from ever being at home in their bodies. It is precisely this primordial difference that Merleau-Ponty will variously term the 'prehuman', the 'one' or the 'anonymous body'.

This enigmatic discussion of a subject both beneath and prior to me is not an appeal to disembodied mysticism. Rather, what he is describing is situated in the realm of phenomenology itself, as he remarks, it is 'the life of my eyes, hands, and ears [where we find] so many natural selves', each of which has 'already sided with the world' (224). Such claims are not abandoned by Merleau-Ponty as his thinking evolves. Indeed, so important is the formulation of the subject as structured by a primordial depersonalized mode of perception that he will return to it at the end of his life. Thus, in a working note from 2 May 1959, he writes as follows:

> I do not perceive any more than I speak. Perception has me as has language. And as it is necessary that all the same *I* be there in order to speak, *I* must be there in order to perceive. But in what sense? As *one*. What is it that, from my side, comes to animate the perceived world and language? (Merleau-Ponty 1968, 190)

What we are faced with in these descriptions of bodily existence is a body that is on the verge of the personal and the impersonal. Such a body never entirely reveals itself, but instead gestures towards a latent depth that in occasional moments – not least in depersonalization and dreaming – takes form as a central structure in the life of a human. Hidden behind the veneer of being a discrete self who is identifiable with 'one's own' body, there dwells another kind of existence, indifferent to the self that assumes a relationship to it. This non-possessable body, which operates at all times as a 'pre-history' of a 'past that has never been present', situates itself at the threshold of experience, revealing itself indirectly as a trace or a symptom, yet a symptom that can never be reduced to the level of lived experience (250–252). We remain, in short, outsiders to ourselves, and specifically outsiders to the bodies, which impart a joint sense of intimacy and alienation upon us. Merleau-Ponty draws to light the strange undercurrent of bodily life. But what he overlooks and underplays is how this impersonal dimension is given to experience, either directly or indirectly, in an affective sense. As we will now discover, we take the impersonal dimension of the body to be central to the experience of anxiety. The reason for this can be formulated as follows: *As a particular kind of affective experience, anxiety is predicated on the idea of a personalized self encountering the impersonal dimensions of corporeal life, such that the impersonal dimension threatens the image of the self as being in possession of itself.* In what follows, we shall unfold this complex claim.

Dimensions of the anxious body

Our excursion into the conceptual framework of Merleau-Ponty reveals the complexity of the body. As we have seen, the narrative that is told in this framework begins with the body in its interdependent relation with the world, before moving to the other side of corporeal existence, which renders this relation possible in the first instance. Despite Merleau-Ponty's appeal to the image of the body as a familiar source of expression and motility, a strangeness haunts his vision of corporeal life, and indeed it is the mood of strangeness that links anxiety with the uncanny (a point already prefigured in Merleau-Ponty's early aesthetics, where he will suggest only 'one emotion is possible for the painter – the feeling of strangeness' [cited in Johnson 1993, 68]). The strangeness inherent in Merleau-Ponty's thought is captured most strikingly in the form of the body as anonymous and impersonal. What is striking about this aspect of bodily life is the level of importance Merleau-Ponty assigns to the anonymous function of the body, as both independent of 'my' existence and also temporally prior to that existence. Yet for all that, Merleau-Ponty underplays the affective dimension of impersonal existence, even though he explicitly notes that this dimension is tied up with a dreamlike quality, which engenders itself towards anxiety. Our reading of Merleau-Ponty, therefore, is against the grain of his intentions insofar as we wish to elicit the disturbing quality of impersonal existence.

As we have seen in the preceding chapter, it is with Levinas in fact that we gain a visceral affective sense of impersonal being. I have elaborated elsewhere on the relation between impersonal being and horror in Levinas, but it is worth noting presently the extent to which Levinas will align impersonal with a suffocating horror, stating that the impersonal existence is what persists, stubbornly and anonymously, once we imagine the 'destruction of things and beings' as having taken place (Levinas 2005, 46; Trigg 2014b). The excess that survives the imagined destruction of things survives in the form of a presence, 'an atmospheric density, a plenitude of the void, or the murmur of silence…[an] impersonal "field of forces"' (46). If this anonymous existence takes flight in insomnia and in nocturnal space, then the 'horror of darkness' also appears in waking life as the structure of consciousness being stripped of its subjectivity, leading to the subject becoming 'depersonalized' (Levinas 2001, 54–56). While his account of anonymity as being a stifling presence seems *prima facie* to describe anxiety, Levinas himself explicitly distances the movement of horror from that of anxiety, at least in a Heideggerian form (58). The reason for this is that Heideggerian anxiety is concerned with 'the fear of nothingness', which in turn brings about the positivism of a 'being toward death', and thus the redemption of anxiety (58). It is an anxiety that is to some extent resolvable through its transformative and disclosive aspects. The scenario in Levinas is rather different. For him, horror 'is an irremissible existence' (58). In other words, horror is both infinite and irresolvable, given that the anonymity of being is not reducible to existence, but instead constitutive of it. It is this idea of impersonal existence as preceding the formation of the (personalized) subject, and thus marking a constant source of danger for the self that we take from Levinas. To this extent, his distance from Heideggerian anxiety only confirms what we wish to demonstrate in the ensuing analysis; namely, that anxiety is not reducible to the conflict within an already existing subject, but is instead framed as the basis of an impersonal existence, which if provoking anxiety, also provides the grounds of selfhood.

To give voice to these conceptual issues, let us return to the stage upon which anxiety is enacted: the supermarket. What is important about this scene is less the locality of the place itself – we might also be in a museum, a zoo or anywhere else where we might feel trapped within a border, visible or invisible. What is important is the transformative power of the place. Whether it derives from the lighting or from the configuration of the space, the place serves to amplify and enact an anxiety, which is tacit as a generalized mood rather than a seizure in the body. As we have seen, the mood of anxiety attests to the intertwining of body and world as co-constituting each other in a dialogical fashion. From a strictly structural perspective, the difference between the mood of anxiety and the mood of jubilation is negligible. In each case, the corporeality of the world is given its experiential feel, as Heidegger has it, 'neither from "without" nor from "within," but rises from being-in-the-world itself as a mode of that being' (Heidegger 1996, 129). In other words, the mood of anxiety is not a mood that is superimposed upon an otherwise neutral world. Rather, it is in and through a mood, taken in a prereflective way, that our interpretations and bodily perceptions take root. The specificity of anxiety as a mood is marked as a rupture in the body's complicity with the constitution of the world.

The key movement in this phenomenology is the self-alienation that transpires when the subject catches sight of himself as a partially unknown and unknowable zone of materiality, manifest in our illustration as the apparition of the reflected face and perceived hand, each of which loses its quality as being one's own and instead becomes an organ of anonymity. Indeed, the entire movement of our phenomenological exploration revolves around the felt transformation of materiality – either in the home or in the body – from the centre of personalized and intimate existence, to the site of an anonymous and foreign life. From the outset, it is important to note that the transformation in question is not a transformation of the body's materiality. Anxiety does not introduce a new facet to the body, but instead unveils that a dimension that is operational, if latently, in both anxious and non-anxious existence. What is transformed is the relation we have with our bodies, such that the concealed dimension of the body in its anonymity becomes visible. We take this experience of a transformation not only as an expression of anxiety, but also as its source. There is much to say on the multifaceted nature of this transformation. To formulate the contours of the experience, at least four interdependent dimensions can be thematized. In the first instance, we are concerned with the question of how there can be a personalized experience of impersonal matter; second, we are concerned with how this experience is taken up as a figure of the uncanny; third, our concern falls with the thematic implication of to what extent the body as impersonal and uncanny can be trusted;

in the final case, our question concerns what kind of materiality is at stake in the phenomenology of the anxious body.

1. Experiencing the impersonal

Our analysis begins with a paradox: how is it possible to conceive of an experience of the impersonal? The question is paradoxical given that any experience of the impersonal presupposes a personalized perspective, from which the impersonal is taken as an intentional object. This paradox is not a logical concern, and that alone. Rather, our concern remains tied to the lived experience of one's body as impersonal. We are remaining with this tension given that the experience of anxiety, as we conceive it, entails the partial transformation of the body from that which is irreducibly personal and intimate to that which is insufferably impersonal and alien. How, then, is it possible for the impersonal and personal bodies to be situated in relation to one another without personalizing the impersonal? In response to this question, let us remind ourselves that in Merleau-Ponty's formulation, the 'advent of the impersonal' is never absolute, but instead marks the 'margin of *almost* impersonal existence [that] appears around our personal existence' (Merleau-Ponty 2012, 86). Merleau-Ponty's emphasis on an '*almost*' impersonal existence proves instructive, as it underscores the fact that what appears as impersonal does so on the fringe of the personal. The liminal status attached to the impersonal dimension of the body means the personal body remains intact throughout, and at no point is it wholly colonized by the anonymity of the body as an organism.

To situate this ambiguity in the context of the anxious body, we can begin by noting that it is precisely because the body is able to host (at least) two different levels of existence at once that anxiety takes form. Were the subject to regress to a level of organic existence, then it would be impossible to conceive of anxiety as assuming the place it does in the subject, given that what remains would be nothing more than inert matter. In the moment of anxiety, a human subject remains present, gazing onwards upon his own body, and it is thanks to this ability to regard the body as both one's own and not one's own concurrently that anxiety emerges in the interstitial space between subject and object, between personalized experience and impersonal materiality. Through the anxious episode, we survive and despite the visceral sense of impending collapse, no such breakdown occurs. Is the collapse a product of an overactive imagination or otherwise a cognitive misreading of one's immediate situation? The answer in each case is no: the prospect of collapse gains the value of reality insofar as we come to the borderland where the body as one's own is put into question. The subject feels himself to be disappearing, as the body in its knowable presence recedes, while the impersonal body as a set of anonymous functions takes over, as Merleau-Ponty has it: 'It can even happen that, when I am in danger, my human situation erases my biological one and that my body completely merges with action' (86). This mergence with action is predicated on the personal body not being sufficiently present to ensure the continuity of self. In such an instance, the anonymity of the body assumes influence, ensuring the brute survival of the subject, irrespective of our own relation to the situation. The experience of the impersonal, such as we are phrasing it, is the experience of oneself sliding towards the anonymity of general existence but without ever losing the conviction (however illusory) of selfhood.

In anxiety, we reach the edge of an *almost* impersonal existence, and it is through this unrealized (and unrealizable) movement that the possibility of one's boundaries being effaced by the impersonal materiality of the body comes to the foreground. The body of anxiety is a body whose edges are no longer clearly delineated, but instead are slithering between divergent levels of existence. In the confrontation with the underside of bodily life, the anxiety provoked is not simply structural – that is, a possible erasure of one's personal boundaries in the face of becoming anonymous – but also thematic insofar as the subject is confronted with a body that is both intimate and alien at once, a body of both interiority and anteriority. Thematically, this encounter with the body's impersonal side operates as a movement of *dispossession*.

Consider in phenomenological terms the significance marking the subject of anxiety when he feels as though his legs will give way. The trembling of the legs is not a mechanical fault in the limbs, but instead the necessary outcome of a broader process of self-alienation from the body. Where the legs are concerned, we are confronted with an especially striking vision of the body as sliding away from the subject. Indeed, what is more alien than the experience of no longer being able to support oneself, but instead of having to rely on props in the world to steady oneself? The gap between the body in its personalized being and the body in its impersonal being is not absolute. The legs remain present, and they do not become phantoms of an otherwise functioning body. Rather, their very trembling accents the overwhelming facticity of being subjected to the body as a unit of matter. The legs become overly abundant, overly materialized in their strangeness. Thanks to this elevated materialization, the sense of the legs as no longer mine (yet precisely for this reason *still* mine) becomes a reality. In the case of trembling legs, we are faced with an excess in materiality, which distorts the subject's relation to his body. The body becomes a site of instability, incongruity and vulnerability. But the dispossession of the body is not only a question of excessive materiality, but also the very unknowability of the body. Yet another way the body becomes dispossessed is through its symptomatic rapport with the world. Nowhere is this clearer than in the symptom of immobility.

* * *

You are in a military cafeteria. There is a space where you will receive lunch; an entire world will be available to you. Following your colleagues, you ascend a series of stairs, proceed through a set of hallways and arrive at the dimly lit space where food is served from behind counters. You cannot be seen clearly in this space, despite the fact that it is full of other people getting their own lunch. Shrouded in the low light, you scan the room, as if looking on from afar. Your selection of food is perfunctory, and for you, the only concern is with getting through the process unscathed by what follows next. The tray of food is assembled and ready to be purchased. As you come to the edge of the dimly lit space, another world opens. It is a world where everyone and everything is exposed to a brutal architecture, wholly indifferent to the welfare of those who eat their lunch in the zone of aggression. Harsh light floods in from above, pierces through the ceiling, through the iron grates, violently interrogating those beneath the light. A spotlight descends on each of the subjects who occupy the space. Dense clusters of military personnel are seated in and around the expansive room, their bodies tightly interwoven not only within each other, but also in complicity with the space. As a mark of respect for these people and the sanctity of their institution, you are instructed to remove your hat and dark glasses, which until now have defended you against this world. Your colleagues have gone ahead, finding their place within the new world despite its apparent dangers. You must follow, yet at the threshold between the dining area and the dimly lit space where the food is selected, you are unable to move. You look outwards, towards the sea of people within the light, and an invisible line divides you from joining them. Your body has assumed the paralysed presence of a monument, lodged in both space and time. A colleague turns her gaze back to you, evidently aware of your breakage in the world of things. Your legs, far from trembling, are instead inert, and it remains for your hands to function where your legs would otherwise act. You are motionless, the tray of tepid rice and chicken held in one hand. The other hand gestures to your colleague to move on, to concede to the impossibility that you will be able to participate in the collective activity of eating beneath the aggressive skyline of the military cafeteria.

* * *

In the act of coming to a standstill before no visible danger, the body evades our grip on the world. A symptom is produced: that of being unable to cross an invisible barrier. From the perspective of empirical reason, the symptom is incongruent within the context of the situation. A human being is unable to move, inhibited by a body that can no longer be deciphered as belonging to the world. Through the lens of anxiety, the body both protrudes into the world through its excessive materialization while also intruding upon the subject in terms of its opaqueness. From where does this symptom derive? For that matter, from where is this danger drawn? To cross the invisible line that demarcates one zone from another is to confront the alterity of the body in its brute materiality. Maintaining oneself within the darkness – behind the column or within a shadow – not only splits space into different parts, it also establishes a series of regions, from which the body's centre of existence can be directed. So long as there remains a relatively fixed perspective, upon which the body can survey the world around itself, then a border remains in place, against which the subject of anxiety can both evade and repel the world. To cross that boundary is to confuse the line between where the body begins and where it ends.

This idea of the body as both not-mine and mine at once might seem at odds with a phenomenological account of the body as being irreducibly mine. Indeed, how can the materiality of the body lose its status as being mine and thus transformed to an alien entity? How, that is, can I experience my body as anything *less* than mine? The question has a specific peculiarity to it given that in a phenomenological context, the body is, in Husserl's words, 'constantly in the perceptual field quite immediately' (Husserl 1970, 107). The body is with us at all times, allowing us to 'hold sway' in the world, and thus maintain a relation with materiality generally, by which our bodies are never truly 'alien living bod[ies]'. Similarly, as we have seen for Merleau-Ponty, the body presents us with a 'primitive spatiality', in turn forming a compact with the world, from which no escape is truly possible (Merleau-Ponty 2012). In the experience of anxiety, we face a rupture in the concordance of the body's being-in-the-world, such that the contingency of this relation is revealed. Indeed, it is notable that when Merleau-Ponty talks about the 'living experience of vertigo and nausea', he refers to 'the horror caused by our contingency' (265). If being a self means being embodied, then what Merleau-Ponty reminds us is that this bodily status is exposed to self-alienation precisely thanks to the intimacy of the body.

The irruption of the body in its uncanniness is not peculiar to the mood of anxiety, but remains an ongoing if often concealed dimension of bodily existence more broadly. In his essay 'L'Intrus', Jean-Luc Nancy reflects on the strangeness of his heart transplant (Nancy 2000). These reflections begin with the classical question, 'what is the enunciating subject?' (2). Against the backdrop of his own heart transplant, Nancy poses a question of the heart's betrayal:

> If my heart was giving up and going to drop me, to what degree was it an organ of 'mine,' my 'own?' ... It was becoming a stranger to me, intruding through its defection ... A gradual slippage was separating me from myself ... My heart was becoming my own foreigner – a stranger precisely because it was inside. Yet this strangeness could only come from outside for having first emerged inside. (3–4)

Nancy traces the inroads leading to the body's dispersal. The strangeness that comes from within does so not as a pathology of the body, much less a deviation of what is otherwise a body of plenitude and certainty. More than this, the empirical fact of the heart transplant reinforces a strange and non-possessable body. The heart comes to the foreground as a broken part. But we would misread the appearance of this broken heart if we were to regard it, in Heideggerian terms, as a mode of being present-at-hand, and that alone. That the heart presents itself as being more present means not an incursion of strangeness, as if strangeness were contingent to the body, but instead an amplification of the intrusion of an already existing (if dormant) strangeness. Nancy's heart gives voice to the body as a site of anonymous and interchangeable functions, a nexus of sometimes living, sometimes dying components, each of which has a history outside of the host subject (a heart that is some twenty years younger than the rest of Nancy's body). Furthermore, as Nancy reminds us, as a gesture of hospitality and intimacy, the transplant of body parts is not without the risk of repulsion, as the immune system of the patient consists of a process of 'vomiting up the heart and spitting it out' (8). Thus, this intrusion that promises to save the patient serves also to render his host body foreign, altering the immune system that is originally designed to fend off foreign attacks. To survive, one must welcome the foreignness, both that of one's own but also that which can never belong to the enunciating subject, as Nancy writes eloquently:

I feel it distinctly; it is much stronger than a sensation: never has the strangeness of my own identity, which I've nonetheless always found so striking, touched me with such acuity. 'I' has clearly become the formal index of an unverifiable and impalpable system of linkages. Between my self and me there has always been a gap of space-time: but now there is the opening of an incision and an immune system that is at odds with itself, forever at cross purposes, irreconcilable. (10)

The strangeness of identity speaks of both anxiety and trauma. The gap of space–time that Nancy speaks is now filled with the occupancy of two bodies inhabiting the same space. This dynamic rapport between different materialities is as evident in Nancy's heart transplant as it is in the case of the bodily experience of anxiety. Each corporeal modality is to a certain extent a privileged one, insofar as it reflects the very limits of identity, the precise point when the gap of identity appears. This *phantom zone* (to employ a previously developed concept) designates a corporeal zone, in which the felt experience of being a self is split between conflicting bodily temporalities (Trigg 2012, 253). On the one hand, there exists the felt sense of time as cohering in the present. Yet on the other hand, another past – conceived in trauma and therefore denied its expression as the event occurs – is sedimented in the flesh, announced only retroactively and even then, indirectly. The phantom zone concerns those brief moments where one's own self catches sight of one's own body being remolded for another past. Such moments fold back upon the almost impersonal horizon of experience, which, as soon as it appears for the perceiving body, is rendered personal. But through this conversion of traumatic and anxious materiality to the consolidated image of the body as unified, that same level of ruptured and fragmented materiality persists. As with trauma, anxiety occupies a phantom presence, at once both visible and invisible, both experiential and non-experiential, but never dissolved nor forgotten.

2. Uncanny anxiety

By way of heartbreak, we are returned to the experience of the impersonal. In speaking in these terms, it becomes necessary to accept the paradox of the body as cannily familiar and uncannily strange. To understand this, we can consider the idea of the 'body uncanny'. The term 'body uncanny' can be traced back to the work of Richard Zaner, an expression that has since been applied in a diverse fashion, not least in the field of the medical humanities (cf. Burwood 2008; Leder 1990; Svenaeus 2000; Zaner 1981). Broadly speaking, we understand the body uncanny as an affective atmosphere, which is not yet anxiety, but instead an underlying sense of the body as not entirely my own. Thus, the uncanny body is linked to the experience of anxiety as a matter of amplifying this sense, with each gradient accenting the corporatization of uncanniness. To say more on this relation between uncanniness and anxiety, it is worth pausing to consider Zaner's reflections on the body uncanny, given that his elaborations on this theme will enable us to approach the experience of anxiety with greater precision.

Zaner's framework consists of four aspects of the body uncanny. In the first modality of the body uncanny, the issue concerns the inescapability of the body (Zaner 1981, 50). As we have already seen in Merleau-Ponty, being a subject means being limited and delimited by our bodies. This does not simply mean that our existence as human beings is limited by the particular bodies we have; more than this, it means that our general existence as subjects is always already given to the world in a corporeal form. To transcend the body would mean to divest ourselves of what it is to be human. Born into a corporeal form, human beings are then faced with the prospect of rendering this set of parts, modules and zones of flesh 'one's own', even though we play no part in determining the bodies we have (51). The inescapable body carries with it an important consequence: if my sense of self is inescapably interwoven with my body, then there is a parallel sense in which the body 'implicates' me. Zaner writes, 'If there is a sense in which my own-body is "intimately mine", there is, furthermore, an equally decisive sense in which *I belong to it* – in which I am at its disposal or mercy, if you will' (52). Merleau-Ponty's concept of freedom and servitude, which we have already glanced at, echoes in Zaner's formulation of being at the mercy of the body. Subjected to the body's anonymous existence, I am also vulnerable to its failures and fault lines. My body serves to both protect me, but as it protects me, it remains unmoved by my own existence, except in terms of assuming a set of biological functions, which enable me to live.

With the idea of the body as inescapable and implicating, we have a specific kind of structure. Such a structure is double-sided, for it is a body that is both available to me while also transcending me. The affective realization of this structure is what Zaner terms 'the chill' (52). The experience takes form as a shudder or shiver one undergoes when faced with the existential realization that I am at all times exposed to the otherness that constitutes me but at the same time deprives me of ever being at home within my own body. That I am both unable to escape my body and implicated by the materiality of the body, instils a fission between my sense of self and the body that I am interwoven with but never identical with. Zaner reflects, 'Inescapable, my embodiment is as well dreadfully and chillingly implicative' (53). In the idea of the chill, we move closer to the presence of anxiety, and this affective dimension is underscored in the felt experience of the body as alien (54).

The underside of the body as an alien presence disembarks from its function as 'me' and assumes the category of an 'it' (54). It is for this reason that we can speak of the body as an 'it', which has its own nature and rhythms, each of which must be accommodated in turn. 'It' lives, and importantly, it does so in spite of me. 'It' is impersonal, and may at times repel the life I give it through my own history, memories and experiences. 'It' remains the same for each of us, a set of discrete organs, the prehistory of which predates my own existence and will proceed to outlive that existence.

For all that, the alien quality of the body is never alien to the point of being wholly foreign. My affective relationship to the body as uncanny is predicated precisely on an ambiguous interplay, in which the body is both intimately my own while simultaneously being that which is most alien to me. If the body appears for me as alien and uncanny, then this is thanks to the fact that something of me still inheres in and through the alien presence that is unveiled in the body. Indeed, the sense of uncanniness that accompanies bodily existence is characterized by a threat to our sense of self, while rarely leading towards the total dissolution of self. It is at the point of betrayal, when the body not only reveals itself as having another life, but also reinforces that alien life, that the uncanny affect intervenes. What is uncanny, therefore, is that the betrayal of the body is only fractional. As a partial betrayal, there is a collision in different orders of materiality existing alongside each other rather than one order supplanting the other.

* * *

In the experience of the body uncanny, we are positioned at the threshold of anxiety. With Zaner, we find the body uncanny presented not as a deviation of an otherwise normal body, nor as an articulation of the body as broken. Such is the Heideggerian reading of the concept framed by Svenaeus and others, which we dissent from (Svenaeus 2000). Uncanniness is not an accident of bodily existence nor is it an affect peculiar to certain psychopathologies. Rather, we find it as a permanent structure of self-consciousness, which is never eliminated, except through a process of concealment. Indeed, the merits of Zaner's analysis is that he ties the body uncanny to the structure of subjectivity itself, rather than reducing it to certain thematic dimensions of existence. Thus, that the body implicates me is a dimension of corporeal life common to us all. We are not disembodied agents autonomous from our materiality. At all times, we hinge upon and are indebted to the primacy of our bodies. To what extent this dimension leads to a sense of the uncanny is contingent on the sensibility of the subject. For the most part, we proceed through life either unaware or otherwise unconcerned with the dimension of our bodies that is not our own. We grant trust to the body that keeps us alive, knowing in advance that its unknowability is neither a source of distress nor something to be interrogated. At times, however, this steadfast confidence comes into question. Illness is only one way this level of the body appears. Anxiety is yet another way, arguably more far reaching. For some subjects, the onsets of symptoms of anxiety are experienced as being separate from oneself, as though deriving from an 'ego-alien' that intrudes upon oneself (Marks 1987, 432). The strategic advantage of assuming this perspective on one's symptoms is that bodily sensations in turn become externalized as a foreign presence, no longer belonging to me, but instead framed as a monstrous invasion to be avoided. For other sufferers of anxiety, symptoms emerge from within and are thus recognized as one's own, but are regarded as deviations that must be eliminated (346). Throughout, our relation to our body alters. On occasion, the body reinforces the sense we have of ourselves, while at other times the uncanny sense that there is something decidedly strange about the body comes to the foreground in the shape of anxiety. In these moments, the uncanny frames the 'I' as being exposed to a fundamental gap between my body and myself.

In Freud's essay on the uncanny, we find additional evidence of this gap between the I and the body (Freud 2003). At the heart of Freud's thinking on the uncanny is a series of ambiguities, each of which undermines the clear and distinct idea of a sovereign and rational self. The theme takes as its point of departure a thought posed in an earlier formulation of the uncanny, as presented by Ernst Jentsch, namely, 'Whether an apparently animate object really is alive and, conversely, whether a lifeless object might not perhaps be animate' (135). Jentsch has in mind bodies such as those of waxworks, dolls and automata. In each of these figures, the motif of the uncanny concerns the prospect that there might be 'vague notions of automatic – mechanical – processes that may lie hidden behind the familiar image of a living person' (135). This blurring between the familiar and the unfamiliar appears in Freud as a recurring motif. Thus, in his analysis of the doppelgänger, Freud comes to the conclusion that what is uncanny about the doppelgänger is not simply the theme of encountering oneself as another, but that the very persistence of this figure belongs to a 'primitive phase in our mental development' (143). The retention of such a sensibility assumes an anarchic place in the mind and body of the contemporary human. The appearance of the doppelgänger as a specific kind of belief is thus uncanny in that it forms a discord with an existing idea of the self as rational and resistant to superstitious avoidance patterns. In this sense, the uncanny is announced not as a radical departure from the subject, but instead as a confirmation of a presence that was already there. As Freud has it, 'this uncanny element is actually nothing new or strange, but something that was long familiar to the psyche and was estranged from it through being repressed' (148).

This temporal ambiguity mirrors the bodily ambiguity, where we are faced with different levels of existence coexisting in the same body. What Freud brings to this analysis of uncanny is an affective dimension that is for the most part lacking in Merleau-Ponty's account of the body. This affective dimension reconnects us with our question concerning the experience of the impersonal. As we have seen, this movement involves a sliding towards the impersonal aspect of bodily existence without ever entirely encountering that aspect. Anxiety finds its genesis in this space for two reasons. First, the movement of descending towards the impersonal involves a deformation of boundaries, and thus marks a threat to the structure of the subject; second, anxiety presents itself here as a confrontation with the unknowable substrata of the body. There are several thematic implications that derive from the anxious experience of the body uncanny. A central theme is that of *trust*.

3. Bodily trust

A body that is prone to collapse, and which presents itself as a strange artefact, never fully possessable by the subject, is a body that forms a discord in the life of a person. We have already established contact with this body throughout the book. As we recall, on the outside of a place – be it the place of the bridge, the supermarket, or, as we will see in time, on a bus or a plane – the subject experiences himself as a locus of integration, and thus able to survey space from a relatively fixed site. To put it another way, the pre-anxious body conforms to the Husserlian zero point of intentionality, stretching out towards a world, which is taken from the centrality of the subject. In a word, there is a relation of certainty placed in the body's perception of things. All of this changes once in the supermarket or on the bridge. At first, there is a tension in the head, which then morphs into visual disturbances. Throughout this, there is a vigilance over bodily sensations, a constant monitoring as though to bring any wayward sensations into order. Before long, the subject's vigil over the body falters, and the body reveals itself in its brute or naked facticity. In response, self-alienation ensues, which then intensifies anxiety as both being expressed by the subject and also further provoked by the body as an object of anxiety. As a dispossessed body, which threatens to give way at any point, revealing therein another side to its appearance that undermines the integrity of the subject, such a body is experienced as no longer being *trustworthy*.

To speak of the body in terms of being trustworthy or not trustworthy gives us two very different sides of bodily existence. Once more, it is in concert with Merleau-Ponty that these differences can be voiced. Despite his insistence on the body as ambiguous, as both bearer of time and object of time, *prima facie* the body that appears and reappears in Merleau-Ponty's earlier phenomenology does so as a unity, writing in *Phenomenology of Perception* of the body as 'a work of art' (Merleau-Ponty 2012, 152). As we know, the body synthesizes the world as a whole thanks to the trust implicitly placed in the body's alliance with the world. As Merleau-Ponty indicates, the synthesis of the world cannot be understood in causal terms, or in strictly empirical terms, but is instead as a movement that takes place in a prereflective way. This rapport between trust and a prereflective affirmation of the bodily world appears elsewhere in his writing as central to love, where Merleau-Ponty will speak of a 'trusting tenderness which does not constantly insist upon new proofs of absolute attachment but takes the other person as he is' (Merleau-Ponty 1964b, 228).

This sense of trust as being outside of empirical proof is reinforced in the recent literature on the phenomenology of trust, where the affective experience of trusting one's body is variously described in terms of a 'unity' that supersedes any bodily ambiguity, from which a taken-for-granted sense of bodily certainty emerges, allowing us to exist in the world without the need to question our body's ability to act (Carel 2013). Either through habit or through repetition, the trusted body that emerges in this literature is characterized as a body that is able to act, providing a background context, against which the subject propels him- or herself through the world. On an affective level, the implicit trust placed in the body is thought to generate a sense of familiarity and bodily continuity, devoid of concern insomuch as the body presents itself as a fulcrum of stability, which thus lacks any compelling reason to be interrogated (180). Importantly, the continuity of the body is stipulated on a capacity for it to adapt to situations and sensations in and through ambiguous modes of bodily existence. To speak of bodily continuity, then, means speaking not simply of the continuity of the body as an organic structure, but also of the continuity of a relation with the body as being trustworthy. In remaining intact through the ambiguities and ambivalences of human existence – whether it be fatigue, illness or disorientation – the tenability of the body as trustworthy is contingent on the capacity to renew trust through and beyond these situations. From this stance, trusting in the body does not simply mean placing trust in the body's capacity to act and function; more than this, the experience of trusting the body serves to establish a trustworthy relation with the world more broadly, such that we could speak of a generalized mood of trust.

Formulated in these terms, the body as trusted is a body that is aligned with a level of 'normalcy', even if that felt experience of normality is conditioned at all times by what Havi Carel terms 'epistemically ungrounded beliefs' concerning the reliability of the body (192). Notwithstanding the epistemic vulnerability that grounds our beliefs about the body, in much of the phenomenological literature, we find that the trusted body is equivalent to the healthy body, such that 'belonging to the world' is grounded in 'bodily certainty' (180). In this reading, the body that is untrustworthy and subject to doubt is a body that presents itself not simply as a dysfunctional obstruction, but in fact 'unnatural' (193). To speak in terms of natural and unnatural embodiment, as they relate to the affective experience of the body as trustworthy, is to presuppose a particular constitution to bodily life. Even if, as Carel argues, bodily certainty is a construct that functions irrespective of its epistemic status, then by pairing this 'achievement' with the felt experience of normalcy, everyday experience is presented as hinging on a certain mode of comporting oneself to the body. Seen in this way, instances of bodily doubt and uncertainty are framed as both unnatural and unhealthy deviations of an otherwise normal existence.

There are two points to mention in response to this account. The first is to recognize the validity in this description of the body from an experiential perspective. Without the tacit belief that our bodies persist with a minimal regularity, there can be no question of functioning in the world, at least not without the risk of inhibition and disintegration. Fictitious or not, such a belief in our bodies is what enables us to restore our relation to the world, despite the contingency that underpins that relation. But while accepting the necessity of this tacit trust, we do not need to follow Carel in assigning a 'natural confidence' in the body, such that the body subject to doubt delineates an 'unnatural' body. The risk inherent in such a move is to further pathologize bodily instances of 'abnormality', not least anxiety, as intrusions upon a subject. Indeed, Carel goes as far as to describe the 'failure' of bodily doubt as giving 'rise to a kind of anxiety' (185). Yet at the same time, she avoids conflating anxiety and bodily doubt, given that for her, the noetic content of bodily doubt is 'neither irrational nor meaningless', but instead tied to the 'true beliefs' regarding the possibility of collapse (186).

The second point proceeds from this marginalization of anxiety: to give a complete account of whether or not the body gives itself to experience as something to be trusted will depend in large upon what constitution the body has. To begin from the perspective of the body as unified means phrasing doubt and anxiety as interruptions in an otherwise integrated framework. This vision situates anxiety within the realm of a particular concept of the subject, such that anxiety is ultimately reducible to a conflict in what is an already constituted subject. Indeed, in Carel's vision, anxiety is read in a strictly Heideggerian guise as concerning the loss of 'practical coherence' (189). For this reason, at no point does anxiety risk collapsing and destroying the subject, given that it is from the subject that anxiety appears.

* * *

Against Carel, there can be little doubt that in our formulation of the anxious body as the site of uncanny mechanisms, we are contending with a body that is both beyond possession and, in some sense, unknowable. If there is a side of the body that is knowable to us in personal perception, then this experience of the body as one's own does not exhaust it of its broader significance. The hidden dimension of the body is thus uncanny in that it is both partially known and unknown, visible and invisible at once. At times, the body confirms the image we have ourselves as subjects while at other times it betrays that image. Already in Freud's etymological analysis of the term 'uncanny', this reversibility between the known and the unknown is evident (cf. Freud 2003). Thus, he will speak of the uncanny as that which is 'concealed, kept from sight, so that others do not get to know about it, withheld from others', while at other times, he will speak of the uncanny as 'that class of the terrifying which leads back to something long known to us, once very familiar' (129). Throughout this interplay between the known and the unknown, formal knowledge alone does not lessen the affective force of the uncanny. To know in abstract that one's body is constituted by a set of impersonal organs that will likely never be perceived first-hand, or to otherwise study the body in an anatomical manner, does nothing to assuage the original strangeness of the body itself. Thus, to speak of alleviating the uncanny through the acquisition of intellectual certainty is to misunderstand the nature of the uncanny.

Given the close rapport between anxiety and the uncanny, a particular relation to the issue of trust emerges. Already in Freud's essay, a connection is made between the hidden and secretive dimension of the uncanny and a sense of untrustworthiness (153). To what extent we can entrust a body that is prone to partial collapse, not simply as an accidental or pathological deviation of an otherwise normal and natural set of functions, but as the very constitution of bodily subjectivity, is central to the phenomenology of trust. To approach this issue, two aspects of the anxious body merit attention: discontinuity and betrayal. These themes take place against a broader mood of anxiety, which curtails, inhibits, and shapes the movement the subject. As we have seen, the anxious experience of being-in-the-world is framed by a cautious vigilance, such that the body presents itself as an organ with, if we may say paradoxically, a mind that appears to be of its own. Against this atmosphere of disquiet and trepidation, the theme of distrust emerges.

In the first case, we are concerned with what we can call the discontinuity of the anxious body. If there is a certain predictability in how the anxious body responds to certain situations and events –

harsh light, enclosed spaces, exposed spaces, to name but a few of what are misleadingly termed 'triggers' – then this foresight does not domesticate the rupture that emerges when the body becomes anxious. This advent of anxiety breaks suddenly and often violently from the non-anxious body, such that how one comports oneself to the body and the body is fundamentally altered. Not only is there a felt discontinuity between the anxious and non-anxious body, but in the aftermath of anxiety, a fatigued body remains in its wake. The apparently paradoxical mention of an 'anxious body' rather than an anxious subject is employed deliberately to accent the felt quality of the body as the organ of anxiety. Of course, this experiential dualism is not a substance dualism, but an indication of the subject's experience of their body as a site of betrayal. As a site of potential betrayal, the different modes of bodily existence frame the identity of the anxious subject as one of temporal and narrative discontinuity. In fact, we are faced with at least three modalities of selfhood: a pre-anxious self, an anxious self and a post-anxious self. We take the pre-anxious self as the source of self-identification for the subject. It assumes the role of a centre of orientation, vigilance and avoidance, and is able to survey the potential onset of anxiety from afar. The anxious self erases this distance, and thereby renders the precarious image of the self as non-anxious an illusion. In the aftermath of anxiety, the post-anxious self turns back upon his experience, now unable to consolidate how anxiety and non-anxiety can coexist in the same body without undermining the integrity of the subject. Each of these three delineations thus carries with it a specific way of being-in-the-world, and while they can all be considered as contributing to an overall arc of anxiety, these movements are nevertheless discontinuous in that they do not constitute a unity, but rather divide the self into discrete parts given that each of the parts contradicts one another.

This sense of affective and narrative discontinuity reinforces the sense of the body as being trustworthy only in certain contextual situations. The body, as it is experienced when in the home is markedly different from the body that is in the midst of a crowd of people while waiting to board a plane. Likewise, the agoraphobic person's experience of an urban environment is radically different when accompanied by the presence of a trusted person than when travelling alone. As we have seen, and as we will continue to see, beyond the confines of the home, the body becomes the bearer of a different kind of materiality, and this transformation requires interrogation not only to verify that the hand of the subject is the same one that belongs in the home, but also to ascertain that the hand is *my own*. When away from the home, the homebody becomes an unhomely body, a body that is no longer irreducibly mine, but instead a body that cannot be relied upon as reinforcing the sense of self I identify with.

The temporal structure of the discontinuous body serves to accent the futural orientation of anxiety. Anxiety appears for the subject as a possible threat on the impending horizon. Indeed, from Freud up to contemporary clinical literature, anxiety is framed as an anticipatory mode of being directed at all times towards an unwritten future (cf. Barlow 2004; Marks 1987). Seen in this way, the experience of discontinuity is not only lived from the standpoint of the present; it is also embedded in a projection towards the future. Prior to the onset of anxiety, the subject has an experience of himself in the present. For the most part, it is an image he affirms *as* himself. But from all sides, this precarious – indeed, fictitious – image he has of himself as a non-anxious subject is framed by the possibility of rupture. As the future presses down (imagine our subject must leave the home in order to travel somewhere unfamiliar), so the future becomes a canvas upon which anxiety is cast, defined by the phrase emblematic to the experience of anxiety: *what if*.

The phrase *what if* is registered here in terms of the subject's urge to domesticate if not repress alterity. To ask in concrete terms what if my body gives way while travelling from one point to another is to ask on a more fundamental level: what if the body I trust when at home betrays me when outside the home? Likewise, to ask in very specific terms, what if the underground train stops between stations, exposing the passenger to an indefinite darkness, is also to ask: what if the world betrays my expectation of how it ought to work? In this concern over the future, we are faced with a counterpart to the vigilance directed towards the uncertainty of the body, in its independence and otherness. In each case, the motivation is to reduce and localize the otherness of time and embodiment to the image of that which is most familiar (even if, as Freud taught us, this image is itself a product of anxiety).

Alongside this anticipatory awareness, the function of *ritual* transpires as key in the mastery of anxiety as an unbridled and formless presence, whether it takes form in the body or in the alterity of time more broadly. Most obviously, the role of ritual in domesticating anxiety is at work in obsessive–compulsive disorders, whereupon the subject devises a series of rules in order to localize anxiety, much in the same way an agoraphobe localizes his or her anxiety to a discrete object, be it a bridge or, in classical terms, a broad plaza. Enacting the ritual serves to confer an atmosphere of familiarity upon what is otherwise unknown and unknowable. Seen in this way, it is not by chance that the image often associated with the sufferer of obsessive–compulsive disorders concerns the door both into and away from the home. Time and again, we are told of various rituals performed at the door: opening and shutting the door, using gloves to touch door for fear the handle is ridden with germs, and most frequently, compulsively checking to see if the door is locked (cf. Abramowitz 2005). As the boundary line between inside and out, personal and impersonal, the door becomes the ambassador for a set of anxieties either contained within the home or otherwise dispersed through the world, and to proceed in each direction requires the intervention of this boundary as the guarantor of safety.

Both phobic anxiety and obsessive–compulsive disorders concern behaviour that is, objectively speaking, at odds with a sense of self. The obsessive and compulsive drive, which can motivate a subject to expend his or her energy on a series of Sisyphean tasks – collecting dust particles, counting sand grains, hoarding pinecones – only appear meaningless if we subtract these acts from a broader context. The precise manifestation is less important than the need to localize the vortex of anxiety, which, in the absence of the obsessive act, emerges as an all-consuming, violent force that threatens to destroy the subject. In the act of cultivating a phobic relation to a bridge, or in the insistence on ritualistically sitting on the aisle in a plane, we are confronted with a similar relation to how the obsessive–compulsive subject insists on checking to see if a door is locked. At stake in each of these modes of comporting oneself to the world is the motivation to neutralize the otherness, which underpins the existence of both the phobic and obsessive subject. That cleaning and scrubbing oneself is another key trope in the literature on obsessive–compulsive disorders is yet more evidence for this attempted neutralization of otherness as a kind of possession or infection, now manifest in literal form.

* * *

As we have seen, the reduction of time and embodiment through anticipatory awareness and ritualistic behaviour strives to control the extent to which the pre-anxious self, anxious self and post-anxious self fragment, while also developing the means through which anxiety can be localized to a specific image. If the uneasy relation between anticipation and expectation disturbs the trust we have in both the body and the world, then this futural direction about uncertainty is also mirrored with fixation on the past as a point of *betrayal*. To speak of betrayal in the sense of one's own body as the betrayer seems odd if not paradoxical. When invoking betrayal, we do so usually in intersubjective terms. The betrayer is the one whom I place my trust in only for that trust to be abused. In this way, the act of betrayal requires a certain degree of deliberation on behalf of the betrayer. But can we say the same of our relation to ourselves, and especially to our bodies? In speaking of the experience of rock climbing, Anthony Steinbock touches upon this issue:

> Now, the rock beneath my foot slips, or my fingers get tired and they lose their grip. Do I experience a violation of trust? Did the rock betray my trust? Did my fingers violate my trust in them? I do not think that we can meaningfully speak of violation or betrayal in this instance, and likewise of trust in a genuine sense. (Steinbock 2010, 88)

Steinbock is surely correct to resist assigning the status of betrayal and trust to inanimate objects, but the concept of the body as being immune to self-betrayal is tenable only if we grant the body the affective status of being irreducibly my own. The phenomenology of anxiety provides us with a different impression of the body. From the perspective of the anxious subject, the paradoxical and uncanny status of the body deprives us of the means to unreservedly trust it as a site of stability and self-affirmation. Indeed, the anxious body is an existence that presents itself as having an independence from the subject him- or herself, and to this extent, can never be possessed so long as it transcends me. We maintain our position on the high ledge, but change our perspective through Sartre's analysis of vertigo.

> Vertigo is anguish to the extent that I am afraid not of falling over the precipice, but of throwing myself over. A situation

provokes fear if there is a possibility of my life being changed from without; my being provokes anguish to the extent that *I distrust myself and my own reactions in that situation.* (Sartre 1998, 29. Emphasis added)

Against Steinbock, Sartre gives us a different account of self-betrayal. The relationship here between vertigo and anxiety does not concern the materiality of the precipice itself, but instead one's own boundaries in the face of the fall. The distrust I have within myself is nothing less than an expression of the contingency of the self as indeterminate, and, of course, for Sartre, radically free. If the materiality of the precipice exists as a more or less stable object of fear in the world, then what remains entirely unpredictable is how *I* respond to this object, whether that object is a cliff or another person. Moreover, the freedom that derives from this situation, which is to be contrasted at all times with a localized fear of the precipice as an objective danger, is dizzying, and in this height, anxiety emerges in the impossibility of tying myself down to a fixed relation with the precipice.

The mistrust in one's own boundaries is not peculiar to Sartre's illustration, nor by any means unusual. Clinical cases of patients terrified of how they will respond to situations of danger, such as crossing bridges and fearing they may 'become crazed and, in panic, jump over the rail' are recurring motifs, especially for agoraphobic subjects (Chambless and Goldstein 1982, 131). Likewise, in a case from 1890, the same compulsion reappears on a boat: 'This feeling [of anxiety] is at times so strong that even when on a steamboat or a vessel, I cannot bear to look across any wide expanse of water, feeling almost impelled to jump in and out of sheer desperation' (cited in Marks 1987, 326). What Sartre brings to the foreground in such circumstances is the opacity of the body. Of course, what Sartre is describing is not the anonymous body as the site of an autonomous agency, but instead the radical contingency of the subject as lacking a fixed essence. In each case, the possibility of throwing oneself over the precipice, together with the anxiety this prospect entails, involves a movement of self-betrayal, insofar as we take the betrayed and the betrayer as a distinction between the fixed and radically free subject. The free subject enters the stage in the shape of anguish, displacing the role fixed upon the subject in a gesture of bad faith, and thus is experientially given as a betrayal of the image of oneself as stable. In this context, the question posed by phobic patients in this situation is telling; namely, what if I go mad in this situation and throw myself off the cliff or bridge (132)? At stake in this madness is not a psychotic breakdown of the subject, but instead a confrontation with madness as a level of subjectivity ordinarily concealed in waking life.

Metaphysically, we are not in the realm of a Cartesian dualism, in which different selves demarcate two substances. Indeed, it is precisely because we maintain a phenomenological commitment to the subject as a *bodily* subject that the very experience of alienation and anxiety is possible. If we were approaching anxiety from a Cartesian or Lockean perspective, then arguably the detachment of mind and body would be the grounds of relief rather than anxiety. What matters is that the experience of interrogating the body both as an organ of perception and as the expression of my being-in-the-world leads to the destruction in the integrity of self. This interrogation emerges from the broader history of the body, with a special appeal to cases of what we term 'self-betrayal'.

As we have already seen, for Freud, the anxious dimension of agoraphobia is rooted in '*the recollection of an anxiety attack*' (Freud 2001a, 81). Past experience emerges here as a pivot, against which the agoraphobic subject is able to measure the likelihood of encountering a given situation without being faced with a threat to the image of self, thus one patient writes, 'When the time comes I fortify myself by recalling my past victories, remind myself that I can only die once and that it probably won't be as bad as this' (cited in Marks 1987, 346). In circumstances where the subject takes a leap into the unknown only to be met with panic upon finding him- or herself in the middle of a bridge, both unable to proceed to the end while also incapable of returning to the beginning, and so stuck in the hinterland between places – in such a situation, the ensuing shame is directed at the body, which materializes as the betrayer of a trust (naïvely) placed in it. The body thus becomes inscribed with a litany of near disasters (along with some victories), from which the agoraphobe is negatively educated in Kierkegaard's model of anxiety as a 'school' (Kierkegaard 1981, 156).

The significance attributed to rituals as a way of ordering anxiety finds another expression in the usage of so-called props. Already we have encountered the prop as the means of generating a sense of self-integrity, otherwise lacking in the troubled mistrust placed in the body. Think back to the role the cart plays in the supermarket and the lamppost plays on the bridge. In each case, the object functions not only as a means of steadying balance, but also of maintaining a relation with the world above and beyond the subject's transformation in the world. The object – emblematically and historically that of an umbrella or a bicycle – is both steady in its essential and unwavering quality as a distinct object, but also steadying in terms of allowing for a relationship with the world despite the body's vulnerability to collapse.

'The presence of a cart', so we read in a case study from 1884, 'even a stick or umbrella in the hand, persons, or trees, gives a sense of confidence when walking an unknown road' (White 1884, 1140). To be clear, out concern with objects such as umbrellas is not with their status in empirical terms, less even with the factual prospect of the object as being able to physically support the subject. For the agoraphobe, the umbrella enters the horizon of

FIGURE 2.2 *Rue Chanoinesse, Paris.*

experience as an entrusted other, providing therein a familiar and reassuring presence. We can refer here to a case study from 1898, in which a medical doctor, Dr Headley Neale (and fellow sufferer of agoraphobia), writes as follows:

> I have referred to the possibility of recognising the 'agoraphobic' as he walks along the street. Apart from the coarser evidence of his suddenly pausing to lay hold of a paling or to place a hand upon a wall, he will hardly ever be without a stick or umbrella, which you will notice he will plant at each step at some distance from him, in order to increase his line of support. (Neale 1898, 1323)

The distinct gait of the agoraphobe – cautious, uneven, erratic – testifies to a reliance upon props to guide the body through the world. Lacking trust in his body as both an objective thing positioned in the world and a centre of perception through which the world is experienced, the agoraphobe converts this instability through a transference to the objects around him. As his body extends to the umbrella, undermining a strict distinction between the two, so the prop becomes enshrouded with a totemic and ritualistic significance elevated beyond its mere existence as a device to fend off rain.

The individuation of a zone of safety in the form of a prop such as an umbrella reflects a much broader tactic for survival, which is played out in the agoraphobe's rigid way of being-in-the-world, adhering at all times to a need to be near the exit, on the margin, behind the column, within proximity of a beacon of escape and stability. In the case of an open umbrella, we have a particularly striking expression of both the agoraphobe's refusal to face the world on its terms, and instead to filter it through the perception of a screen, as well as a means to conceal oneself from the intrusive gaze of others. Once more, the screen serves to divide the subject from the world, establishing a distance that prevents him from getting too close to the world as the site of an anonymous if not hostile existence. To see the world through a screen (and note the invariant presence of dark glasses for the agoraphobe) is to gain the illusion of being able to editorially select content that either reinforces the subject's standing in the world or otherwise risks destroying it (cf. Marks 1987, 338). In turn, this selective perception of the world extends beyond localized objects and becomes invested in the surrounding environment along with the people in that environment. Thus, in one of Westphal's patients, Mr C, the following observations are made:

> The same feeling of fear overtakes him when he needs to walk along walls and extended buildings or through streets on Holiday Sundays, or evenings and nights when the shops are closed. In the latter part of the evening – he usually dines in restaurants – he helps himself in a peculiar way in Berlin; he either waits until another person walks in the direction of his house and follows him closely, or he acquaints himself with a lady of the evening, begins to talk with her, and takes her along until another similar opportunity arises, thus gradually reaching his residence. Even the red lanterns of the taverns serve him as support; as soon as he see one his fear disappears. (Knapp 1988, 60–61)

With Mr C, we bear witness to an extension of the trusted object into the presence of another person, able to guide the patient through the world in the same way an inanimate object does. We shall have more to say of the agoraphobe's relations with others in the following chapter. In the meantime, consider how the agency of the other person is rendered a mere prop for the patient. If there is a trust involved in this relation, then it is a trust that is stipulated on the agoraphobe's insistence on framing objects as having a fixed essence to them, incapable of betraying their own nature. This objectification of the other person serves to portray him or her as corporeal expressions of home, where we take the homely dimension to typify the 'safe' world, which at all times reinforces and mirrors the patient's sense of self. To succumb to panic in the company of the trusted companion means being able to survive the bodily metamorphosis from a centre of meaning to a site of impersonal existence without entirely undergoing a loss of self. More precisely, that the companion ensures the 'survival' of the subject means surviving the onset of panic *as* a self, rather than enduring as a biological and organic body. All of which is possible thanks to the fact the other person becomes a surrogate prop for the agoraphobe to reinforce and solidify a body, which, lacking something or someone to hold onto, risks collapse.

4. Nausea and slime

Sealed off from the surrounding station, the waiting area of the Eurostar terminal in the Gare du Nord is an enclosed world. In it, there is a small space marking the transition from the cultural milieu of Paris to that of London. Passing from the French to the British passport control, the traveller will drop their baggage through the security check before reclaiming it on the other side. There, one can take a seat in the waiting area at the lower end of Gare du Nord before boarding the Eurostar. At 250 feet beneath sea level, the train will journey through the darkness separating the two countries. Finally, the passenger will emerge in Great Britain on the same train boarded in Paris a mere two hours before. Such a miracle of transport remains for you a figment of your anxious imagination, forged while you still occupy the waiting area of this transitional place.

A vast window overlooks the Rue du Maubeuge. It runs parallel to the waiting room, marking another life outside of the Gare du Nord. You are positioned as close to the window as is possible, as though the mere sight of an exterior world in all its clarity will become more accessible to you, despite being sealed off by thick glass. There is no escape other than through the way you came, backwards through the passport control, once more passing from British to French hands, before returning to the streets of Paris. Other people come and go on Rue du Maubeuge, and you view them from above while they remain entirely oblivious to your gaze. As the train nears its departure, the space becomes crowded. The once deserted seats that surrounded you on all sides are now filled with passengers, each of whom locked in their own world will eventually board a train just as you plan to.

These moments of anticipation are charged with the pathos of drama. In the minutes separating you from the train, you have no idea whether you will survive the wait. You cannot be trusted to retain your composure and the presence of other people sitting in and around you only underscores the unpredictability of how your body will respond to this situation. Very often, you will flinch without provocation. A trail of sweat will form on your forehead before dripping on your cheek. You will grip the collar of your shirt; a button will shoot off, landing in a remote region of the waiting room. But no matter how much you tear at your clothes, the anxiety cannot be rid off. It remains beneath the skin, within you, yet registered as an invasive presence. When your anxiety escalates and you panic – that sensation of needing to be *anywhere* aside from here – then it will remain for you an unvoiced and silent presence. It will occur solely within the interior of your existence, and other people will merely witness the surface expression of a disquiet that forms a fundamental discord in you.

The anxiety possesses you, betrays you. Manifesting itself in and through your body, the anxiety seizes control, constricting your breath and rendering you mute. Now, it is you that are subjected to the clairvoyance of your body, which senses a danger inaccessible to your own reflections. Thanks to some invisible arrangement, the waiting room at the Eurostar terminal in Paris has set these sensations alight. The place has exposed you as a forgery, no longer identifiable with your personalized body but instead a stranger within your own skin. That you are able to conceal and maintain a semblance of composure outside of the station is due merely to good fortune. This appearance, however, is an achievement rather than a given, and the revelation of your existence as a contingent image superimposed upon what is otherwise a largely formless mass is irreducibly *nauseating*.

* * *

Anxiety is both in the world and beneath our skin. Because of its liminal status – as neither belonging to one space nor another, but instead converging on the ever-changing terrain between borders – anxiety proves an elusive phenomenon. Upon emerging, it disappears; in disappearing, it reappears. Unable to be tied down, anxiety belongs, to paraphrase Heidegger, in the *nowhere*. All of which we can discern from the lived experience of anxiety. Part of the destabilizing quality of anxiety is its resistance to sedimentation and certainty. Can we, after all, ever be sure that the experience we are having is, without question, anxiety, and not some other phantom of our waking lives? Anxiety distorts and repels our attempt at drawing a frame over it. Thus, any phenomenology of anxiety remains a liminal one, a method that pursues the mood without ever dwelling alongside it, except as a form of resistance. Our attention is drawn to the slippery shadows where anxiety derives and gravitates. One way to conceptualize this shadowline is through Sartre's notion of nausea.

The rationale for turning to Sartre's concept of nausea is that with it, we find a conceptual vocabulary that complements Merleau-Ponty's distinction between the personal and anonymous body of perception. Yet while Merleau-Ponty presents the bodily subject as being structured by a series of boundaries between the personal and impersonal, those boundaries nevertheless exist in a porous and dynamic relation with one another. To this end, anxiety as a phenomenological experience remains impossible so long as the body's different levels of exist in an ambiguous if ultimately unified relation with one another. With Sartre, the boundaries and levels structuring the body do not interact in a fluid and dynamic way, but instead appear as rigid delineators, which, in coming into contact, destabilize the image of the subject as sovereign. We have, then, two different accounts of the subject, each of which shed light upon the other. Yet what is vital in Sartre's analysis is not his account of the ontology of the subject, but the visceral and affective sense of the body's capacity to melt – a dimension that is arguably necessary to any phenomenology of anxiety – which is present but not explicit in Merleau-Ponty's account. To get a sense of the visceral affectivity inherent in Sartre's concept, let us plunge into the murky world of Antoine Roquentin.

'Something has happened to me', so Sartre writes at the beginning of *Nausea*, 'I can't doubt it any more' (Sartre 1964, 4). As is well known, what had happened to Antoine Roquentin is that both his body and his world were transformed from a solid and reliable mass to a nauseous thing, which is both constantly wavering and wholly unfamiliar. 'It came as an illness does', so Sartre notes before continuing his reflections:

> [T]here is something new about my hands, a certain way of picking up my pipe or fork … just as I was coming into my room, I stopped short because I felt in my hand a cold object which held my attention through a sort of personality. I opened my hand, looked: I was simply holding the door-knob. This morning in the library, when the Self-Taught Man came to say good morning to me, it took me ten seconds to recognize him. I saw an unknown face, barely a face. Then there was his hand like a fat white worm in my own hand. I dropped it almost immediately and the arm fell back flabbily. (4)

The opening lines of *Nausea* are striking on several levels. In the first case, the hand appears to be strange, and therefore obtrudes into the consciousness of Roquentin. In response, Roquentin considers to what extent this strangeness inheres in the hand or in the pipe. Yet again, the same disturbance creeps into the door-knob. We ask the same question as that of our existence in the supermarket: does the hand bring its strangeness to the door or was that strangeness already there? We discover that Roquentin is witnessing this increasing nausea spread to the world more broadly. Now, in the face of another person, ten seconds must pass before the man can be identified as having a face of his own. In each case, both body and thing begin to lose their irreducible and singular identity as 'one's own' and now become impregnated with a sense of the uncanny.

The sense of the uncanny in Sartre's novel recurs time and again, each time finding a new mode of expression. From objects in general, to the face, to the division between inside and out, and then towards space and time, Sartre's book can be read as a mediation on the uncanny, which, though manifest in innumerable ways, always finds

FIGURE 2.3 *Rue du Prévôt, Paris.*

its root in the body itself. Indeed, the body that appears and then disappears in *Nausea* extends beyond the caricature of 'existentialist hero' by defining itself quite precisely in phenomenological terms as a body at the intersection of the I and the non-I, the personal and impersonal, and the specific and anonymous at once. It is a body that betrays the Husserlian account of the body as being a 'zero point' of orientation, and presents itself instead as a series of parts and fragments. More than this, it is a body on the verge not simply of inhumanity, but also of an animality. Time and again, the body appears as fishy or in other occasions, crabby. The hand 'lives – it is me. It opens, the fingers open and point. It is lying on its back. It shows me its fat belly. It looks like an animal turned upside down…like the claws of a crab which has fallen on its back' (98). Throughout, there is a porous interchangeability between body parts and objects, with each thing rejecting the name arbitrarily imposed upon it and, as a result, liberated from having a form. Take the face as it appears in this novel. It is a particular kind of face, one that finds its origins in human flesh, but a face that nevertheless appears to deform the flesh. 'There is', so Sartre writes, 'a white hole in the wall, a mirror. It is a trap' (16). Unable to resist taking a look at the 'grey thing' reflected in the mirror, Roquentin draws in closer:

> It is the reflection of my face. Often in these lost days I study it. I can understand nothing of this face. The faces of others have some sense, some direction. Not mine. I cannot even decide whether it is handsome or ugly…At heart, I am even shocked that anyone can attribute qualities of this kind to it, as if you called a clod of earth or a block of stone beautiful or ugly…Obviously there are a nose, two eyes and a mouth, but none of it makes sense, there is not even a human expression…When I was little, my Aunt Bigeois told me 'If you look at yourself too long in the mirror, you'll see a monkey.' I must have looked at myself even longer than that: what I see is well below the monkey, on the fringe of the vegetable world, at the level of jellyfish. It is alive, I can't say it isn't…The eyes especially are horrible seen so close. They are glassy, soft, blind, red-rimmed, they look like fish scales. (16–17)

Sartre divests the face of its human attributes and renders it a set of discrete parts, no longer bound by anything in common, except for occupying the same patch of flesh. With this decomposition of meaning, the face can no longer be understood in aesthetic terms. To confer the quality of ugly upon it is already to presuppose a certain knowledge of the face. But in this nauseous face, bodily knowledge is lacking, and the face becomes a part of the same world as blocks of earth, of which it would be equally absurd to cite as 'beautiful'. Throughout this fragmentation, the body in its brute materiality persists. The parts that constitute the face do not vanish at the moment their meaning is put into question. Instead, they transcend that loss of meaning, but only now reveal their underside as anonymous and nameless. As understood from a nauseous perspective, things resist the human attempt at being tied down to how they appear for consciousness. As Sartre indicates, life goes on – 'It is alive' – but it is a life reduced to the level of a gelatinous lifeform, amorphous in its structure, and lacking any fixed essence.

Sartre's concept of nausea runs strikingly close to the formulation of anxiety as involving a transformation of the body towards an anonymous materiality, no longer irreducibly human, but instead, suggestive of what Sartre describes as a 'dumb, organic sense' (17). As with anxiety, nausea assumes either a tacit, free-floating mood that shapes our experience of the world in a pre-cognitive way, or, it becomes thematized explicitly in our experience of the body as a site of disintegration and alienation. Here, too, we find a similar double-sided structure to Sartre's account of nausea. On the one hand, nausea is diffused through the world as a vague and non-specific movement of disquiet: 'It came as an illness does, not like an ordinary certainty not like anything evident' (4). On the other hand, and more often than not, it announces itself sharply as a gradual transformation of the world, such that 'the Nausea seized me, I dropped to a seat, I no longer know where I was; I saw the colours spin around me, I wanted to vomit' (18–19). Of this seizure, it is, of course, the body that becomes the foremost place of nausea. The body, as Sartre presents it, is an amorphous body, a body that has been hollowed out and inverted. This hollow deprives the body of a discernible affective form, be it pleasure or pain, and in this absence, nausea comes to light as an apprehension of the body's contingency. Several years after *Nausea*, Sartre returns to the theme of the hollow body in *Being and Nothingness*, writing that:

> Coenesthetic affectivity is then a pure, non-positional apprehension of a contingency without color, a pure apprehension

of the self as a factual existence. This perpetual apprehension on the part of my for-itself of an insipid taste which I cannot place, which accompanies me even in my efforts to get away from it, and which is my taste – this is what we have described elsewhere under the name of Nausea. A dull and inescapable nausea perpetually reveals my body to my consciousness. (Sartre 1998, 338)

True to his phenomenological heritage, the nausea that embeds itself in Sartre's account of the body also finds expression in the world more broadly, thus he writes, 'The Nausea is not inside me: I feel it *out there* in the wall, in the suspenders, everywhere around me. It makes itself one with the café, I am the one who is within *it*' (Sartre 1964, 19–20). In describing street scenes, Sartre extends this world: 'The Boulevard Noir is inhuman. Like a mineral. Like a triangle' (26). We are witnessing the extension of the body's mutation in spatial form. It is a world in-itself, whereupon people are also subjected to a loss of personalization: 'Here are some people. Two shadows. What did they need to come here for?' (26). Time, also, is subjected to the fate of nausea, as temporal order is stripped of its fixed structure: 'Nothing happens while you live. The scenery changes, people come in and go out, that's all. There are no beginnings' (39). Objects as innocuous as books come into question, their presence reduced to a derealized screen of appearance, no longer situated within the context of a referential whole: 'Nothing seemed true; I felt surrounded by cardboard scenery which could quickly be removed…I looked at these unstable beings which, in an hour, in a minute, were perhaps going to crumble' (77). Against this ever-present possibility of collapse, it is only through 'laziness that the world is the same day after day. Today it seemed to want to change. And then, *anything, anything* could happen' (77). The utter contingency of things, compounded with the sense that anything could happen at any time, gives rise to the vertiginous aspect of nausea. When the nausea strikes Roquentin, it does so with a dizzying force, disempowering not only his relation to his body, but also to his immediate surroundings and the objects within those surroundings, which now gain a supernatural quality divorced from the meaning superimposed upon them:

A real panic took hold of me. I didn't know where I was going…As long as I could stare at things nothing would happen: I looked

at them as much as I could, pavements, houses, gaslights; my
eyes went rapidly from one to the other, to catch them unawares,
stop them in the midst of their metamorphosis. They didn't look
too natural, but I told myself forcibly: this is a gaslight, this is a
drinking fountain, and I tried to reduce them to their everyday
aspect by the power of my gaze. (78)

The passage presents us with a compressed attempt at forging a
home (parallel to that of the panic room we encountered in the
previous chapter), upon which Roquentin can regain his perspectival
bearings. This passion is taken up in the simple act of gazing at
things. Here, we have an especially striking image of the attempt
at keeping things in place through fixating upon them visually,
enacting what Merleau-Ponty would term the 'narcissism of vision'
(Merleau-Ponty 1968, 139). This gesture is already familiar to us
as a mode of surveying the body's response to the world through
a vigilant gaze. So long as things – not least the human body –
are surveyed by sight (ostensibly the most rational but also violent
of the senses), then the meaning given to those things stands a
better chance of remaining placed. Through a forceful reduction,
vision restores what objects themselves reject: their existential
meaning. This gesture of monitoring things in order to forestall
their metamorphosis is taken as the ultimate statement of egology,
consisting of nothing less than a conversion of the alterity of things
to the sameness of the I. As such, the attempt fails and Roquentin
finds himself once more haunted by the world around him: 'Doors
of houses frightened me especially. I was afraid they would open of
themselves' (Sartre 1964, 78).

Passages such as this give us indication of the two salient
features of anxiety: the mistrust placed in things together with the
formlessness of things. 'As long as I could stare at things nothing
would happen.' With this indictment of a thing's autonomy, the
world becomes a site of potential betrayal and discontinuity, in
which anything could happen and at any time. This loss of trust
in things is intertwined and interdependent with the lawlessness of
matter itself. That things exist means that they do so on the verge
of almost (but never entirely) being dissolved: 'Things are divorced
from their names. They are grotesque, headstrong, gigantic and
it seems ridiculous to call them seats or say anything at all about
them: I am in the midst of things, nameless things' (125). In his

venerated account of the root of a chestnut tree, we witness the final expression of the impenetrable resistance of things existing in an infinite cycle of forming, deforming and reforming:

> T]he root, the park gates, the bench, the sparse grass, all that had vanished: the diversity of things, their individuality, were only an appearance, a veneer. This veneer had melted, leaving soft, monstrous masses, all in disorder – naked, in a frightful, obscene nakedness…This root, with its colour, shape, its congealed movement, was…below all explanation. Each of its qualities escaped it a little, flowed out of it, solidified, almost became a thing…This moment was extraordinary. I was there, motionless and icy, plunged in horrible ecstasy. (127–131)

In the forever shifting boundaries that both veil and unveil things, Sartre locates the specificity of anxiety in material terms. At stake in this moment is not an abstract recognition of factual contingency, but a 'vision' that leaves one 'breathless' (127). As a disordering of boundaries, anxiety spreads in and through the world, defamiliarizing and depersonalizing the everydayness of habitual experience, and rendering it the site of an unhomely alienation. The anxiety that emerges in the mood of nausea does so, therefore, with a horrifying and visceral presence. Such an anxiety departs from the contemplative mood one finds in Heidegger's account, and situates us, instead, in an 'obscene' world, where even the thought of one's own death reinstates the stubborn and elemental persistence of indifferent matter, which can never be possessed: '*In the way*, my corpse, my blood on these stones, between these plants, at the back of this smiling garden…my bones, at last, cleaned, stripped, peeled, proper and clean as teeth, it would have been *In the way*' (128–129). What is in the way is the superfluous excess of the body, which, despite being constitutive of the self, is nevertheless other than, and in certain situations, even against selfhood.

Here, Heidegger comes to an agreement with Sartre: 'In anxiety beings as a whole become superfluous. In what sense does this happen? Beings are not annihilated by anxiety, so that nothing is left. Rather the nothing makes itself known with being and in beings expressly as a slipping away of the whole' (Heidegger 1977, 104). But Sartre goes beyond Heidegger in his emphasis on a movement of slipping by returning this theme to that of the body itself. Let us not be surprised, therefore, that Sartre will talk of things as *oozing* and *melting* in response to the imposition of meaning (Sartre 1964, 130–131). What is repelling (if also compelling) about anxiety is the movement of interstitial being that opens up in the gap between the experience of oneself as coherent and knowable and the realization that this level of familiarity is only an image. The gap is not a static or neutral space waiting to be colonized or excavated. Rather, the space emerges in the form of a fundamental threat to the image of selfhood as a sanctuary from the insecurity of the world.

Sartre's conception of a psychoanalysis of slime articulates the repugnant and horrifying quality of interstitial space as having both a moral and ontological dimension to it (Sartre 1998, 604). At stake in the image of slime is a 'fusion of the world with myself', only the fusion is not a co-dependent harmonious synthesis, but instead involves an 'outline of appropriation' (606). The slime enters my horizon as an amorphous materiality, as a *'leech sucking me'* (606). The oozing quality of slime derives neither from myself nor from naked materiality, but instead from an 'ontological expression of the entire world', which individualizes itself quite precisely in the amorphous mass of slime. Sartre's elaboration of this expression is both incisive in-itself and also pertinent to our study of anxious corporeality.

There are a number of points that Sartre mentions, each of which contributes to the overarching quality of slime as a zone of pure interstitiality. In the first case, the slime is beyond possession. Unlike water, which Sartre utilizes as a counter-example, slime 'rolls over us' in an 'infinite temporality' (607). Thus, in distinction to the lucid image of constant becoming suggested in the Heraclitean river, slime appears in 'slow motion', marking the 'agony of water' (607). For these reasons, slime occupies the disturbing (and disturbed) terrain between solidity and liquidity, as he writes, 'Nothing testifies more clearly to its ambiguous character as a "substance in between two states" than the slowness with which the slime melts into itself' (607). In its lassitude and density, the slime does not lend itself to being captured, or otherwise slowed down to the point of becoming a solid thing, despite appearing as though it can be possessed thanks to this slowness. Rather, the non-possessable dimension of slime is taken up as the unfolding of constant becoming that neither ends nor begins, but instead folds back upon its own materiality, forging an increasingly complex layer of existence, which, in expanding its sphere of influence, appropriates things within its embrace. Sartre contrasts this hideous formation with that of a drop of water 'touching the surface of a large body of water' (607). Almost instantaneously, the waters converge and become one, without any boundary dividing them. Here, there is no struggle to speak of, and no excess produced, which would threaten the stability of the pool of water. The same is also true if I myself jump into water, boundaries remain intact, as does personal identity: 'I experience no discomfort, for I do not have any fear whatsoever that I may dissolve in it; I remain a solid in its liquidity' (610). Where the slime is concerned, any such absorption of foreign matter is met throughout with resistance: 'In the slimy substance which dissolves into itself there is a visible resistance, like the refusal of an individual who does not want to be annihilated in the whole of being' (608). The 'softness' that accompanies this movement does not eventually integrate itself into a moment of solidity or liquidity, but instead is preserved as softness, much like, to use Sartre's formulation, 'a retarded annihilation' (608). The slime is not a passive backdrop, against which I can propel myself from it. Rather, to fall into the slime risks becoming lost within it, 'like the haunting memory of a *metamorphosis*' (610).

The creeping movement of the slime, venerated in the genre of classical horror for its ominous quality, is not a pure fiction, but instead a mode of formulating the nature of matter itself. As with the body in its anxiety, there is a duplicitous structure to the formulation of slime: 'Only at the very moment when I believe that I possess it, behold by a curious reversal, *it* possesses me' (608). Here, the slime turns, revealing itself not only to be experientially slippery, but ontologically, too. Sartre's hand has become immersed in a pool of slime: 'I want to let go of the slimy and it sticks to me, it draws me, it sucks at me' (609). The more the hand tries to free itself of the slime, the greater it becomes entrenched within it. The slime, this 'poisonous possession', gets under the fingernails, within the cracks of the hand, without at any point fusing with that hand (609). There is no evasion, less even a destruction of the hand. If the slime breaks apart upon the removal of the hand, then it only reconfigures elsewhere. This pure interstitiality is the spectre of an indifferent superfluity.

In the figure of slime, we find the consummate expression of both the structure and the thematic content of the anxious body. In no uncertain terms, slime indexes a materiality that is not only between states, but also attaches itself in the manner of a leech to those states. In the attempt to free ourselves of the slime, we only become more entangled within it. And so, the slime deprives the image of the bodily self as autonomous while reinforcing its quality as being beyond possession. In this, the slime proves repugnant and horrifying. At the heart of this horrific affect is the power of slime to deform boundaries while leaving the subject intact, if paralysed. To speak of a slimy body is to speak of a body that is tied down by its own thickness.

We speak of the anxious body in the same way: it is a body that is in the first instance situated between different if not contradictory states. As both mine and not-mine, personal and impersonal, specific and anonymous, the anxious body's malleability reflects its slimy nature. Moreover, because this movement is listless rather than dynamic, the interstitial quality of the anxious body invokes repulsion rather than delight. A body that is in the process of transforming itself suggests affirmation so long as that transformation takes as its point of departure a desiring subject. In the case of the anxious body, the metamorphosis is experienced as an invasion, which threatens to destabilize rather than reinforce the subject. Hence, just as the slime leaves a trace upon its departure, so the fragmentation of the anxious self is only realized once the moment has passed.

Furthermore, the materialization of the slime upon the body – to think here of the hand – finds form in our accent on the anxious body as a self-alienated body. In the moments before the body has been re-constituted and re-identified as *my* body, it appears for the subject in a fleeting moment as residual, alien and elemental. The anxiety that frames this movement of self-alienation does not *de facto* carry with it a sense of 'panic'. Rather, we are in the midst of an uncanny expression of anxiety, an anxiety subtended to by a noiseless disquiet, which is exposed nevertheless at all times to the possibility of paroxysm, such that the body ceases to function as a human body. Anxiety, like slime, leaves a mark upon the subject, and this mark is not an innocuous memory destined to vanish, but a presence that continues to exert an active presence upon the structure of the subject. As with the slime, moreover, anxiety dwells under the skin, possessing and haunting the subject even when the subject is unaware of its presence.

* * *

From a seemingly innocent journey to a supermarket – surely, the exemplary 'non-place' – we have been led through the complex, multidimensional topography of the body's anxious being-in-the-world. This journey, which began with the sense of the body as one's own, has ended with a very different incarnation of bodily existence. Indeed, the body that emerges in anxiety does so on the fringe of experience. Such a body issues a challenge not only to our sense of self, but also to phenomenology's treatment of the body as a largely invulnerable locus of unity. The body as we find and experience it in anxiety, transforms human subjectivity into an almost impersonal thing, no longer one's own, yet at the same time, not entirely alien. In and of itself, what is anxiety inducing about this transformation is not the existence of impersonal, non-possessable and unknown aspects of bodily existence themselves. We can readily imagine a relationship to the different levels of the body, such that anxiety does not come to the foreground. When one of my limbs is burnt, I do not experience the process of healing – which is, after all, an impersonal process that occurs irrespective of 'my' relation to the body – as inducing anxiety. The reasons for this non-appearance of anxiety centre on the fact that the healing of the body reinforces my sense of self rather than dissolving that sense. Structurally speaking, the ambiguous and duplicitous side of the body does not 'cause' anxiety. Rather, the emergence of anxiety takes form in a specific relation to the body, such that the encounter with the impersonal dimension of the body invokes a destabilization in the self, thus rendering the experience of anonymous bodily life an experience of uncanny matter.

Seen in this way, the experience of anxiety and nausea does not mark a departure from an otherwise normal or stable life, but instead amplifies and accents structures, themes and dimensions, which are there all along in non-anxious life. The unstable transition between the personal and the impersonal is not peculiar to anxiety, but is an invariant structure of the body more broadly. What is specific about anxiety is that the experience of this impersonal dimension threatens the image of the self *as a coherent and fully mastered self*. We have described this threat in terms of the uncanny, given that the expression and materialization of anxiety involved in this movement renders the body both present and absent at once. As the body undergoes doubt, so an insistence on rituals and props enters the frame. Yet if we have so far described these props as inanimate objects elevated in their symbolic value, then we have also seen how other people function in a similar way for the subject of anxiety. What remains to be said is how other people are not only ambassadors of a homely presence, but how in turn, they can also assume a hostile role in the life of the phobic subject. In what follows, we will attend to this intersubjective dimension.

CHAPTER THREE

Two Ocular Globes

Everybody who passed by looked at him, stared at him, all those faces, pallid in the evening light. He tried to concentrate on some thought, but he could not. All he felt was an emptiness in his head. His whole body trembled and sweat ran down him. He staggered, and now I am falling too. People stop, more and more people, a frightening number of people.

(EDVARD MUNCH)

The bus journey

It is two o'clock on a grey Tuesday afternoon and you are standing at a bus stop on Boulevard Henri IV waiting for the 86 bus. The bus will take you over the Pont de Sully, through the hustle of Saint-Germain-des-Prés, where you will get off before connecting to the 39 bus. Once on the 39, you will travel deep into the southern edge of Paris. Along the way, you will cross Sèvres-Babylone, which delineates one edge of Paris from another. There, you will twist gradually into the depths of Rue de Vaugirard, before reaching Rue Lecourbe in the abyss of the 15th arrondissement. Having arrived, you will then walk along the Boulevard Victor before coming to your destination: the now disbanded Centre de Recherche en Épistémologie Appliquée.

Perched on a seat, you scan your immediate field of perception, giving special attention to places to retreat to, should the anxiety escalate. Although you are unable to visually see your home, you detect its proximity on Rue Saint Paul as a reassuring warmth in your body. When you stand up to gain a better view of incoming traffic, you experience a surge of dizziness pulse through your head. The dizziness is only abated when the bus approaches. You exhale slowly. When it arrives, you are reassured that the bus is comparatively free of passengers. Those passengers that have boarded the bus are either gazing out the window or otherwise buried in newspapers. You take a seat by the window, focus on the outside world and continue to breathe slowly.

The electric doors close and the bus recommences its journey. At the next stop – on the Quai de Béthune – a flux of passengers enters the bus. Despite your best effort to will them away, one of the passengers sits next to you. He is a middle-aged man carrying a suitcase. He takes his seat and begins reading a newspaper. Experiencing the person as trapping you in the seat, you immediately tense your fist and feel a thrust of hostility directed towards the passenger. A transformation is beginning to take place in your experience of the world. Every heterogeneous marker that you pass – a square, a monument or a notable building – becomes further evidence of your distance from home. Indeed, you measure space less in geometrical terms, and more in respect of how anxious your body has become.

When the bus passes over the Pont de Sully, you feel the ground beneath you swell with vertiginous force. As though you are floating in mid-air, you grip the man next to you tightly with the aim of rooting yourself in place. But before you have the chance to murmur an apology, your body has begun another series of involuntary reactions and spasms. You grasp the collar of your shirt so tight that three of the buttons proceed to pop off in a comical fashion, landing somewhere on the floor of the bus. As the vehicle turns a sharp corner, you automatically fix your hand on the window, as you feel your inner organs judder violently with every turn in the bus's course.

Beyond the bridge, the bus is now in dense crowds and traffic-infested roads along the Rue des Écoles. It stops in the midst of congestion. The large windows open upon a stream of people. At times, you cannot even be sure that these beings are indeed human,

FIGURE 3.1 *Boulevard Henri IV, Paris.*

such is the intense aura of unfamiliarity permeating the enclosure of the bus. The trembling you experienced when crossing the bridge is now accompanied by intense pangs of hunger and thirst. Sensing that you might imminently slip into unconsciousness, you wade through your bag in a frenzied state looking for a bottle of water. The respite afforded by the water is only momentary. As the bus surfaces from the traffic, it journeys through a series of alleyways near the Rue de l'École de Médecine. The seemingly high walls, enclosed darkness and lack of view gives you the impression of being swallowed at sea by mounting waves and thunderous clouds. All that prevents you from succumbing to a primal urge to flee is the thought of being abandoned in an unfamiliar part of the city. That you are able to maintain the course is only because you are now clutching your phone, braced to establish contact with the world of familiarity.

With your phone to your ear, you mutter words through trembling teeth, 'On the bus…can't breathe…feel like I'm going to die …'.

The voice on the other end of the call is familiar and calming. As the person begins to talk you out of an anxious state, you become aware of the incongruity of the situation, as though the reassuring tone of their voice were mutually incompatible with the alienness of the bus journey. But the two realms are joined in the space of the bus. In being reminded of the need to breathe slowly, you absorb the calmness of the other person's tone into your body, as though you had previously forgotten to breathe and were instead relying on an external cue to activate your breathing apparatus. Slowly you begin to resume a non-anxious mode of being. Only instead of returning to a pre-anxious body, the post-anxious body you have now fallen into is drained of energy, depleted of spirit and in the midst of an intense migraine. Looking around the interior of the bus, the wariness you previously felt gives way to a numb exhaustion. You sink into the chair in a state of deflated gloom.

The problem of other people

Until now, our attention has been drawn towards the individual experience of anxiety. However, whether it be in the rapport one has with the home or with the body, this experience is mediated at all times with our relation with others. In this chapter, we will explore the multidimensional way other people contribute to the experience of anxiety. Indeed, the question of how the other constitutes our sense of self is not a novel one. While it is true that the 'question of the other' has a rich history in the phenomenological tradition, gaining a clear sense of the relationship between the experience of the world and the experience of others remains a complex issue despite this heritage.

In what follows, we will see two things. First, intersubjectivity is essentially an issue of intercorporeality. This claim can be taken in the context of the 'problem of other minds'. Instead of accessing knowledge of other minds through analogical reasoning or abstract theorizations, our relations with others is already established in the primacy of the prepersonal body, a point we shall see through Merleau-Ponty. This primacy is as much an active force in infancy as it is in adulthood. What this means is that despite the idiosyncrasies and neuroses of adult life, evading or withdrawing from the other remains structurally impossible so long as we remain bodily subjects.

Second, the necessary relation with others defines our thematic and affective experience of the world. Far from a formal connection with others, the corporeal basis of intersubjectivity means that our lived experience of the world is mediated via our bodily relations with others. The implication of this is that our bodily experience of the world cannot be considered apart from our relations with others. Rather, the thematic and affective experience of the world coincides with the structure of intercorporeality. In this way, intercorporeality reveals the body as having being dynamically receptive to social interactions with others.

To get a sense of the thick complexity at the heart of our intersubjective relations, let us return to our case study. How can we begin to make sense of this experience of being on a bus? Thematically, the following observations can be made. First, the subjective orientation during the journey hinges at all times on the reference of a fixed point: *home*. As we have seen (and will continue to see), the idea of 'home' is inherently ambiguous, ranging from a particular building or room, to a general neighbourhood that assumes the appearance of being familiar. In each case, as the anxious subject becomes distant from this fixed point in space – home – so his anxiety escalates. This relation between anxiety and the home colours the subsequent experience of self and other. What follows is a series of intersubjective moments, each of which is determined by the increased distance of home.

The first intersubjective moment is manifest as the experience of being trapped by the other. To be trapped in this way is not only a spatial prohibition, but also a threat to the tightly wound space the agoraphobe has cultivated in the bus. As a threat, the other assumes the appearance of being a danger to general well-being, and thus something the agoraphobic body recoils at. The second intersubjective moment almost immediately reverses this hostile space when the forearm of the other person is gripped in a heightened flurry of anxiety. This transition between hostility and vulnerability is played out in the body shifting from a withdrawn state to a dependent state. The third movement in this arc of intersubjective exchanges focuses on the anonymity of the crowds. If the first two movements give a precise definition to the other, then here we are confronted with a resistance to ascribing any form of affective character. Together with an adjoining sense of unfamiliarity, what remains is a total alienation from the visual materialization of other people's bodies. The final moment in this narrative involves the trusted other. Central to this stage is the fact that the precarious calm opened up in the presence of the trusted other is not limited to the experience of bodily sensations, as though those sensations were autonomous entities interfering with the world. Rather, the presence of the other restores the world to a place that assumes some semblance of being 'homely'.

'One single intercorporeality'

From hostility to intimacy, the role others play in the lifeworld of the agoraphobe is complex and ambiguous. This ambiguity is not limited to instances of pathological embodiment, but instead is incorporated into our everyday experience of the world. For Merleau-Ponty, far from an additional component of lived experience, the coexistence of the other person is implicated from the outset. Ordinarily, so he argues in 'The Child's Relations with Others', we begin our lives as children who are able to recognize the gestures of others in a prereflective way (Merleau-Ponty 1964a). As he goes on to say, when a baby is born, the baby will smile if smiled at by another. Or the baby will open its mouth if another person pretends to bite it. In such a case, the baby 'perceives his intentions in his body, perceives my body with his own, and thereby perceives my intentions in his body' (Merleau-Ponty 2012, 368). Likewise, when hearing the cries of another baby, another baby will also cry. This 'phenomenon of the contagion', as M. C. Dillon puts it, testifies to the synchronicity between different babies, with each baby sharing in the same discomfort (Dillon 1997, 121). Lacking the advantage of perspective, the crying babies attest to a 'pre-communication, in which there is not one individual over against another but rather an anonymous collectivity, an undifferentiated group life' (Merleau-Ponty 1964a, 119). Thus, whereas traditional accounts of subjectivity tend to begin with the solipsistic subject entrenched in what Husserl would term a 'sphere of ownness', Merleau-Ponty begins from the view of the infant's consciousness as lacking the distinction of different perspectives (Husserl 1977). It is not, then, a problem of establishing the existence of other minds, but instead of learning to 'distinguish his experience of himself from his experience of others' (Dillon 1997, 121). All of this takes place on a prereflective way. The baby does not orchestrate these gestures, but experiences the body of the other baby as being incorporated into his own self, as Merleau-Ponty says: 'What is true of his own body, for the child, is also true of the other's body. The child himself feels that he is in the other's body' (Merleau-Ponty 1964a, 134). As we grow older, this lack of independence is replaced with a self-conscious distance between ourselves and others. The body becomes an object, at once separating and distinguishing self and other. Yet despite the independence that maturity confers upon us, our bodies remain prepersonally bound with other bodies. This prereflective bodily reciprocity between ourselves and others, originally experienced in childhood, retains a presence in our ability to recognize ourselves in others. Merleau-Ponty again: 'It is the simple fact that I live in the facial expressions of the other, as I feel him living in mine. It is a manifestation of what we have called, in other terms, the system "me-and-other"' (154). Because of this dialogical structure, it becomes possible to 'place' ourselves in the perspective of the other person's bodily experience. When we witness someone in shock, then we do so not as detached observers, but as subjects who share in that shock. We feel the other person's tremor through our own bodies, as though their experiences were reverberating through us. This we are able to do because the body has a potentiality that enables us to project ourselves beyond the limits of our flesh.

In moving away from the objective account of others, Merleau-Ponty is able to put forward an account of others that calls upon 'the opacity of an originary past' (408). What this means is if I reflect upon my own experience of the world, and there discover a 'primordial setting in relation to the world', then what is to prevent me from regarding other bodies as sharing in this primal relation? As he puts it simply, 'why should other bodies that I perceive not be equally inhabited by consciousness?' (367). Merleau-Ponty's question presents a challenge to the positivistic account of others, which takes things of the world to either exist as mental or physical. For Merleau-Ponty, the body assumes 'a third genus of being', problematizing this division (367).

What Merleau-Ponty has in mind when he is talking about other bodies is not simply the phenomenal appearance of the body as mine. What enables me to recognize the existence of another person through their body is not the idiosyncratic characteristics of a particular body, or otherwise, a style of bodily language. In fact, 'another person is never fully a personal being', given that what structures bodily existence is an anonymous, prepersonal being, which we have been tracing in the previous chapter (368). As he writes, 'Insofar as I have sensory functions – a visual, auditory, and tactile field – I already communicate with others, themselves taken as psycho-physiological subjects' (369). Because world and body belong together, other bodies, and not only my own, also belong to the world. Here, the reference to 'my' body is not me the personal subject, but instead the anonymous and prepersonal subject that inheres in all bodies. Merleau-Ponty writes:

> Henceforth, just as the parts of my body together form a system, the other's body and my own are a single whole, two sides of a single phenomenon, and the anonymous existence, of which my body is continuously the trace, henceforth inhabits these two bodies simultaneously. (370)

This is a key passage. In it, Merleau-Ponty deprives the egocentric subject of an ontological centrality, replacing it with it an anonymity that belongs to all bodies. In turn, this privileging of the prepersonal body means that self and other partake of the same world, cohere in the same space and reveal the possibility of a shared understanding of bodily experience. That I already have a human body necessarily puts me in contact with other things of this world that also have human bodies. As bodily subjects we belong to the same ontological and thus corporeal order. To this end, the experience and behaviour of the other person can, in potential, also be my own experience and behaviour, given that our bodies dovetail into the same plane of existence. The 'miraculous prolongation' of the body cements my subjectivity with that of the other, cojoining each of us in a 'single fabric' of being (370). What we see in Merleau-Ponty is that intersubjectivity is really an issue of *intercorporeality*. That I am in a world of others is thanks not simply to the superimposition of an abstract idea, which would give agency to other people. Rather, 'he and I', so he writes in the essay 'The Philosopher and His Shadow', 'are like organs of one single intercorporeality' (Merleau-Ponty 1964b, 168). This union of flesh places each of us in an 'interworld', whereupon having a body means necessarily being open to the experiences of others (Merleau-Ponty 2012). It means, moreover, sharing in the world of the other, a world that is taken up in the materiality of the lived environment.

The alignment between intersubjectivity and intercorporeality points towards a third union; that of *interspatiality*. If our experience of the world is mediated by the presence (and equally absence) of others, then such a mediation is not limited to the realm of the lived body. Instead, the relation we have to others extends to the materiality of the world itself. But consider at the outset how our experience of the world is fundamentally affected when we are distant from those we love and our dear to us, such as when loved ones die or are far from us. Those who mourn for the loss of loved ones do not carry that pain within their own bodies alone. Rather, the grief breaches the walls of the body, and reaches into the world itself. In the absence of those loved ones, the world and others become distant, and thus impregnated with a level of unfamiliarity that parallels our own estrangement from the world.

Merleau-Ponty has shown us that relations with others are primordially bodily in structure and involve a level of prepersonal existence that is resistant to the contingences of personal life. In a word, we are *always already* in touch with others long before others are visually in our frame of perception. The body's intentional relation with others is not only structural but thematic, too. In the complexity of their look, movement and language, people's bodies *affect* us. People's bodies affect us not only in terms of being able to physically interact with us, but also in the sense of bearing influence upon the experience of our own bodies. This we can already see in an especially visceral way in our example of being an agoraphobic subject on a bus. There, the very presence of another's body instigates a transformation not only in the agoraphobe's experience of their own bodily sensations, but also of the spatiality the agoraphobe shares with others. How can we understand this double transformation of space and sensation? Let us return to the specificity of the agoraphobe's body.

In common with all anxiety disorders, the body of the agoraphobe is conditioned by a highly sensitized mode of being. That the body of the agoraphobe is receptive to such intense sensations means that their body is already attuned to the world through the primacy of the senses. As we have seen in the preceding chapters, the sense we have of the agoraphobe's experience is a constant vigilance over any unfamiliar or undesirable sensations, as though those sensations could be arbitrarily activated from any source. In order to domesticate these sensations, the agoraphobe strives to retain absolute control over his body, and thus of his surroundings. Through a highly regulated and ritualized life, the agoraphobe's self-control presents itself as an attempt to insulate his body from the contingences of the world.

The emphasis on the phobic reaction coming from any source (and, just as importantly, at any *time*) positions the locus of control out of the agoraphobe's body and into the body of other things. While those other things might include any environmental factor such as a shift in temperature, a particular configuration of space or a certain type of lighting, where the issue of control is concerned, the body that concerns the agoraphobe the most is the body of the other person. Unlike the lighting and temperature – both factors that can influence our bodily sensations – establishing control over the thoughts and perceptions of another person's body is not possible. Precisely for this reason is the alterity of the other's look the focal point of anxiety – to phrase it in Levinasian terms, the look of the other resists all comprehension, and thus, in the agoraphobe's interpretation, presents itself as a threat to identity (Levinas 1969). Here, we must confront a critical question: *why* should the look of the other cause the agoraphobe to lose partial control of their bodily sensations, and in turn feel their sense of self fragment? What exactly endangers the security of the agoraphobe in the face of the other? To answer this question, we must tackle the issue of the body as objectified by the look of the other.

Agoraphobia and the look

Let us return to the bus journey. Let us recall that when the bus becomes populated with passengers, a transformation takes place in the overly sensitized body. The agoraphobic person's body tenses up before moving into an anxious state when he feels entrapped by another person. More than an issue of just being unable to escape, the presence of the other person's body amplifies the agoraphobic person's anxiety through reinforcing the reality of their anxiety. The other person is not a mass of materiality, and that alone. Their body is an active field of force that draws other bodies into its sphere of being. If a suitcase were placed where the fellow passenger was

FIGURE 3.2 *Saint Germain des Près, Paris.*

sitting, then instead of feeling trapped, the agoraphobe would feel both enclosed and protected by the barrier established. Likewise, on the metro, the agoraphobe feels insulated by a series of glass screens, rather than entombed. Where a human body is concerned, protection is replaced with penetration. Without even directing the visual gaze towards the agoraphobe, the other person's body penetrates the already porous boundary of the agoraphobic person's flesh. The presence of the other's look attests to the reality of the agoraphobe's sensations, and thus heightens those sensations.

If there was any doubt that the agoraphobic person was anxious, then in the look of the other person, all doubt has been erased: the other person confers a distinct material reality upon the agoraphobe's anxiety. It is for this reason that hostility is the natural response to the other passenger. In the prereflective interpretation of the agoraphobe, the arrival of the other is causally linked to the development of anxious sensations and is thus at least partly assigned responsibility for these sensations. In a word, for the agoraphobe, the arrival of the passenger is experienced as something external that triggers anxiety, as though anxiety was floating freely in the air, even though the 'trigger' belongs neither to the self nor the other, but the world between the two. Given this all-encompassing totality, the 'look' of the other does not mean that intersubjectivity is reducible to the visual gaze. The other is other for me, not simply through the meeting of flesh on flesh, but instead through the dynamism of his or her behaviour. The other does not depart from the world of things and become other through facing me as an autonomous entity. He encircles and surrounds me, precisely because we are both joined in our intercorporeality. To this end, at no point can we withdraw or resist the other's being. We may experience it as strange or alarming, but it is through that response that our bond with the other is reinforced. At all times, we are in a relationship of being-with-the-other, even if the other is physically absent. Consider, as Merleau-Ponty does, how the materiality of the world is constituted by the trace of the other. In a cultural and historical sense, things sculpt themselves to the existence of other people, which are then rediscovered in their anonymity later on, as Merleau-Ponty has it:

> In the cultural object, I experience the near presence of others under a veil of anonymity. *One* uses the pipe for smoking, the spoon for eating, or the bell for summoning, and the perception

of a cultural world could be verified through the perception of a human act and of another man. (Merleau-Ponty 2012, 363)

Merleau-Ponty reminds us that the very materiality of the world is indented with the anonymous residue of others. Long before there are other people in the visual horizon, their look is felt in the instruments and objects created and defined by human engagement. At the same time, the things that populate the world are imbued with a silent anonymity, deprived of their personal presence, as he puts it: 'An Objective Sprit inhabits these vestiges and these landscapes' (363). Such a discovery of the other is re-enacted in our intersubjective relations, whereupon, as bodily subjects, we necessarily partake of an intercorporeal realm. That the intercorporeal realm is anonymous means that it occupies a structural rather than thematic role. Indeed, in distinction to Sartre, who, as we will see, portrays intersubjectivity as being marked by alienation and violence, Merleau-Ponty leaves us somewhat in the dark about the thematic content of the intercorporeal realm, indicating broadly that his is a philosophy of harmony and peace. The evidence for this can be sourced from his use of language. Thus, he will write of a 'common ground' between self and other, with each 'inter-woven into a single fabric', resulting in no less than a 'being-shared-by-two [whereupon] we are collaborators for each other in a perfect reciprocity' (370). Only as adults is the 'perception of other people and the intersubjective world problematical' (370). In contradistinction to the adult, the child 'is unaware of himself, and for that matter, of others as private subjectivities' (371). This retention of an 'unsophisticated thinking' means that intersubjectivity entails a commonality and tacit reciprocity.

From a Merleau-Pontean view, how can we account for the agoraphobic experience of the other, given that what we seem to be faced with in this world view is a complete rupture of intercorporeality? Phrased another way, how can we retain Merleau-Ponty's emphasis on bodily intersubjectivity as occupying a transcendental relation to appearances while account for the lived experience of estrangement from that relation to appearances? Each of these questions points to the issue of whether or not Merleau-Ponty's account of intersubjectivity allows for pathological instances of embodiment. The danger here is of falling into a dialectical account of intersubjectivity, in which the other person enters my horizon with an already determined strategy to oust or deny me. In fact, it is precisely because Merleau-Ponty grounds his account of intersubjectivity in the primacy of intercorporeality that the experience of anxiety and alienation can be accounted for.

According to Merleau-Ponty, when I am confronted with a stranger's look, the objectification I experience is 'unbearable only because it takes the place of possible communication' (378). Communication is the transcendental condition of intersubjective relations, and to this end, is ontologically prior to alienation. In distinction to the Heideggerian and Sartrean model of subjectivity, Merleau-Ponty does not begin with being thrown into the world. That I have a 'natural body and a natural world' means, for Merleau-Ponty, that a series of 'patterns of behaviour with which my own interweave' is mapped out in advance (374). On this point, it is worth remembering that for Merleau-Ponty, the fact that 'I have sensory functions, a visual, auditory and tactile field' puts me in contact with others 'taken as psycho-physical subjects' (411). On this psycho-physical level, we necessarily enter into a relation with others. And yet, such a relation is strictly prepersonal and anonymous. At no point, does the relation foreground the personal 'I'. In this respect, for Merleau-Ponty, the impersonal is at the 'centre of subjectivity' (414). Thus, we see a double displacement of agency: at once intracorporeal and intercorporeal.

Our previous chapter considered the bodily experience of anxiety, and demonstrated how the structure of the anxious body is organized around the shifting terrain between personal and impersonal materiality. The recession of personal boundaries brings about an instability in the image of the self as in possession of itself, and thus deprives it of its sovereignty. In the present chapter, we are witnessing this disturbance in agency from the perspective of intercorporeality. In implicating me in the field of other people – irrespective of 'my' own standing on the issue – the body betrays any attempt at being autonomous from other people. In what remains of the chapter, we wish to provide a phenomenological account of the destabilization of agency that occurs in the (anonymous) face of the other.

The body's boundaries

The case of agoraphobia presents us with a special instance of intersubjectivity. If the 'psycho-physical' body described by

Merleau-Ponty necessarily puts us in a relation with others, then for the agoraphobe this level of bodily subjectivity is problematic insofar as the natural body is beyond personal intervention. At all times, the body expresses a receptivity to other bodies. The body is porously interwoven with the world, necessarily conjoined with other bodies, each of which seeps into the intercorporeal space of the personal subject. Quite apart from the idiosyncrasies of the subject's psychological characteristics, being a subject means being exposed to and in touch with the bodies of others. Here, we can formulate an overarching thesis: *With the agoraphobic experience of anxiety, the relation between the anonymous structure of intersubjectivity and the irreducibly personal experience of intersubjectivity effectively fractures.* Let us consider the different levels of this claim.

To begin, let us turn to the body's porousness. For the agoraphobe, the porousness of the body is a problem for at least two reasons. First, the very fact that the body's boundaries resist closure positions corporeality outside of the agoraphobe's control. Confronted with anxiety, it is as though the body has betrayed him by allowing itself to be affected by the encroachment of the other's body. As this movement unfolds, the agoraphobe loses control of the boundaries of his intercorporeal space and thus experiences the other as a threat to ontological security. Second, because his relation to the body is one of control (and dominance), in the experience of anxiety and panic, the agoraphobe's body ceases to be identifiable with the personal subject and instead assumes an objectified quality, which we have explored in the previous chapter. This is no longer a body that the agoraphobe can recognize as being 'mine', as the world view of the agoraphobe fails to negotiate with gradients of ambiguity (relying instead on regularity and ritual). The failure to incorporate ambiguity and alterity leads to a bifurcation of the body. *Either* the body is controllable and thus retains a sense of ownership, *or* the body is beyond control and accordingly divested of a sense of ownership. When confronted with the latter option, the body of the agoraphobe presents itself as having an objectified relation not only to the surrounding world but also to the agoraphobic subject.

In both modes of bodily comportment, the structure of the natural body not only retains but also asserts its ontological primacy. The agoraphobe's experience of being out-of-joint in the public sphere is predicated on the fact that the expression of communication has been ruptured precisely because its possibility remains intact, as Merleau-Ponty has it. Far from destroying or denying the other, the agoraphobe's anxiety accents the lived relation to the other. That the agoraphobe undergoes a transformation in the presence of another body is evidence of a tightly wound relation to that body. The body retains a special and privileged significance. Only now, the significance has assumed a negative quality, in which the possibility of communication has become obtruded by a body maladjusted to the intersubjective realm.

Agoraphobia thus demonstrates the ambiguities and tensions in Merleau-Ponty's account of intersubjectivity. In non-pathological embodiment, the anonymity of the body's relations with others is that which enables us to communicate with other people, and is thus taken for granted. In pathological instances of bodily existence, where intersubjectivity is a threat rather than a source of reassurance of subjectivity, the body's relations with others is a flashpoint for anxiety. This is especially clear in the case of the agoraphobe, where bodily existence is subject to a series of rituals and regulations, all of which strive to domesticate the body's relation with the world of others. We see, then, that the agoraphobe's ownership over his sensations is exasperated by the presence of others in close contact. Not only does the other person intensify the presence of anxiety, but he also strips the agoraphobe of their agency by reducing him to a thing – a material mass of raw nerves with no discernible subject to control them. All along, of course, the other person is unaware of the role he is playing in shaping the agoraphobe's experience, and indeed, likely unaware of the agoraphobe. But for the agoraphobe, a complex and yet silent dialogue is occurring with the other person.

'This constant uneasiness'

If the anxiety of the agoraphobe arises from a prepersonal orientation towards the other person's body, then what happens if we begin again with another perspective, a perspective that positions us not in touch with the other but at odds with their presence? It is through Sartre that such a perspective can be sourced. As with Merleau-Ponty, Sartre begins by distinguishing the body as it is lived from the body as it is understood as an object. Understood as an object, the body can be broken down in such a way that it never reveals to me anything of my experience. The body in its interiority – the mass of organs that keeps me alive – is quite different from the body that enables me to have a meaningful relation with the body. And yet, from time to time, we see our own bodies projected on medical screens and presented to us in terms of quantifiable data. Still here, my body taken as a thing to be analysed medically is situated in the midst of other things, as Sartre writes: 'I was apprehending a wholly constituted object as a *this* among other *thises*, and it was only be a reasoning process that I referred it back to being *mine*; it was much more my property than my being' (Sartre 1998, 304). In this way, the body necessarily evades us. To apprehend the body as an object is to efface what is central to it: its experiential structure.

Let us see how this evasion is played out for Sartre in our relation with others. Under the category 'body-for-others', Sartre refers to the way the other's body appears for me as an object, just as I myself appear for the other as an object. How does the other appear for me? Sartre suggests there is an extension of sorts of the other's body into things of the world more broadly. Thus, in an empty room where Sartre waits 'for the master of the house', the surrounding furniture, desks, ornaments, and even the way the light shines through the window and illuminates objects in the room, all conspire together to form a sense of the other long before the body of the other is physically present. What this means is that the body of the other is always involved in a meaningful relationship with the world. The body is not an isolated unit of space nor is it a chunk of materiality atomized from other chunks. Rather, the body presents itself 'in terms of a total situation which indicates it' (345). Not only this, but the body that appears does so within its own referential totality. Thus, to perceive the body of the other is not to perceive a discernible set of limbs working independently from one another, but is instead to bear witness to a total subjectivity articulated in and through the body. As if to prove this point, Sartre draws our attention to the phenomena of experiencing 'the horror we feel if we happen to see an arm which looks "as if it did not belong to any body"' (346). The result is a 'disintegration of the body', given that we take it as pregiven that a body presents itself to us as whole, and it is only within this context that it can be understood.

This disintegration becomes central in Sartre's account of intersubjectivity. Intersubjectivity, for Sartre, is not simply a reciprocal encounter between two or more similarly structured subjects, each of whom stands in a neutral or indifferent relation to one another. Rather, what happens in this encounter with the other is that I become an object for something unknowable, insofar as I am taken primarily as an object of the other's world, the result of which is a 'concrete collapse of *my* world' (352). This alienation of my body is stipulated on the sense of it being perceived in a world '*outside of my subjectivity*, in the midst of a world which is not mine' (353). Already in this account of my body being taken as an object for the other, Sartre sees the relevance for phobias and anxiety, writing as follows:

> This constant uneasiness, which is the apprehension of my body's alienation as irremediable, can determine psychoses such as ereuthophobia (a pathological fear of blushing); these are nothing but the horrified metaphysical apprehension of the existence of my body for the Others. (353)

Here, we face a critical aspect concerning the relation between phobia and embodiment. First, the structure of phobia is interwoven with the structure of non-phobic existence. This is clear in Sartre's sense of ereuthophobia as 'nothing but' a different kind of apprehension of my relation with others. This relation is, of course, beyond transcendence, but only now presented in a metaphysical guise as horrifying. Indeed, that Sartre refers to a 'constant uneasiness' strengthens this bond between phobic and non-phobic existence, such that there is a continuous arc between each pole. In each case, uneasiness and horror mark two aspects of intersubjectivity, which, if there all along, are nevertheless manifest in varying ways.

Here, Sartre draws our attention to the intercorporeal structure of phobia. To experience oneself as being phobic towards a particular thing or particular affect is to be phobic in the face of the other. This is not a contingent aspect of affective existence, but is instead a structural feature of bodily subjectivity, such that we cannot conceive of the body-for-us without also considering the body-for-the-other; indeed Sartre goes as far to say that 'the body-for-the-Other *is* the body-for-us' (353). In order to demonstrate this claim, let us return to the phenomenology of agoraphobia, and, specifically, its relation to the spatiality of the look.

The case of 'Vincent'

Our resources for this analysis come from a short document titled 'Confessions of an Agoraphobic Victim'. The author of this testimony is named simply, 'Vincent', and we must assume the anonymity of the text bears witness to the refusal of the subject to be seen by the other person, a point that links both the writing of agoraphobia with the body of agoraphobia (Vincent 1919). We begin at the onset of Vincent's illness. He reports that the condition was prefaced with a 'coldness that produced a very unusual sort of sensation, or perhaps, a *lack* of sensation' (296). This confrontation with frail health at an early stage leaves our subject with a melancholic disposition and a heightened sense of danger. Around this time, Vincent encounters a tragedy. At the age of eleven, a friend of his disappears, the presupposition being that he had drowned or kidnapped (296).

Some time later, the body of the friend is found on a riverbank. But instead of being drowned, as was thought, the boy's throat had been cut, and then dragged to the river afterwards. Vincent is traumatized by the experience, and now suffers from an anxiety in certain spatial situations, not least the crest of hills where the symptoms of agoraphobia become acute. Thereafter, he avoids hill-tops (297). In turn, this formative experience with anxiety and death spreads itself beyond hills, and now finds expression in 'wide fields...of crowds of people, and later of wide streets and parks' and even 'ugly architecture' (297). Despite being amplified by certain places and situations, the dread remains implicitly. In a chair talking with a friend, he soon finds himself 'gripping the arm of the chair with each hand. My toes curl in my shoes, and there is a sort of tenseness all over my muscles' (298). For all this, the anxiety is never constant, but instead fluctuates in its intensity. Moreover, at times, the anxiety is alleviated by certain things, such as darkness or a snowstorm, 'probably because one's view is obstructed' (298). For the same reasons, stormy days for him 'stand out as bright spots in my life' (298). As for walking, it is manageable but only if he is carrying something such as a suitcase. Without such a prop, Vincent finds himself 'suffer[ing] agony' in the very act of walking (298). The extent of this anxiety over walking is so great that when Vincent sees 'a man hobbling past my house on crutches, a cripple for life…I actually envy him. At times I would gladly exchange places with the humblest day-laborer who walks un-afraid across the public square or saunters tranquilly over the viaduct on his way home after the day's work' (299).

What is striking about Vincent's case study is precisely the lack of reference to the other. For all his clarity, the one thing Vincent fails to touch upon is the intersubjective dimension of his anxiety. This blind spot is perhaps not by chance. Indeed, perhaps this omission is even necessary insofar as it is consistent with his refusal to incorporate the other into his existence, be it textually or corporeally. Yet if we return to his confession with a view of seeking the presence of the other, either visibly or invisibly, then we find another layer of meaning embedded in the text, a layer that reveals in terms of what is not said. Far from absent, the look of the other is there from the outset. From his fear of being alone, to the persistence of his anxiety even when in company on top of the hill, to his body recoiling when being seated in the company of the other, and then onwards to the full blown fear of crowds he develops – in all this, the anxiety of Vincent takes as its point of departure the look of the other. To appreciate this, it is necessary to insert the presence of Sartre in the midst of Vincent's confession. Let us, then, think alongside Sartre's phenomenological exploration of the experience of the other.

Sartre with Vincent

Sartre is in a public park. From where he is sitting, he observes another man passing by some benches. As this happens, Sartre reflects on his experience of the man as both man and object. How is this dual perception possible? It is clear that the man is not simply an object, and that alone. If that were the case, then, as Sartre suggests, his presence in the world 'would be that of a purely additive type' (Sartre 1998, 254). In other words, if he were to disappear, then there would be no consequences with respect to his relation to other objects. Of course, this is not the case. When we are confronted with the experience of a person entering our visual horizon, our experience of space alters, such that this new thing – the other – becomes a centre, around which my subjectivity now revolves, without at any point augmenting the objective aspects of space, as Sartre has it: '...the lawn remains two yards and twenty inches from him, but it is also as *a lawn* bound to him in a relation which at once both transcends distance and contains it' (254). What happens in this movement is that the presence of the other redefines the relational aspect of space: space becomes the province of another presence, and because of this intervention, 'there is now an orientation *which flees from me*' (254).

The key point that Sartre makes in this initial observation is that this reorientation of space is not affectively neutral, but instead carries with it a certain 'element of disintegration' (255). As the other comes into view, I experience myself as an object for them, thus altering my own experience of myself as a subject and my world. The presence of the other is the presence of another kind of spatiality, a spatiality that obligates me to re-perceive all the objects within my immediate world, including myself. Sartre's account of intersubjectivity thus takes as its point of departure a primordial

FIGURE 3.3 *Jardin de l'Hôtel de Sens, Paris.*

experience of the world as a world precisely *for me*. It is *my* world insofar as it derives from, belongs to and orients itself around my gaze. That the other alienates me from this world is only possible because of the special status attached to the other's look. For Sartre, this collision of self and other is not a localized interaction, but instead attests to a 'decentralization of the world which undermines the centralization which I am simultaneously effecting' (255). As the other imposes their look upon my own look, so the world shifts away from me, becoming, in Sartre's characteristic formulation, a 'kind of drain hole in the middle of its being' (256).

For all his emphasis on the view of the other, Sartre's account of the look does not reduce itself to a study of 'the convergence of two ocular globes in my direction', nor even to a straightforward account of intersubjectivity (257). If the look has a sensible or material expression to it, then this does not mean it requires an ocular gaze to instantiate it, less even an actual person. In an important move, and one that has a direct impact on our study of agoraphobia, Sartre extends the look beyond that boundaries of the body itself, writing how: 'The look will be given just as well on occasion when there is a rustling of branches, or the sound of a footstep followed by silence, or the slight opening of a shutter, or a light movement of a curtain' (257).

How is it that the material world can embody the look of the other, even if the other him- or herself is physically absent? When we are confronted with a lone house on top of a hill at dusk, the chill we might experience is not simply due to a certain set of contingent dimensions conspiring together to produce a ghoulish atmosphere. Rather, the impression of being looked at stems from a probability that embeds itself in the materiality of the house, a probability that cannot be reduced to the empirical situation in and of itself but instead attests to an invariant structure of intersubjectivity, whereby we must make a distinction between the look as something belonging to the eye and the eye that is represented in things other than itself, as Sartre has it: 'the eye is not at first apprehended as a sensible organ of vision but as the support for the look' (258). In other words, because the look is ontologically primary to the eye as an organ, it thus becomes possible to detach the look from the eye, establishing in theory a look without eyes. That the look is not reducible to the eyes means, therefore, the same eyes are organs of expression among other such organs, be it abandoned houses or dense forests. In this respect, the question of the other for Sartre is not defined simply as a relation between myself and another person. It is also a question of my relation to an alterity that can embed itself in things more broadly, thus assuming a pervasive and all-encompassing status, which is not only a presence in the world, but also an 'omnipresence' (353).

In all this, there are significant implications for our study. We see already that Sartre's account of the look is marked by at least two central features. One, the look is not neutral, but instead inscribed with value. To perceive the other is to experience oneself being looked at by the other, be it the other as another person or the other as an ambiguous if not unknowable presence lurking in the world more broadly. Moreover, to be looked at is to experience oneself in a particular way: no longer a subject of perception, but instead a perceived object, and thereby to recognize that 'I am vulnerable, that I have a body which can be hurt, that I occupy a place and that I can not in any case escape from the space in which I am without defense – in short, that I *am* seen' (259). To be seen is to be seen from a perspective outside of myself, a perspective whose spatiality, perception, and values do not simply disorient me, but actually disintegrate my experience of being a subject. In this sense, to be seen is to necessarily experience myself as a stranger to myself, to which I have no control over, and, in the case of agoraphobia, respond to with anxiety.

Let us return to Vincent's blind spot. Vincent is there, reflecting on his anxiety, calm and poised. On first glance, it looks as though he is more or less an autonomous subject, reflecting on his relation to his own anxiety, as if it were a thing of the world. Throughout, there is a tendency to reduce his anxiety to something to be understood solely in physical terms (to be cured at times by a 'vigorous rubbing of my body with rough towels', or, to provide an explanatory context for the condition in terms of something predestined: 'I was born with an active, nervous temperament' [Vincent 1919, 296]). As we have also seen, aside from this objectification of his anxiety, the complimentary tendency is to situate his disorder in a narrative. But such explanations, although valuable, provide only half the picture so long as we overlook the role others play in the structure of Vincent's anxiety.

By situating the Sartrean framework in the context of our study of agoraphobia, we can see how certain idiosyncratic aspects in

Vincent's report gain a thematic clarity when considered from the perspective of the look and the accompanying desire to conceal the look. Let us consider two examples, each of which demonstrates in an especially vivid way the structure of the look:

> Later, perhaps a year or so, I commenced having a dread of wide fields, especially when the fields consisted of pasture land and were level, with the grass cropped short like the grass on a well-kept lawn. (297)
> I dread going out on water in a boat, especially if the surface is smooth; I much prefer to have the waves rolling high. (298)

From land to sea, we follow Vincent in his melancholy journey from a horizon of smooth space to a landscape marked by edges and rolling heights. Given his nervous temperament, why would he prefer being out at sea in stormy waves to smooth sailing? Why, for that matter, would a level and maintained field induce anxiety whereas a field of uncut grass would not? In each of these situations, we have to position ourselves in the place of Vincent. In this gesture of placing ourselves within a visual horizon, we see a certain commonality between the seascape and the field. Namely, both are spaces of exposure that present themselves as fundamentally homogeneous in their character. Without the presence of an object to break the homogeneity of the view – be it in the form of a lone tree or in the form of a tumultuous wave – space assumes the impression of being infinite, while the subject in the midst of that world becomes the centre of a look that cannot yet be placed other than in the form(lessness) of anxiety. Because of this lack of definite features, much less a place to conceal oneself in, there is no place to position oneself in relation to and thus in opposition to.

Lacking a place to be concealed in, the other is both everywhere and nowhere. Indeed, the absence of the other in Vincent's text, and more specifically in these two spatial illustrations, is entirely consistent with the omnipresence of the other. In both the seascape and the open field, the anxiety at stake concerns the non-localizable look of the other. In the absence of a place to hide, the other is permeated through the world, and spatiality itself becomes the medium through which this permeation of otherness takes place. In and through space, the agoraphobe defines his relation to the other (as Vincent says disingenuously but nevertheless tellingly:

'Ugly architecture greatly intensifies the fear', as if ugliness were something that belonged to the building and not to his relation with the others who inhabit space [297]).

Here, it is not a question of homogeneous space as being the site of a multiplicity of looks, as if Vincent were contending with several different eyes gazing at him from nowhere. What is exposed is not the possibility of other human beings empirically lurking within the sea and the field, with each of those beings directing their attention to the solitude of our agoraphobe. Vincent's anxiety on the calm seas and in the open field concerns an inability to integrate alterity and ambiguity into his bodily subjectivity. In both examples, the phenomenon of homogeneous space expresses an all-consuming threat to the stability of the agoraphobe. The other is everywhere, embedded not only in regions of the world that render the agoraphobe ill-at-home in the world, embedded even less in the visual gaze of another person, but now constitutive of the totality of the world itself. Without darkness and without division – without a place to hide behind and within – the spatiality of the world becomes expressive of the otherness of the other.

More than an incidental gesture, this theme of concealment, darkness and shadows runs throughout the confession, with each illustration attesting to Vincent's desire to constrict the look of the other. We are told, for example, how he feels better 'in the evening…partly because the darkness seems to have a quieting effect on me' (298). As we have also seen, for him, snowstorms and storms produce a paradoxically calming effect precisely because 'one's view is obstructed' (298). In fact, despite his professed love of storms and waves, his ideal place is 'a wood, where there is much variety in the trees and plenty of underbrush, with here and there low hills and little valleys, and especially along a winding brook' (298). These rich examples serve as a compressed overview of the agoraphobe's relationship to spatiality. The view obstructed is not simply that of empty space, nor is it an anxiety directed towards the objective properties of space itself, as if those properties could be detached from the other that inhabits space. Rather, the look of the other is always already embedded in the world, but nevertheless revealing itself in altering ways depending on the particular way in which spatiality appears for the subject. This is why the expressive role of space is never an incidental aspect of our relation to the other, be it for the agoraphobe or the non-agoraphobe. In each case, there is a specificity in our relation to space that reveals the place and the absence of the other.

Thus, if there were waves for Vincent to hide in or grass to position himself in relation to, the other would find their place. Whether or not the other would still inspire a sense of anxiety is less important than the fact that the other has a place in the first instance. Once in place, Vincent is able to establish a relationship with the world, such that he is able to 'conceal … the disease … most cunningly' (299). This insistence on concealing his anxiety, as if it were an accident in an otherwise prosperous existence, is not only manifest during anxiety itself, but also possesses him throughout his life, such that by the end of his confession, Vincent is seeking a way to justify himself according to contingent social values: 'My credit is good at the banks. But I have deliberately told lies to avoid embarrassing situations and have even changed my plans to have my lies "come true" … I have never been refused a policy by any life insurance company' (299). This final attempt at normalizing his existence in accordance with an imagined set of social values marks the natural extension of Vincent's concealment of the other person as other by filling the gap of the unknowability of the look with the knowability of a defined set of values. As we have seen in this chapter, this veiling of the other serves to contain and constrict the anxiety accompanying the 'decentralization of the world' central to both phobic and non-phobic subjects alike (Sartre 1998, 255).

CHAPTER FOUR

Lost in Place

[She] never has suffered from any other fear so great as that of getting lost or turned around in bed; in every strange place this fear keeps her awake; she has always been haunted with fear that she should lose her way from school and go off in the wrong direction, although the ground was very familiar; the fear of getting the wrong classroom always haunts her; she can never enter the smallest forest, and can never turn a corner or curve without fearing it is wrong and painfully fixing the angles in her mind.

(CITED IN HALL 1897)

The forest

Winter has come and you are alone in a forest. Before you, an avenue of trees cramps together, forming a series of erratic patterns in the road ahead. Their branches hang perilously above the ground, dangling towards the floor of the forest, forming a shadow in the path you tread. Within this dense space, you are able to locate the origin of the forest; that place from where you began your journey. The beginning of the forest is visible, but also felt within your flesh, and if you were to suddenly decide that the forest assumed an oppressive presence, then you would easily be able to retreat from this enclosed world. A small inroad breaks off from the surrounding environment, and the forest begins to thicken in its density. You are in the midst of this thickness, yet you remain a centre of existence. All around you, you see not only where the forest begins but also where it might end. On this cold afternoon, the forest reveals itself to you as a world of potential. Here, you see a pathway leading to a river; there, the forest gives way to a small clearing. Sections of trees – stray wood, old branches, fallen leaves – compel themselves to be grasped, sensed and grappled with. Your hand rummages through a pile of leaves, you feel them cracking upon touch. With another hand, you prod the moist ground with a piece of bark. Light shines in from above, and the forest gains the quality of a world removed from the commotion of urban existence.

Night draws its murky presence over the forest ground. Shards of the fragmented moonlight puncture the heights of the treetops, casting ominous shapes on the floor below. You are caught up in those shadows, as if watched by a force above, unseen but nevertheless present. In turn, the obscurity of the night conceals the clarity of the forest, disorienting you from your point of beginning and smothering you in the thickness of trees. You feel the trees press down upon you, as if they were shifting in the thick ground, swerving into your body and disorienting your already tremulous sense of location. In response, you glance at your phone. In the oceanic darkness of the forest, the light of the phone serves as a beacon of familiarity. You raise it to the night's sky, but its underpowered beam is not sufficiently bright enough to light the way. Too thick in this world, the phone is no longer able to receive the network, which connects it and you to the surrounding world. As such, its function as a source of navigation is useless. In the midst of this experience, the memory of being lost comes back to you. As a child, you were once separated from your home. Unable to find your way back, you mistook a stranger's home from that of your own. Yet again, another memory returns to you. Once, you fell asleep on a train and missed your stop. When you awoke, the entire world had become defined by an absolute unfamiliarity, such that even the people surrounding you assumed a strange aura. These memories reappear for you in the forest as that unknowable dimension of the world that is ordinarily masked in our waking hours but which is illuminated in all its clarity in the forest at night.

Your heart is beginning to palpitate, and just as you feel an urge of paroxysm in your body, you spot what looks like the edge of the forest in the treeline ahead. You run to the clearing. As you get closer and closer to the boundary line, the horizon of the forest spreads itself in space, expanding the closer you get to it. The same trees that appeared to offer freedom from this enclave have undergone a transformation, becoming a series of homogeneous units, with no distinguishing features to orient you. Each tree is a clone of the other, each marked by the same configuration of branches and moss rising up the trunk. In the absence of the sun, the moon offers no respite for this disorientation. It is remote and alien, and serves less to place you in the world and more to displace you from your surroundings. Despite the receding horizon, you are compelled to run in any direction, to break free of this relentless homogeneity and to discover within this primal anxiety a landmark, no matter how insignificant, that can orient you. Against this spatial marker, you

FIGURE 4.1 *Forêt du Maïdo, La Réunion.*

would be able to cultivate a sense of place, thus forging a new sense of beginning from which to depart from this insufferable realm. Until then, you remain lost in the forest. Your inability to find your way home is not only a spatial disorientation, however. More than this, it is disorientation with respect to the notion of being itself.

The real dwelling plight

In everyday experience, we generally know where we are. Familiar objects and markers clothed with a personal meaning ensure that we are always already located in the world in a habitual and integrated way. As we move through the world, we retain a sense of being at the centre of things, even if on an objective level, we know this is counter-intuitive. When confronted with an unfamiliar place, our attention might be heightened to novel features in the landscape, such that we are able to get placed. To know where one is thus to know on a bodily and prereflective sense how (and where) one finds their way in the world. To be lost, on the other hand, is not only an atypical experience; it is also a radical departure from our everyday experience of being-in-the-world.

Where am I? Such is the question one typically asks when confronted with the prospect of being lost. In response to this question, spatial cognition and an abstract understanding of where we are is not a guarantee of recovering our sense of familiarity and orientation. For Freud, the experience of being lost in the woods is registered as a specific instance of the uncanny, which defies intellectual comprehension: 'One may, for instance, have lost one's way in the woods, perhaps after being overtaken by fog, and, despite all one's efforts to find a marked or familiar path, one comes back again and again to the same spot, which one recognised by a particular physical feature' (Freud 2003, 144). To be lost means being surrounded on all sides by the indistinction of space, and it is only when the homogeneity of space is broken that we can get re-placed. A discernible object in the landscape – a broken tree, a telephone mast or a discarded set of books – punctuates space, creating a pivot around which perspective is regained. In the midst of the forest, we pause in our tracks when confronted with fog. The fog is a presence that smothers us, as the night does, denying us of our identity, as we become part of the elements. In all this, the fog gets under our skin, enclosing itself upon us, deforming the very boundary line that allows us to return to the place from whence we came.

To be lost in this way – in the fog, in the forest – is to invoke primal anxieties over being removed from home. Left vulnerable, the experience of being lost is forced upon us in a movement of oppression. But let us not discount that other modes of being lost are framed by an element of pleasure and seduction. To be lost in the world of aesthetic discourse is to wilfully submit oneself to the rapture of losing one's bearings. Intoxicating and overwhelming, the 'sacrifice of subjectivity' (to use Mikel Dufrenne's expression) involved in the aesthetic experience of the sublime entails a partial dissolution of one's sense of subjectivity (Dufrenne 1989, 61). In place of subjectivity, a collusion forms with that of the object, be it an unbound ocean, a deserted landscape or an ominous mountain. A moment emerges, where the subject of experience is pushed to the brink of a boundary, without that boundary ever fully dissolving. This 'beginning of terror that we are barely able to endure' does not threaten to annihilate us, but instead situates us at the centre of an ordered disorientation (Rilke 2009, 3). To be lost in the sublime is thus to know in advance that a return from the sublime remains intact.

For agoraphobes, this sense of being lost in a limitless place is especially pertinent, and time and again, we often read of patients who experience themselves as being disorientated, or otherwise 'caught in the middle of nowhere', as though a fog were encircling them (cf. Sadowsky 1997). At stake in these episodes is a sense of being lost not simply in geometrical terms, but in the more fundamental sense of being *lost to the world*. We would like in this chapter to consider the phenomenological implications of being lost in place. We would like, moreover, to phrase this experience of being lost in place as central to the precarious relation the agoraphobe has to home. As we will see, to be lost to the world is to be exposed to the sense of never again being able to return to the world. For agoraphobes, there exists a fundamental discord between the body and the surrounding environment. Space is problematic, and 'dwelling' is achieved only in the most marginal and restrictive of ways, as one of Westphal's patients has it: 'He cannot visit the zoo in Charlottenburg, because there are no houses' (Knapp 1988, 60).

With this mention of dwelling, we are invariably drawn to Heidegger and the 'real dwelling plight' (Heidegger 1977, 339). As he will present it in 'Building, Dwelling, Thinking', this plight 'lies in this, that mortals ever search anew for the essence of dwelling, that *they must ever learn to dwell*' (339). We shall remain with Heidegger, finding within this essay the means to frame our analysis of agoraphobia and its relationship to homelessness. Written in the context of post-war housing shortages, Heidegger's remarks are directed against the idea that 'man's homelessness' can be resolved in material terms alone. For him, the 'real plight of dwelling does not lie merely in a lack of houses', but instead involves a relation to those houses 'that calls mortals into their dwelling' (339). Although 'home' is seldom mentioned in the lecture, the relationship between home and dwelling is tacit throughout. When the issue of home and homelessness is mentioned, then it is all the more striking, as when he writes, 'What if man's homelessness consisted in this, that man still does not even think of the *real* plight of dwelling as *the* plight?' (339). For Heidegger, thinking is not the inward expression of dwelling, but the very basis of dwelling. Thinking belongs to dwelling, as he has it, insofar as it serves to remind us of our homelessness. To give thought to our relationship to dwelling is to remember that relationship in a new light, and in the process to rediscover what it is to be at home.

Today, the production of prefabricated houses, with their lack of origins, built in what are increasingly homogenized towns and cities appears to stand in direct contrast to the Heideggerian idea of dwelling, with its association of eighteenth-century farmhouses set against the backdrop of Germanic forests. Indeed, much of what Heidegger says in this lecture, which was written in 1951, is lost in the context of contemporary culture. Yet Heidegger's lecture is not an invitation to mourn a lost past, even if a tone of lamentation and nostalgia permeates his writing. At stake in the attempt to think of home is not a plea for a specific mode of architecture, but a call to (re)think our relation to home in the first instance. Here, Heidegger's question is critical: 'Do the houses in themselves hold any guarantee that *dwelling* occurs in them?' (324). That Heidegger responds to this question in the negative testifies to the complexity of dwelling. To dwell – that is, to be *at home* – means more than occupying space: it means not only being at home in the locality of the house, but being at home in the world more broadly.

If the materiality of the house is itself not a sufficient condition of being at home, then what else is involved in the act of finding home? Here, a series of sub-questions emerge. Where in the world is home? To what extent is the materiality of the world implicated in the home? How is the home as a place different from the non-home? Already in earlier chapters, we have seen how home delineates a place in a subject's world, which carries with it a sense of ownership, intimacy and an irreducible link to the mood of the body, such that in the absence of the home, the bodily experience of the world shifts accordingly. In this chapter, we will give attention to the home, not only as a place within the world, but also as a mood that is enacted throughout the surrounding world. We will see that the place of the home has its origins in the body, such that home cannot be considered apart from the body, and, likewise, the body cannot be considered apart from the home. From this foundation, we will consider the home as a centre. Instead of being a single monolithic centre, home involves several mutually entwined aspects, which together constitute a complex and dynamic whole. We will give attention to two such centres: an ontological and worldly centre. This distinction can also be rephrased as a centre of reality in the first case, and a centre of familiarity in the second case. Each of these aspects is not autonomous from one another, but instead constitutes a union, with each aspect forming an inseparable whole.

To take these distinctions in concrete terms, consider how the centre of the home is what allows us to journey into the world in the first place, and without that centre, defining a journey *as* a journey would be impossible. In this respect, one has a centre insofar as one has a *place to go to*. The centre of the home is the original place, and thus instrumental in establishing a sense of familiarity and directionality in the world. Consider also the sentiment, 'the centre grounds you'. In some sense, this is true. The centre is not a metaphorical device used to elevate the home to an idyllic fantasy. Rather, it is the source of our relationship to the ground and the Earth, a bearer of meaning, and for these reasons, a condition of being in place. Without the centre, we would not only be lost, we would be *placeless*. To speak of the centre in such a way does not mean that the centre is reducible to the materiality of the home. The home as a centre is the principle manifestation of value and familiarity in a contingent world. At the centre of our world, the home is at once a reassuring source of familiarity or a stifling reminder of our habitual existence. In each case, home and centre coexist on the same plane, with each marking a condition of the stability of selfhood in the first instance.

'Shadows dancing on the dark walls'

Let us proceed by *getting back into place*, to use Edward Casey's memorable phrase (Casey 1993). Phenomenology's attention to the body, in its depth and richness, is rivalled only by its focus on spatiality. In its focus on the dimensional and lived aspects of spatiality, phenomenology has revealed to us that far from the 'milieu (real or logical) in which things are laid out, [space is] the means by which the position of things becomes possible' (Merleau-Ponty 2012, 253–254). Spatiality, as understood in this way, is not the backdrop, but is rather the ground upon which the distinction between background and foreground can be established. It is thanks to the primordiality of spatiality that we are able to have a relationship with the world, as both abstract and concrete possibilities (a relational dimension that both empiricism and intellectualism overlook). As we know from his analysis of the body, for Merleau-Ponty, perception is an act of synthesis, both spatial and temporal, which apprehends things as a totality, prior to those things being understood in their parts. 'Space', he writes, 'is essentially always "already constituted"' (262). As such, we can never understand the nature of space by withdrawing from it, given that 'being is synonymous with being situated' (263). This understanding of spatiality as being informed and structured by a primordial spatiality means that a dimension such as depth is framed from the outset in terms of a 'primordial depth', which gives sense to an abstract comprehension of depth (278). Our spatiality, therefore, is tied up not only with the primordial and non-thetic consciousness; it is also rooted in the lived and affective experience of being-in-the-world (293).

We have already seen in earlier chapters how bodily subjectivity is constituted at all times by our intersubjective and interspatial relations. This 'inherence in the world' is stipulated on the world presenting itself to me as a set of affordances, which is given dynamically (293). The dynamic character of spatiality is a theme pursued incisively in the work of Edward Casey, for whom the 'body continually *takes me into place*. It is at once agent and vehicle, articulator and witness of being-in-place' (Casey 1993, 48). The twofold role of the body serves to both structure and give content to our experience of being placed. Thus, if the body puts us in place, providing us with a sense of orientation, then it also gives life to place as it is lived. At stake in this twofold role is the co-constitution of body and place. To have a body means being in place; likewise, to be in place means having a body. This relationship between the body and place is not homogeneous, but instead involves a complex arrangement of different influences, all of which alter the body's presence in the environment.

Consider how we tend to think of some places such as airports as disorientating the body, and thus putting us out of place. During the experience of interstitial places, we rely less on our intuitive bodily navigation – less, that is, on our *footing* – and more on a series of signs directing us where and where not to go. In other places, such as those we are intimately familiar with, our bodies tend to cohere with the environment, affording us a seamless continuity between the materiality of the place and the materiality of our bodies, as Casey writes: 'Body and landscape present themselves as coeval epicentres around which particular places pivot and radiate' (29). Throughout, body and place remain in a co-constitutive relationship with one another. Even where the environment disorients and displaces us, the primordial act of being placed is never entirely dissolved.

In the place of the home, this close rapport between body and place is given an especially vivid expression. One obvious reason for this privileging of the home is that our fluid relationship with place is often predicated on the experience of intimacy. With the experience of intimacy, our bodies relax into the environment, such that body and place form a union. In the absence of intimacy, by contrast, we become more aware of our bodies as being 'inserted' into the environment, as though occupying an arbitrary position in the world, and thus assuming a more present point of focus (cf. Leder 1990, 34). Traditionally, it is the home that is thought of as a centre of intimacy in our spatial lives, and thus a place where the body has a special relation.

For Bachelard, '[t]he house is a refuge, a place of retreat, a center' (Bachelard 2011, 75). As a retreat, the home is a place marked by privacy and protection from the outside world. In entering another person's home, it is customary to first be invited, and, having entered, the guest is then expected to respect the tacit norms and rules of the household. In this way, inviting another person into one's home is to expose the home to a level of vulnerability that is not often associated with public space. This vulnerability does not only belong to the spatiality of the house as a place in which one lives and thus occupies a history, it is also bodily in structure.

On a similar note to Bachelard, Kirsten Jacobson describes the home as a 'second body' (Jacobson 2009). Invoking Merleau-Ponty, Jacobson suggests that the home assumes this secondary role by dint of its ability to 'ground the "absolute here" of our body insofar as it allows the body a settled territory in which it finds itself... in its "here-ness"' (361). This emphasis on the 'absolute here' of the home means that the 'always retreating "there"' is held in abeyance, forever deferred. The anchoring role of the home is thus not only a spatial notion. Instead, the here-ness of the home orients us, such that we are able to find our way in the world in the first instance. But how convincing is the distinction between a first and second body? After all, if we are able to talk of a 'home-body', then how do we draw a distinction between each body? Just as bodies are porous in their experience of the world, so too are the homes in which those bodies dwell. In material terms, bodies and homes interact and entwine, flecks of skin and flesh peel off into the surface of the home, giving the home an organic composition to it. Equally, the physicality of the home becomes inscribed in the habits of the body, giving the body an identity that is co-constituted by the world of the home. Consider here Bachelard's well-known account of the 'first stairway' as an example of how the home is 'physical inscribed in us':

> After twenty years, in spite of all the other anonymous stairways; we would recapture the reflexes of the 'first stairway'... We would push the door that creaks with the same gesture, we would find our way in the dark to the distant attic. The feel of the tiniest latch has remained in our hands. (Bachelard 1994, 14–15)

Bachelard's notion of 'organic habits' refers less to motorized memories mechanically reproduced by external stimuli, and more to the symbiotic union of home and body, which in turn, co-constitute each other. Home and body each retain their identity through housing a memorial relationship with one another, with each aspect establishing a 'passionate liaison of our bodies... with an unforgettable house' (15). Against this backdrop, Bachelard performs a phenomenological study of the house, finding within it a series of invariant structures that orient us conceptually and thematically. Accordingly, the house is divided into a horizontal and vertical plane, with the cellar and the attic marking the principal poles of the home's material existence between darkness and light, anxiety and reason (18). This vertical division etched into the home's structure is important, insofar as it allows Bachelard to domesticate the uncultivated aspect of dwelling. Indeed, for Bachelard, the cellar is the site of the unconscious. This literal domestication of the unconscious brings home the central function of the unconscious as a structure in both our psychic and spatial existence, with no clear divide between them. Never simply a geometrical unity, spatiality for Bachelard is the means in and through which time is compressed and memories are retained, as he says in a haunting formulation: 'The finest specimens of fossilized duration concretized as a result of long sojourn, are to be found in and through space. *The unconscious abides*. Memories are motionless, and the more securely they are fixed in space, the sounder they are' (9. Emphasis added).

FIGURE 4.2 *Rue de Birague, Paris.*

As the unconscious abides, it thus finds itself 'housed' (10). True to Bachelard's felicitous orientation, he breaks away from psychoanalysis in phrasing the unconscious in a 'space of happiness', writing how the 'normal unconscious knows how to make itself at home everywhere, and psychoanalysis comes to the assistance of the ousted unconscious, of the unconscious that has been roughly or insidiously dislodged' (10). This distinction between a psychoanalytical idea of the unconscious as the site of division and the 'normal' unconscious as the nexus of stability necessitates Bachelard to split the home into a vertical and horizontal plane of being, assigning to the role of the cellar the 'dark entity' of the home, the 'one that partakes of subterranean forces' (18). Up above, meanwhile, Bachelard demarcates the 'upper' zones of the home – those of the attic especially – with the space of reason and 'intellectualized projects' (18). If fear exists in the attic, then it does so with the potential to be mastered by the dweller (rats scamper into corners upon their master's arrival, so Bachelard reminds us). The cellar, meanwhile, becomes imbued with an irrational and terrifying force. That this domestic depth constitutes a space of unconsciousness means that it departs from the 'normal unconscious' that is otherwise a space of repose (19). In the cellar, the fears and anxieties easily repressed in the attic return to the surface:

> In the attic, the day's experiences can always efface the fears of the night. In the cellar, darkness prevails both day and night, and even when we are carrying a lighted candle, we see shadows dancing on the dark walls … the unconscious cannot be civilized. It takes a candle when it goes to the cellar. (19)

Bachelard's rigid delineation between the upper and lower parts of the home reinforces the underlying topophobia in the midst of his topophilia. The distinction also carries with it implications for our understanding of agoraphobia. As we know, the home of the agoraphobe assumes an unrivalled centrality, such that places outside of the homeworld are characterized as not only deficient, but also anxiety inducing. Having considered how Bachelard divides the space of the home into different levels and layers, we wish to now consider how this management of the 'dark entity' is played out in the world more generally. We find evidence of

Bachelard's 'dark entity' in the case of agoraphobia, and our study will revolve around the manifold disturbances that both distort but also reinforce the centrality of the home for the phobic subject.

'A black sky of horrible intensity'

Our being-in-the-world is structured at all times by the experience of place as a constellation of interconnected meaning and affordances. As Heidegger demonstrated, the world reveals and conceals itself according to the pre-cognitive way in which we comport ourselves to the world (Heidegger 1996). Objects of all sorts, from vast columns lit by the moon to domestic appliances marked by childhood memories, present themselves within the context of an entire world. Each thing, each object protrudes or recedes from us depending to any number of circumstances. Let us consider here the wakefulness of depression.

A human being is unable to rise in the morning, their body is tied up with the weight of lassitude, and their desire to emerge into the world is partly destroyed. They remain motionless in the bed, waiting for time to pass, but unable to sculpt that time into the work of productivity. Daylight is an affront to their existence, and the long stretch of time from dusk till dawn is marked by an irreducible emptiness. The knowledge of the world outside the room does nothing to spur the person to action, but only reinforces their felt inability to exist within an exterior space. Into this vast space, the human subject lacks all potentialities and all motivation to fill in these pockets with time with their own being. It is a time of longevity, a longevity without potential. The immediacy of the person's surroundings are oppressive in their familiarity, and every object that is situated within this space seems to express the same apathetic atmosphere felt at the core of the body. The room becomes a flat horizon, a landscape with no definable features, except for the singular quality of total homogeneity, in which subject and room form an uneasy and unwelcome composite.

To give a full description of an experience such as depression, one would indeed require not simply an analysis of the depressed person's experience of their own body and their relations to others. More than this, an intervention would need to be made into their relation to things, specific and discernible objects in the world, each of which expresses the core of their depression (cf. Ratcliffe 2015). The spatiality of the depressed person is a spatiality removed and isolated from that of the world. It is a world, as with the world of illness more generally, from which others enter the horizon of the depressed subject rather than the depressed subject entering the broader horizon. A different spatiality can be described for the anorexic subject, for the schizophrenic subject, for the neurotic subject and so forth. In the case of the schizophrenic patient, J. H. van den Berg speaks of patients hearing 'that a revolution is about to come ... in the voices of people, in the blowing of the wind' (van den Berg 2001, 46). Likewise, in a report from Jaspers, we read of various distortions in space. One patient's bed 'became longer, wider and so did the room, stretching into infinity' (Jaspers 1997, 81). This quality of space becoming infinite reappears again in other patients: 'I still saw the room. Space seemed to stretch and go on into infinity, completely empty' (81). In one especially striking illustration, we read of a total inversion of spatiality:

> Suddenly the landscape was removed from me by a strange power. In my mind's eye I thought I saw below the pale blue evening sky a black sky of horrible intensity. Everything became limitless, engulfing ... I knew that the autumn landscape was pervaded by a second space, so fine, so invisible, though it was dark, empty and ghastly. Sometimes one space seemed to move, sometimes both got mixed up ... It is wrong to speak only of space because something took place in myself; it was a continuous questioning of myself. (81)

Is this 'second space' not that level of spatiality, which is beneath the subject, and which can never be fully possessed by the subject? This second space is marked as the nauseous, constantly shifting and always-slimy spatiality witnessed in Sartre. As the patient indicates, the second space is not a static backdrop, but is instead a dynamic realm, which crosses over into other spaces, and in doing so, forces the patient to question his own boundaries. We are reminded of the interdependent and impenetrable alliance between body and world. The partial dissolution of spatial form does not take place in abstraction, but instead aligns with what Merleau-Ponty termed the 'intentional arc' (Merleau-Ponty 2012, 137). We are now witnessing the lived

FIGURE 4.3 *Rue des Ursins, Paris.*

dysfunction of the arc, as personal – and personalized – existence loses its orientation in the world. Against this lack of primordial orientation, what remains is an abstract understanding of space. A schizophrenic patient cited by Merleau-Ponty offers striking evidence of this failure to apprehend the world except as a set of discrete events: 'A bird is chirping in the garden. I hear the bird, and I know that it is chirping, but that this is a bird and that it chirps are two things so far removed from each other…there is an abyss, as if the bird and the chirping had nothing to do with each other' (295). The patient's failure to synthesize events in the world (itself, a strange philosophical victory, in the sense of demonstrating a radical version of Hume's critique of causality) leaves those events stranded in a non-relational impasse. Thereafter, the spatiality of the world ceases to function as meaningful so long as the 'knowing body' that prehends our existence is reduced to a body of abstraction, incapable of instituting the intentional arc, which gives meaning through a non-thetic intentionality.

Home as ontological centre

If a schizophrenic experience of spatiality is marked by a spatiality of persecution, taking place within a paranoiac landscape, then for the agoraphobe, the experience is conditioned at all times by a troubled relation to the home, either in its proximity or in its distance. This tendency is evident in van den Berg's central patient, who is described as daring not 'to leave the house during the daytime' (van den Berg 2001, 8). In the face of the outside world, the patient reports that 'the street seemed very wide and that houses appeared colorless, gray and so old and dilapidated that they seemed about to collapse' (9). When outside his home, it is notable that other homes belong in a certain sense to a different order of reality, thus van den Berg tells us that for the patient, other houses were 'closed up …'

> [A]s if all the windows were shuttered, although he could see this was not so. He had an impression of closed citadels. And, looking up, he saw the houses leaning over toward the street, so that the strip of sky between the roofs was narrower than the street on which he walked. On the square, he was struck by an expanse that far exceeded the width of the square. He knew for certain that he would not be able to cross it. An attempt to do so would, he felt, end in so extensive a realization of emptiness, width, rareness and abandonment that his legs would fail him. He would collapse. (9)

With this account, we are introduced to the first principal feature of the home as a centre: its function as securing a felt sense of reality. Let us introduce a nuance here in our understanding of what is meant by felt reality. To phrase the phenomenology of home as involving the felt experience of realness is to make a distinction from that of reality itself. We are not concerned with reality, if we take this term in the objective and positivistic sense of *what is real*. Rather, our concern falls to the sense of realness, insofar as it is constituted in a relational manner. In this manner, we find at least two variations of the experience of realness. In the first case, we have the experience of realness as that which reinforces the subject's place in the world. What is real is that which engenders a sense of continuity, unity and integration within the subject, and thus reinstates what was already established within a given horizon of experience. A phenomenological analysis of agoraphobia situates this understanding of realness within proximity to the home, and thus, for want of a better term, is marked as the *really real*. In contradistinction, the felt experience of realness beyond the confines of the home (and thus in the midst of either burgeoning or paroxysmal anxiety) is what we term the *unreal real*. In speaking of the unreal real, we wish to draw a distinction from the experience of place as being *not real*, so long as we understand 'not real' to mean the absence of reality. In fact, the felt sense of reality *as* unreal is amplified rather than diminished during anxiety. Outside the home, the landscape bends and contorts, as though imposing itself upon the subject. Spatiality is not only distorted, but also disintegrating. This uneven and unpredictable world offsets the patient's experience of reality within the home, such that the world beyond the home is marked in its unreality. At no point in this dizzying realness is the reality of the world put into question, and this experience of an unreal reality is not the product of imagination, nor a delusion: 'A reality defined his actions', as van den Berg continues to remark:

> The objects of his world were frightening and ominous, and when he tried to establish that the house, the street, the square and the fields would have reasonably retained their former shape and nature, and that, therefore, his perceptions must have provided him with a falsification of reality, this correction, in which he wanted to believe, if only for a moment, seemed unreal and artificial to him. It was more unreal than the direct, incorrect observation which was so frightening that it drove him back to his room. (10)

Here, van den Berg's patient gives us exceptional insight into the fabric of the unreal real as a distinct kind of reality. In the attempt to enforce a rational if not 'true' perception of reality upon the world, the patient is only more alienated from what is intuitively real to him; namely, the world as anxiety inducing and terrifying. Even with the knowledge that his perception of the world as toppling over is, objectively speaking, a 'false' perception, this abstract knowledge imparts no significance upon his experience. What is 'artificial' is the reconstruction of a reality from the basis of an error in perception. Time and again, this inability to rationalize the spatiality of the world into a *really real* locus of orientation falters for agoraphobic subjects.

FIGURE 4.4 *Bibliothèque Forney, Paris.*

Further evidence of this relation between home and realness can be sourced from Westphal's patient. We recall that for Mr P, crossing the street and entering an open space, there emerges 'a feeling of uneasiness [which] occurs in his heart region as if one were terrified' (Knapp 1988, 70). Alongside this uneasiness, the materiality of the world assumes a parallel presence to this inward state, such that 'he perceives the cobble stones melting together' (70). Keeping with our theme of unreal realness, let us pause to consider the meaning of melting cobble stones. There are at least two ways in which we can understand why the patient experiences the cobble stones as melting. First, we can understand the melting of the world as a 'side effect' of the patient's anxiety. According to this line of thought, the melting cobble stones would be nothing more than an expression of the agoraphobe's insecurity causing a more generalized instability in the world, with the cobble stones becoming an extension of the patient's anxious body. This interpretation captures the entwinement between the body and the materiality of the world, with each folding into the same atmospheric mood. Persuasive though this interpretation might be, what it does not give credit to is the actual experience of the world *as* unreal. After all, to suggest that that melting cobbling stones are a 'symptom' of the agoraphobe's anxiety is to underplay the lived experience of the world as unreal and real quite apart from the aetiology of those symptoms.

Much will depend here on our understanding of symptoms. A phenomenological approach to psychopathology serves to remind us that a symptom is not an isolated object, but instead a gestalt that is situated within a much larger context. Let us think of the melting cobble stones as a phenomenal experience of the world as a gestalt. To think in this way involves the totality of the subject rather than treating symptoms as if they were independent of the subject. A world that is melting is a world that lacks a constant foundation to stand on; lacks, that is to say, the 'absolute here' of the body. For this reason, the felt experience of the world as ontologically

FIGURE 4.5 *Square Vermenouze, Paris.*

stable depends upon the body's placement in the world. For the agoraphobic patient, body and place only synthesize harmoniously in the context of home. In the absence of this anchoring device, the outside world becomes a dizzying, melting spatiality. A melting world is a world that encompasses an entire relational context in its fundamental instability. It is a world that slips away from us, exceeding the control we have over it, and dissolving the image we confer upon it. The result is that the habitual sense of the really real is augmented with an appeal to the unreal real.

Against this melting backdrop, the home presents itself as an image of solidity and fortification. 'In a sense, a phobia', so writes Allen Shawn, an American composer and agoraphobia sufferer whom we shall discover more about in the following section, 'can be seen as a kind of fissure in reality, opened up by a reaction that is either out of sync with what stimulates it or, as with the fear of open spaces and heights, overly sympathetic to it' (Shawn 2007, 124). In the face of this fissure in reality, the intimacy, interiority and insularity of the home is welcomed as a restoration of reality. The result is that the division between home and non-home becomes a divisive distinction rather than a mutually beneficial one, with the non-home marking a threat against the stability of the home. Shawn finds a counterpart in Bachelard, for whom the elevation of the home carries with it a diminishment of the value of the outside world, as he has it: 'Memories of the outside world will never have the same tonality as those of home' (Bachelard 1994, 6). Never having the same value as the home, the outside world thus plays not only a less central role for both Bachelard and the agoraphobic patient, but also a less *real* presence.

Home as world centre

The analysis we are in the midst of consists of describing the multi-centred structure of the home. If the home serves to define and restore the felt experience of realness for the subject, then let us now consider how journeying beyond the home expands upon this dimension. The thematic experience we are concerned with is that of familiarity and unfamiliarity. As we have seen, for the agoraphobic person, the home is a definite, localized place, set in the materiality of the world. He does not carry the home with him, as a bodily practice that unfolds in each new place he finds himself. Rather, the home is left behind, sealed at the door and rigidly affixed to a specific location in the world. Unable to carry home with him, the home becomes materialized and statically emplaced in the most concrete way. All of which is a way of saying that the home is a centre of the world, insofar as it *orientates* him at all times. At stake in this relation between being at home and being orientated is the role of the home as able to confer a sense of familiarity upon the world.

What role does the home play in orientating us in the world? To answer this question we need to journey beyond the home, since it is only when we are removed from the home that the value of the home as a point of world orientation becomes clear. Usually – that is to say, in non-agoraphobic instances – we proceed from the domain of the home before making our way in the world. There, we move from place to place without needing recourse to the locality of the home as an anchoring point that we must refer to time and again. Instead, the home falls into the background of our everyday experience. Forming a silent context against which our security in the world is grounded, the home allows us to move between places, to journey in the world without any ontological or existential risk of self-fragmentation. Trusting our bodies thus means placing a trust in the world.

For the agoraphobe, the point of departure for leaving the home and journeying into the world is altogether different. As we have seen, the agoraphobic patient's relationship to home is divisive rather than harmonious. The home serves to entrap rather than free him into the world, and thus an unhealthy reliance on the home as a beacon of stability in a contingent world is established. Together, this combination of dependency and anxiety means that the home is not only the guarantor of reality; it is also the spatial centre around which the *unfamiliar world* revolves. This mention of unfamiliarity is vital. For the agoraphobe, journeying through the world is generally characterized by the repetition of patterns and familiar routes, with any deviations from these patterns liable to produce anxiety or the urge to flee (cf. Marks 1987). Being able to predict what lies beyond the home in a mode of anticipatory anxiety is the principal way in which the unfamiliarity of the world is repressed, therefore allowing the agoraphobe to journey into the world, albeit with severe restriction.

To spell out the relation between unfamiliarity and the home as a world centre, let us turn to the memoir of Allen Shawn. We join Shawn as he is discussing his experience of driving and journeying beyond the familiar homeworld of his Manhattan streets. Consistent with the agoraphobe's need to anticipate the world beyond the home, Shawn admits that he will often 'rehearse the drive first to see if I can handle it' (Shawn 2007, 126). This act of familiarizing himself with the journey ahead is not simply a question of *knowing* how to get from place to place. Rather, the act of venturing into the unfamiliar world is a 'test' of the very reality of that world in the first place. Such an idea of testing the outside world points back to the sense that outside world is somehow less real than that of the home. To test the outside world means *at*-testing to both the materiality of the world and to how the lived body will respond to this uncertain world. 'Sometimes', so Shawn writes, 'I have to try a ride many times before I get past the point where I am stuck, a stretch of steep mountain, say, bounded on all sides by layered slabs of rock ... or the beginning of a bridge whose length I can't judge from the available view ...' (126). This lack of trust in both the materiality of the world and the materiality of the body – for it is, after all, a body that could give way at any moment – leads to a different relationship to home and non-home. Now, the non-home becomes something that must be verified before it can be taken as having a reality of its own.

At stake here is a problematic relationship with orientation, which manifests itself in a form of travel sickness. Moving beyond the home means being confronted with the interstitial space between places. These are the spaces that join us to other places: motorways, elevators, squares, subways. What these spaces have in common is that they encourage movement more than rest. If the elevator ceases to move between floors or if a car stops on the highway, then these places become dysfunctional. This emphasis on motion and travel means that once a person enters the highway, they are then limited in their means to abandon their journey. Likewise with the elevator, to stop between floors would not be possible, except as a break from the really real: the elevator traveller is required to see the journey to its end. In each case, the problem with such spaces is not only the possibility of being stuck on the motorway, but of being lost in the world.

Part of the problem here is that, for the agoraphobic subject, the lack of heterogeneous features in the landscapes means that measuring the space from and to the home becomes impossible. A landscape disrupted by markers – a line of trees, a lone monument, an abandoned discotheque, a strip mall, a colossal stadium – is a world that can be navigated in terms of clearly delineated sectors. In the absence of such markers, the agoraphobe must rely on his felt experience of nearness and distance, and it is precisely this dependency on the body's prereflective orientation in the world that cannot be called upon. The anxiety, then, is not a question of being lost in the geometrical sense. After all, in principle one could be lost in an elevator or even – especially perhaps – in one's apartment. In a report from 1879, we read of a patient who 'could never go the shortest distance across lots, no matter how plainly she could see across, without getting confused and turned around'(Hall 1897, 161). The loss involved is less geometrical and more ontological: more, that is to say, a loss of familiarity, orientation and, above all, of being *lost to the world*. As an example of this, consider Shawn's method of 'testing' the outside world. He writes, 'Sometimes I keep a log on a yellow pad next to me on the drive to a new place, to help me cope with the experience' (126). On that notepad, Shawn will write down the places he passes by way of testifying to the very existence of those places. It is worth quoting them to get a sense of the specificity of the places in question:

> Quail Hollow Inn …
> Yankee Pet Supply ('Got Pups? You bet') …
> Cold River Industrial Park …
> Sign: 'Corn' …
> Chuck's Auto …
> City Auto …
> Tom and Dale's Auto …
> Church (sign: '"Everybody's doing it" doesn't make it right')
> Noise 'R' Us Fireworks …
> Wendell Marsh … .
> (126–127)

This extraordinary list is important for several reasons. First, the very act of recording the names of these ostensibly prosaic places certifies their existence in the form of written evidence. Given that the materiality of the world is not in itself a sufficient condition of stability or realness for the agoraphobe, documenting it becomes a necessary stage in 'getting placed'. The act of making a note of the place names is the genesis of establishing familiarity in the world, thus implying that the list were somehow more real than the places itself. This entwinement of testimony and place underscores the second reason for composing the list: it not only situates the world in place, but also orientates Allen himself in the world of Tom and Dale's Auto and Cold River Industrial Part, as he writes, 'When I see these same signs on the return trip, I am deeply reassured and also surprised that everything has stayed put' (127). This radical doubt places the world in a state of perpetual flux, a flux that can only be assuaged by comparing the notes written on the pad with that of the outside world. Such is the disquiet of the agoraphobe's relation with the non-home that the existence of the outside world emerges as an affront to the very fabric of his existence, as Allen puts it: 'The place-specific notations seem to demonstrate an effort to maintain a sense of reality and a sense of identity while in transit, as if my identity and sense of control were at risk ...' (127). In one clear sense, Allen's identity *is* at risk, insofar as that identity is inextricably bound with the fixed locality and familiarity of the home. In the face of an unfamiliar world, the reality of the world decomposes, and in doing so, all means of bodily orientation are replaced with a strictly topographical understanding of where things are.

At this point, we can observe how the two aspects of the home centre converge: *unfamiliarity coincides with unreality*. For the agoraphobe, departure from the home carries with it a double threat. One, we discover a threat to the reality of the material world. Two, we notice a threat to the familiarity of the material world. These threats are not independent of one another, but instead are co-constitutive. Each centre converges in the lived experience of the agoraphobe's homebody, which becomes the expressive organ of both unreality and unfamiliarity. But does this formulation of unfamiliarity coinciding with unreality mean the opposite; namely, that reality necessarily entails familiarity? The answer is clearly no. The reason being: the specificity of the agoraphobe's body occupies a special relationship to the issue of unfamiliarity that assumes a less prevalent role in a non-agoraphobic subject. For the agoraphobe, unfamiliarity is not one phenomenological feature among many. Instead, unfamiliarity forms a direct correspondence with the appearance and disappearance of reality.

For Allen Shawn, the unfamiliarity of the open road or an 'environment of wilderness' leads to a Pascalian confrontation with 'the eternal silence of infinite space', which invokes a terrifying sense of disorientation and a 'sensation of abandonment' (123). This union of unreality and unfamiliarity points to a broader problem in the agoraphobe's relation to home: no matter how much the agoraphobic patient 'desensitises' himself to the outside world by means of 'testing' it, the familiar reality of the world will forever elude him so long as he regards the physical site of his home as the centre of the world. The unfamiliarity of the world is thus not a problem of becoming acquainted to the world or of remembering the details of a particular route, etc. The world is unfamiliar insofar as it resists being dwelt in, and to this extent, is *constitutionally unfamiliar* so long as the locality of the home retains its fixed placement in the world.

CHAPTER FIVE

Through the Mirror

*We find these feelings so close to the
ultimate vertigo unbearable.*

(BATAILLE, *EROTISM: DEATH AND SENSUALITY*)

The plane

An artificial walkway elevated above the ground. On it, you will
proceed in order to board a flight from Paris to Oslo. Those in
front of you cramp together, each taking their turn to pass from the
walkway to the interior of the plane. Your turn has come. As you
approach the door to the plane, you look through the grilled floor
of the walkway towards the concrete below. A small opening in
between the walkway and the side of the plane will allow you to
see the wing and the engine, the two main organs that will render
this phenomenon possible. As the view passes, you enter the plane,
passing through the door, which before long will be sealed shut
35,000 feet above the surface of your home planet. You exchange
glances with the flight attendant, ensuring she is made aware of
your anxiety by dint of the look in your eyes. Indeed, you feel it
necessary to forewarn not only the staff aboard this flying vessel of
your hazardous condition, but also the passengers, some of whom
will have the misfortune to be seated next to you.

Able to walk, you take a seat in anticipation of the flight. This
triumph of exploration is matched only by the triumph of your

body, able to adapt itself to a foreign terrain that does not belong to the ground of stability. And you remain a master of your domain; remain, that is, master of your home. You look through the window of the plane; scan the world around you from this advantageous perspective. A world lit by the city lights emitting a series of sparks in the distance. Yet as the doors to the plane seal shut, the mood alters and you begin your own series of rituals. You are inside a pressurized environment, both atmospherically and affectively. The place requires that you adjust your own sensual and perceptual relationship to the world. Now, light and sound have been torn from your control. In response, you distance yourself from your surroundings by withdrawing into dark glasses, hats, scarves and headphones, as though these implements will curtail the spread of your anxiety. The less of you that is in the world of flight, the more of you that remains tied up with the Earth.

The plane is released from the departure gate and begins its slow march towards the runway. A series of craggy indentations is traversed in the taxing area between the airport and the runway. The plane makes a succession of erratic bumps on the surface of the Earth before situating itself in a queue of other planes waiting to leave. It is inevitable that the plane you are seated in will, in a few brief but painful minutes, be in the sky. There is nothing you can do to prevent this from happening. To leave one city and to arrive at another means subjecting yourself to the anxiety of flight.

From nowhere, the plane surges forwards. The force pushes you back into your seat, causing you to seize the armrests around you. Then the plane begins to tilt upwards, the nose of the machine now pointing towards the skyline. The Earth that your body once belonged to is left behind, and beneath you an entire abyss opens up. When the plane banks sharply to the right, the organs of your body undergo a series of violent pulsations; each vital organ is felt to be shifting back and forth, with no centre to align them. Peering out from your dark glasses and hat, you see that a series of dense clouds is pressing down upon the plane's body. Upon contact with the clouds, the plane responds by shifting its mass across space, striking itself against the new terrain with an unsteady force. The great machine jitters up and down, as if being torn by the clouds. At any point, you expect the structure to dissolve.

When the plane surfaces beyond the clouds, you are surprised the floating ark has survived the struggle from ground to sky. But

FIGURE 5.1 *Princess Juliana International Airport, Saint-Martin.*

there is no respite. Throughout the flight, you will depend upon two principal props. The first device is a half-filled water bottle that you will position on the table in front of you. Lacking trust in your perception of movement, you rely on the water bottle in order to objectively 'measure' the stability of the plane. Very frequently, you will stare at the bottle, as though your identity and security were contingent upon this makeshift spirit level. The surface of the water moves gently up and down inside the plastic bottle, a motion that betrays the movement you experience from within. Your relationship to the water bottle is complimented by your attention to the screen affixed to the back of the chair in front of you, which tracks the course of your flight in real time. You study the curve of this movement carefully, monitoring the specifics of the plane's altitude, wind speed and estimated time of arrival meticulously. The visual sight of the virtual plane represented on the small screen in front of you presents you with a reality preferable to your own. With these props, your sense of time can be dissected. The first zone of time is defined when the seatbelt sign is turned off. Until then, you experience the movement of ascent as a time of tremendous uncertainty, a region in which anything is possible. You know in advance that you will have to wait about ten minutes for the plane to level out, but your ability to measure time is offset by the disorientation of your body. With the drag of time, you rely solely on the objective presentation of movement, both spatial and temporal.

Nothing deprives you more of the illusion of self-control than the encounter with turbulence. The body is broken down, gripped by something outside of itself, an uncontrollable and elemental force, which is trapped in the plane. You are buckled up, hemmed in, entrapped, but your body is sprawled out. Parts of it fall in one corner of the plane; other parts group together in another sphere of the space. To speak of *panic* is to speak of a lack of interiority. For there is no place to conceal oneself, no room to withdraw into and no wisdom to be gained in the failure of your rituals. Your reconstitution of your fragmented body to the unified objects around you – be it half-empty bottles of water or virtual representations of the plane's movements on the screens in front of you – fills the gap your body can no longer endure. In the absence of your living body, those things become surrogates for a body that has otherwise been rendered a crystalline reflection of the strange formlessness that is both your own and not your own simultaneously.

When the plane jilts from side-to-side, your body loses all sense of self-possession, becoming an assemblage of fraying limbs, each of which is seized with a paroxysm of anxiety. You interpret not only the violent jolting of the plane as a signal of distress, but also the milder bumps that appear from nowhere. Indeed, so attuned are you to the plane's turbulence, that you feel you are able to pre-empt the arrival of rough air, as if you were possessed with an awareness beyond reason and experience. Knowing all of this is the work of illusion does nothing to deter your conviction that with turbulence comes grave if not mortal danger. This dissolution of self-mastery is amplified in the face of other people, for whom none seem concerned with the instability of the plane. Precisely because of their apparent lack of concern, you experience their presence not only as a violation of your space, but also as a means of amplifying your own anxiety. Against the background of other people's calm, your anxiety appears all the more visible, and thus renewed before the face of other people.

Eventually, the plane journeys beyond the ocean, rediscovering the land from whence it came, and thus begins its descent. As soon as the landscape regains a human scale, your anxiety lessens and your body returns to you. The landscape beneath you is foreign and unknown – indeed, nothing more than a grey, anonymous mass of space – but its very presence as a visible boundary line between yourself and the sky immediately assuages your anxiety. In sight of land, you care nothing for turbulence, so long as the Earth beneath you is situated in a relational context to your body. The plane lands and you disembark. Before you exit the gate, you return your gaze back to the shell of the plane, towards the wings that caught your attention when you first boarded. Despite your episode on the plane, it is fundamentally impossible to accept that the structure you are now looking at with your own eyes was moments before situated in the sky with you inside of it. Impossible to accept that what took place was anything less than a dream. Fundamentally impossible, moreover, to accept that the person on the plane in the grip of anxiety was in fact *you*.

A phenomenology of vertigo

Beyond being the pinnacle of anxiety, the experience of air flight presents us with a visceral recapitulation of the main features of our study. On the one hand, we have a broad set of themes that structure the experience of anxiety, principally: body, others, home. On the other hand, we have a set of sub-themes that constitute these broader categories: impersonality, anonymity, alienation, homesickness and so forth. Each of these features appears and reappears through the experience of anxiety, as we understand it, and assumes a pivotal place in the experience of air flight. What characterizes the anxious dimension of flight is the total effacement of boundaries, save for those artificial edges constructed through rituals and props. Beyond these devices, the interior surface of the plane unfolds in its relentless consistency as a place fundamentally lacking an outside, except for that of the infinite skies, which offers no room to gain a perspective on things. With no outside, the pressurized spatiality of the plane draws everything inwards, towards the world of the cabin in its borderless and edgeless materiality. In response, the human body has to forge its own boundaries, synthetically fabricating the image of a world that is consistent with the Earth below. The mantra of ritual serves to enact – if not conjure – a phantom world that has no place in the cabin. But while these practices operate efficiently on *terra firma*, in the world above, those rituals fail to domesticate the undeceivable nature of anxiety. In all this, *anxiety cannot be contained*. The failure to contain anxiety dismantles the image rendered of the body as being in possession of itself, and this breakage carries with it radical alienation from both one's own body and the others who perceive that body. Other people are presented as beyond comprehension, inhabiting a world somehow estranged from anxiety. All that curtails the infinite terror of anxiety is the re-connection with the visibility of the Earth. Upon first sight, the Earth's very presence as a zone of solid matter instantly assumes the symbolic quality of being homely, irrespective of the factual status of the ground itself, may it be the Sangre de Cristo Mountains of Colorado or the rolling heights of the English countryside.

Together, these features – body, others, home – characterize central themes amplified in phobic experience, but present throughout in non-phobic experience. Seen in this broad and relational context, the phobic object does not gain its quality from its objective standing in the world. Rather, a bridge, plane or a subway serves as expressive mediums for a wider set of themes, not least the effacement of identity encountered in the face of these objects. For this reason, we are able to learn from these places, as they give form to the multidimensional nature of anxiety. Indeed, such is the methodological approach we have assumed in the course of our study. Where air flight is concerned, a phenomenological approach remains legitimate. To approach the experience in this way would mean to consider what is peculiar to a vertiginous world.

Already the issue of vertigo has appeared in the birth of agoraphobia itself. Originally thought of as a 'common feeling of dizziness', agoraphobia's embryonic transition to 'platzschwindels' (place vertigo) is instructive (Knapp 1988, 74–75). As Danielle Quinodoz tells us in her eloquent study of vertigo, '[t]he word *vertigo* is derived from the Latin *vertere*, to turn; it reflects the mistaken impression that our surroundings revolve round us, but also the opposite false impression, that it is we ourselves who, having lost our balance, keep spinning involuntarily' (Quinodoz 1997, 2). With vertigo, we have at least two illusions: the first is that the subject retains his or her place in the world, and around this fixed site, the world revolves. The Copernican reversal of this view – the second illusion – is that it is we who, having lost our egocentric stability, are the ones floating around in an otherwise stable world.

Anxiety's presence on the stage of vertigo is evident by dint of its sheer force, a point that Freud himself noted: 'In its mildest form [vertigo] is best described as "giddiness"; in its severer manifestations, as "attacks of vertigo" (with or without anxiety), it must be classed among the gravest symptoms of the neurosis' (Freud 2001a, 95). As a grave symptom, vertigo announces itself as the very limit of anxiety, in which the subject feels himself to be pulled from beneath, sinking into a void, where 'he continues to feel that he exists and that he is simply stumbling about in space or in the void' (Quinodoz 1997, 21). This psychic impasse marks the very point at which the subject survives the onset of anxiety, but is held in a suspended impasse, no longer able to reform the image of unity necessary to keep anxiety at bay. In phenomenology, too, we find these sentiments affirmed. Thus, with Merleau-Ponty, we have seen how the 'living experience of vertigo and nausea [is] the consciousness of, and the horror caused by, our contingency' (Merleau-Ponty 2012, 265). Likewise in Sartre, vertigo is also understood as an anxiety tied up with radical contingency, such that vertigo deprives me of the borders and boundaries that normally delineate and reinforce my sense of self (Sartre 1998). Sartre writes:

I am on a narrow path – without a guard-rail – which goes along a precipice. The precipice presents itself to me as to be avoided; it represents a danger of death. At the same time I conceive of a certain number of causes, originating in universal determinism, which can transform that threat of death into reality; I can slip on a stone and fall into the abyss; the crumbling earth of the path can give way under my steps. Through these various anticipations, I am given to myself as a thing; I am passive in relation to these possibilities; they come to me from without; in so far as I am also an object in the world, subject to gravitation, they are my possibilities. (30)

This background serves to remind us of the specificity of vertigo as an essential facet of anxiety. As we see it in both Sartre and Merleau-Ponty, vertigo brings us to the brink of both spatiality and to the edge of our own contingency. The borderless path upon which vertigo is experienced presents itself as both a reinforcement of selfhood as well as a confirmation of its dissolvability, as Sartre reflects: 'I approach the precipice, and my scrutiny is searching for myself in my very depths. In terms of this moment, I play with my possibilities. My eyes, running over the abyss from top to bottom, imitate the possible fall and realize it symbolically' (32). For agoraphobic subjects, the dizzying encounter with the precipice need not be assumed in relation to a cliff top, but instead is given voice in space more broadly. In several of the historic case studies we have considered, the response to the instability of the world is to grip to the nearest surface, as if to transform it to a makeshift centre. One of Westphal's patients again reveals to us something essential:

> Being asked what he would do if he were led to an open meadow and suddenly left alone, he deems that the thought alone is unbearable, that he could not even conceive it, that he does not know what we would do; perhaps he would throw himself face down to the ground and tightly cling to the grass with his hands. (Knapp 1988, 61)

There is much to learn from this action of place-making. Instead of playing with one's possibilities, as Sartre has it, the agoraphobic subject refuses those possibilities, and indeed goes so far as to fuse with the ground as an object of stability. The absence of bodily boundaries is thus not a space for the novel recreation of selfhood, but instead a sinister space that threatens to dissolve selfhood. As seen in this manner, the production of place – a theme that is consistent throughout the agoraphobe's lifeworld – is the construction of a certain kind of place. Such a place is one of insularity, circumspection and stability. We have an exemplary illustration of this in the world that is created when Westphal throws himself 'face down to the ground and tightly cling to the grass with his hands'. If it is one thing to lie on the ground, then it is quite another to lie face down on it, tightly clinging to the earth – an action that not only veils the outside world but also prevents the onset of vertigo by attaching oneself as much as is possible to a fixed site.

Pascal's abyss

To pull this phenomenology of vertigo deeper in the direction of an abyssal anxiety, let us reach further back in time. The case concerns a pivotal moment in the life of Pascal. In 1654, Pascal was nearly thrown into the Seine while crossing a bridge at Neuilly-sur-Seine. At this crossing, his horse bolted, leaving the carriage dangling over the river. While not physically injured, Pascal nevertheless suffered another kind of trauma. Hereafter, he was convinced that an abyss had formed on his left hand side. Such was the extent of his anxiety that for a while Pascal would require a chair beside him to feel reassurance that he was not on the verge of falling. Quite apart from the logical improbability that such an abyss was real, this near miss on the Seine set in a place a reality of Pascal's own, and one that was entirely independent of the objective properties of the world. In a letter written we are told the following:

> His friends, his confessor, and his director tried in vain to tell him that there was nothing to fear, and that his anxiety was only the alarm of an imagination exhausted by abstract and metaphysical studies. He would agree ... and then, within a quarter of an hour, he would have dug for himself the terrifying precipice all over again. (cited in Vidler 2000, 20)

Pascal's abyss is graphic evidence, as if it were needed, of what we have earlier termed 'the discontinuous structure of the anxious self', a structure that sets in place several modes of bodily existence, each of which fails to reconcile into a unified whole. With Pascal, we have what we might term a 'pre-abyss and a post-abyss body'. The creation of the abyss operates from both the body and the world at once, leading Baudelaire to comment, '*Pascal avait son gouffre, avec lui se mouvant*' ('Pascal had his abyss, moving where he moved') (Baudelaire 2008, 342). The formation of the abyss is an exemplary illustration of anxiety as being dialogically structured between subject and world. Circumstantially, we have a specific context and place from where Pascal's abyss emerges. Yet the specificity of this anxiety is neither reducible to the empirical event of nearly falling into the Seine, nor is it explainable in terms of an error in perception, as though reason alone could repair the abyss. As we see in the letter above, it is one thing to agree in abstraction

FIGURE 5.2 *La Seine, Paris.*

with the absence of a void; it is quite another thing to experience it being no longer present.

Pascal's abyss is at once a lesson in phenomenology and psychoanalysis. In phenomenological terms, the abyss extends beyond the location on the bridge, and is now dispersed through the world. In this respect, if Pascal's anxiety takes as its point of departure the event on the bridge, then it does not end with that event. This diffusion helps us to understand the dynamic quality of Pascal's anxiety. As is reported in the letter, the causal explanation for the abyss is an exhaustion induced by too much metaphysics. Formally speaking, Pascal is in agreement with this account. Time and again, however, the abyss returns. In Pascal's case, the justification of an abyss from a rational perspective has little impact on the anxiety that assumes a pervasive hold on his existence. Anxiety's dissent from reason points not only to the structure of lived perception in the constitution of the world, but also to what Merleau-Ponty

describes as a 'deeper life of consciousness beneath "perception"'
(Merleau-Ponty 2012, 295). The deeper life of consciousness is not
an occult level of perception, which can retroactively explain the
phenomenology of anxiety. Rather, it is a level of perception that
operates in and through consciousness itself.

In what follows, we wish to move towards this 'deeper life'. If
we have so far illustrated how anxiety can be read as being a world
in its own terms, then what we need to consider is the structure of
the self that embeds itself in this world. We wish to proceed beyond
the thematic analysis of how the impersonal dimension of the body
generates anxiety for the subject in order to consider the structural
levels operating within experience. To this end, we will establish
a dialogue with psychoanalysis, and more specifically, with the
function of the image as it is understood from this perspective.
We begin by considering the sense of self, after which we will then
turn towards the body image and schema that constitutes our
selfhood, and end by converging with a phenomenological and
psychoanalytical account of subjectivity. Only then, will we grasp
what is at stake in anxiety.

A sense of self

We carry with us a sense of self, which is grounded in a complex
interface between different structures of subjectivity along with
the memories, dreams, imaginations, desires, regrets and so forth,
each of which generates a sense of who we are. These affective
and structural dimensions are assumed on both a prereflective and
reflective level. From a Merleau-Pontean perspective, it is thanks
to the pre-reflectivity of the 'intentional arc" that my existence is
underpinned by a sense of global orientation. I experience myself,
for the most part, as a coherent whole, and self-coherence is not
something I think of in abstraction, but is instead constitutive of
the prereflective self, which in turn serves as a foundation for my
higher-order reflections on *what it is like to be me*. More than
this, the sense of what it is like to be me presupposes what is often
characterized as a quality of mineness. Consider how to be self-
consciously aware of a given feeling – be it vertigo or euphoria –
is to grasp instinctively that the feeling is my own. The feeling of
vertigo is neither derived deductively nor is it inferred on the basis of

what is otherwise a 'neutral or anonymous experience' (Gallagher and Zahavi 2008, 50). The quality of mineness is thus active from the outset of perception, evident in the implicit sense that is I who am undergoing a given experience, even if I myself am not always consciously aware of this mineness of experience. Being unaware that I am the recipient of experiences does not lead to a rupture in our sense of self given that there follows a latent sense for each of us of being a singular person, which is carried with us, even in our attempts to flee that quality.

For Gallagher, this latent sense carries with it two sub-themes: a sense of self-agency and a sense of self-ownership (Gallagher 2004, 2005, 2012). Whereas self-agency indicates the sense of being 'the source of movement or action', a sense of ownership, on the other hand, refers to an implicit sense that it is 'I who am experiencing the movement' (Gallagher 2005, 173). The contrast between voluntary and involuntary movement offers a clear way to conceive the difference between agency and ownership. In drinking my cup of coffee, I do so with the sense that the action of drinking coffee not only derives from me, but it is also I who am drinking the coffee. There are variations of this experience. If I am, for some curious reason, coerced into drinking coffee, then while I may feel that I am still in possession of a sense that it is *I* who am coerced, I may at the same time feel deprived of my sense of agency in being forced to undergo an action against my volitional will. Here, too, we can think of involuntary memories as adhering to the same logic: a memory emerges and is recognized as my own (however loosely), but at the same time, there may still exist a vague doubt that I was the agent responsible for bringing those memories to consciousness. The sense of ownership is thus predicated on a prereflective sense of mineness, which secures the corporeal basis of subjectivity. Here, R.D. Laing provides a rich illustration:

> The embodied person has a sense of being flesh and blood and bones, of being biologically alive and real: he knows himself to be substantial. To the extent that he is thoroughly 'in' his body, he is likely to have a sense of personal continuity in time. He will experience himself as subject to the dangers that threaten his body, the dangers of attack, mutilation, disease, decay, and death. He is implicated in bodily desire, and the gratifications and frustrations of the body. The individual thus

has as his starting-point an experience of his body as a base from which he can be a person with other human beings. (Laing 1990, 67)

Laing underscores the thick involvement with the body and its multifaceted and inseparable immersion within subjectivity. The dangers and desires invoked and confronted by the subject are experienced, not as external sources of agitation or pleasure, but as taking root in the centrality of the body itself. It is from the body as both source of action and ownership that existence springs forth, allowing us to formulate the sense of what it is like to be conscious. Against this backdrop, disturbances of agency and ownership thus involve a disordering of the body. We know from everyday experience that thoughts, memories and images can appear from out-of-nowhere, without yet disturbing the overall coherence of the self. The capacity for these spontaneous thoughts to be integrated into an already-existing and more-or-less stable self means that their quality as 'unbidden' is soon diminished (Gallagher 2004).

In the case of schizophrenia, the situation is different, and the difference reveals to us in a clear sense the relation between agency and ownership. With the schizophrenic patient, the insertion of thoughts into consciousness is conflated with the attribution of action to another person, meaning that the patient is subjected to, 'but not the agent of, the movement or thought' (98). What remains intact, albeit tenuously, is the claim of ownership. It is this partial (but never absolute) effacement of the patient's sense of self that renders the experience of alien possible. The subject feels her thoughts, actions and movements are at times controlled by another agency, yet an agency that impinges upon a still-existing sense that *I* am the one who is being subjected to this alien force.

On a structural level, then, we see here a correlation between the anxious subject and the schizophrenic patient. As we have phrased it in earlier chapters, the anxious experience of the body involves a partial transformation from a centre of unity and personalization to a body that is both disunited and impersonal. This movement never entirely abolishes the sense of ownership of the body, given that it is precisely such a sense that is involved in the production of anxiety. Throughout, the body is not destroyed, nor lost, but instead accented in its inseparable presence. Once more, Laing draws our attention to the affective dimension grounding this structure:

> Socrates maintains that no harm can possibly be done to a good man. In this case, 'he' and his 'body' were dissociated. In such a situation he felt much less afraid than the ordinary person, because from his position he had nothing to lose that essentially belonged to him. But, on the other hand, his life was full of anxieties that do not arise for the ordinary person. The embodied person, fully implicated in his body's desires, needs, and acts, is subject to the guilt and anxiety attendant on such desires, needs, and actions. (Laing 1990, 68)

Laing's reflections are telling. The Cartesianism inherent in the Socratic vision of the body serves to diminish the anxiety involved in experiences of threat or instability. For anxious subjects, the loss of bodily control, not least when it involves the expulsion of one's *prima materia*, is interpreted in apocalyptic terms, precisely for the reason that the body retains a central rather than incidental role in the constitution of selfhood (cf. Kamboj *et al.* 2015). In effect, the hyper-corporeality of the anxious subject is at odds with the Socratic or Cartesian body in the following respect: if the Socratic 'wisdom' in death involves a depersonalization of the body, then where anxiety is concerned, the disturbance in corporeal existence involves an *impersonalization* of one's own body. This exchange between impersonalization and depersonalization is worth spelling out.

In speaking of the depersonalization of the body in the Cartesian or Socratic sense, let us think of a will-towards-dualism, in which the body is regarded as secondary if not contingent in the formation of selfhood. As seen from this perspective, stripping the body of its personal attributes does not invoke anxiety, but instead a peculiar calmness framed by the purported autonomy of the mind. To treat the body as a non-essential appendage to one's sense of self is to depersonalize materiality. The quality of the body as being less real than the mind is carried over into the medical understanding of depersonalization as a disorder characterized by 'loss of emotions and feelings of estrangement or detachment from … thinking, [the] body or the real world' (Sierra 2012, 1). Only here, the detachment from the body is not a space of wisdom and calm, but of anxiety and distress.

As understood from a clinical perspective, the relation between depersonalization disorder and phobic anxiety is compelling, such that the two disorders have been conflated under the title 'phobic-anxiety depersonalization syndrome' (Roth 1959; cf. Sierra *et al.* 2012). The expansive research on depersonalization disorder and phobic anxiety corroborates what we have deduced from first-person experience: principally, that depersonalization, instead of being construed as a 'dissociative' disorder, is, in fact, closer to an anxiety disorder (Hunter *et al.* 2004). Thematically, both depersonalization and anxiety are related to a loss of control, with each disorder provoked by visual disturbances, coupled with a 'specific intolerance to fluorescent lights … the significance and mechanism [of which] is far from understood' (Sierra *et al.* 2012, 126). As we have shown, the mechanism is only mysterious if we abstract it from the context from where it emerges. For these reasons, it cannot be understood in the laboratory but must be situated within the total situation of (inter)subjective existence.

From a phenomenological perspective, the relation between depersonalization and phobic anxiety is evident in their shared symptoms, especially the disturbance of bodily ownership, disruption of agency and heightened self-observation (cf. Sierra 2012, 31). Where they differ, however, is in the loss of affect. Clinical research on depersonalization points to 'de-affectualization' as a major symptom, understood here as an emotional 'numbing', which prevents the patient from either empathizing with others or otherwise being affected by the world more broadly (32). As seen in this way, the anxiety that coexists with depersonalization exists in a strictly 'internal' relation, whereas discernible objects and situations in the world are reported as being less anxiety inducing given that they appear for the patient as unreal (33).

Despite these similarities between anxiety and depersonalization, we have opted to describe the anxious experience of the body in terms of being impersonal rather than depersonal. The reason for this is largely an issue of emphasis. While there is a clear symptomatic correspondence between phobic anxiety and depersonalization, in the case of anxiety the onus rests less on a process of de-personalizing the body and more on the encounter with a body that is already impersonal. The language of impersonalization, therefore, serves to underscore the structure of the body as being both personal and impersonal at once.

The question of how is it possible to conceive of an experience of
the impersonal, which we posed in the previous chapters, is central
to the emergence of impersonalization. Our response to this question
was to employ Merleau-Ponty's mention of an *almost impersonal
existence* that structures personal existence, thus forging a phantom
zone, in which two or more bodies occupy the same space.
As we have understood it, anxiety emerges when the impersonal
dimension of bodily existence disturbs the image of selfhood as
being in possession of itself. The difference, then, between anxiety
and depersonalization returns us to the division of affect. In the case
of anxious subjectivity, the encounter with the almost impersonal
level of existence leads not to a 'de-affectualization', but precisely
towards the *re-personalization* of what is manifest as an impersonal
presence.

This movement of re-personalization emerges as an attempt at re-
integrating the body in the face(lessness) of anxiety. We can conceive
of this action in specific terms. Think here of the very existence of
the object of phobia. As Freud suggested, the rationalization
of anxiety consists of a process of domestication, such that the
object assumes the place of anxiety itself. This metamorphosis of
objects gives an image to anxiety, a face that can be both denied
and confronted. In response, the subject is afforded an impression
of self-mastery, and so long as the object can be avoided, then so too
can anxiety. In a similar way, the function of ritual is to give form
to anxiety, to encircle and contain it. Thanks to the power of the
prop, the world conforms to the image of stability and constancy.
Finally, let us reflect on the brief moment a subject prone to spatial
phobias leaves the place or encounter where their anxiety escalated.
We have seen a movement of turning back, of reflecting on the
doors, glancing towards the façade of a building, with each moment
marked by a sense of disbelief, as though they had been dreaming.
(In fact, we will discover later on that this dreamlike quality is more
than a metaphor). The response of disbelief is curious and telling.
To disbelieve that I was subject to this particular episode of anxiety
is to forge a distance between the anxious and non-anxious self,
as if it were unimaginable that the non-anxious subject could have
succumb to such a disordered state. We know now that this disbelief
is in fact rather disingenuous and is stipulated on the attempt to re-
personalize the body in a unified image, as seen from the idealized
view of a *mirror*.

Body image, body schema

We have in this chapter been considering a provisional phenomenology of vertigo. We have considered a sense of self in terms of ownership and agency. As we continue in this route – a route that will connect us with the figure of Lacan and the theme of the mirror – it is necessary in the first instance to interrogate the meaning of the term 'image', especially as it is understood in relation to the body. In a non-technical sense, we have mentioned images in previous chapters. Indeed, already we have defined anxiety as being *predicated on the idea of a personalized self encountering the impersonal dimensions of corporeal life, such that the impersonal dimension threatens the image of the self as being in possession of itself.* The task now is to explore just what we mean in speaking of the image of the self.

The terms 'body image' and 'body schema' have a complex history in phenomenology. In Merleau-Ponty, the French term is '*schéma corporel*', and has been translated in English as both 'body image' and 'body schema' in the recent translations of *Phenomenology of Perception*. Merleau-Ponty's choice for using the term is embedded in a complicated history, which hinges on previous research by Head and Schilder. Indeed, Merleau-Ponty's usage of *schéma corporel* rather than *l'image de notre corps* (the image of our body) testifies to this complexity (cf. Gallagher 2005; Weiss 1999). As it is presented in *Phenomenology of Perception*, the term refers to an implicit awareness of one's body, in its dimensionality, position and posture. Thus, Merleau-Ponty will suggest that knowledge of his body derives from a body schema that 'envelops' each of his limbs, and that responds dynamically to the environment (Merleau-Ponty 2012, 101). The unity of the body, then, does not derive from a representation of the body as understood as a bunch of associations, much less an empirical understanding of the body as occupying a certain physiological structure. Rather, the body schema takes root in the 'global awareness of my posture in the inter-sensory world, a 'form' in Gestalt psychology's sense of the word' (102).

The Merleau-Pontean idea of body schema as belonging neither to the body nor the world in isolation, but with the reversible and dynamic moulding of the two, finds a voice in the contemporary phenomenological literature. In distinction to Merleau-Ponty, recent research on the issue of body image has sought to distinguish it from that of body schema (Gallagher 2005). The advantage of this distinction is not only to clarify the joint function of each term, but also to consider how these terms can help us understand the nature of atypical bodily experiences. Gallagher characterizes the distinction in the following terms:

> A *body image* consists of a system of perceptions, attitudes, and beliefs pertaining to one's own body. In contrast, a *body schema* is a system of sensory-motor capacities that function without awareness or the necessity of perceptual monitoring. (Gallagher 2005, 24)

As Gallagher indicates, these terms are different but closely related (24). In turn, they provide us with at least two ways to understand how the body coheres. From the perspective of the body schema, the body is understood as being able to move of its own accord, quite apart from any beliefs or attitudes we have about it. This mechanism thus involves what Gallagher and Zahavi term is 'the close-to-automatic system of processes that constantly regulates posture and movement to serve intentional action' (Gallagher and Zahavi 2008, 146). As they see it, a body schema is a largely anonymous set of processes, which are neither intentional nor thematic, but are instead enacted through the 'accomplishment of movement' itself (Gallagher 2005, 24). In contrast, body image is perceptual, and is thus predicated on a 'complex set of intentional states and dispositions … in which the intentional object is one's own body' (25). As perceptual, the body image is informed not only by one's relation to their body, but also by the intersubjective sphere in which that relation takes place. The structure of a body image is thus dynamic, at times becoming visible while at other times receding into an implicit awareness of one's bodily self. Moreover, the image we have of our bodies is manifest in divergent ways. In certain moods, localized parts of the body can be perceived and experienced as more distant than other parts. The body that has been damaged tends to split into parts, with the damaged part offsetting the surrounding area of the non-damaged parts. When damaged, the limb or part draws attention to itself, as it were. In our perception of the damaged body part, we not only have a concept of it as damaged, but also an affective relation with this experience (25). Moreover, the body can obtrude into perception before becoming experientially absent again, reshaping our relation to the environment in the process (Gallagher 1986; Leder 1990).

Prima facie the division between body image and body schema offers us a useful way to approach bodily pathologies, such as loss of motility and proprioception, evident in cases of Anarchic Hand Syndrome, Alien Hand Syndrome, and Unilateral Neglect (cf. Gallagher 2005; Gallagher and Zahavi 2008). Let us take the case of schizophrenia. Alongside delusions of control and disturbances in a sense of agency, schizophrenia also involves what R. D. Laing phrases an 'unembodied' self, and what Thomas Fuchs similarly terms 'disembodiment' (Fuchs 2009; Laing 1990). Fuchs speaks of the schizophrenic patient suffering from a 'loss of automatic processing on the level of "passive syntheses", leading to an increasing fragmentation of perceptual and motor Gestalt schemas, and to a "pathological explication" of the implicit functions of the body' (Fuchs 2009, 553). Here, Fuchs relies on Merleau-Ponty's notion of the intentional arc, such that the global breakdown in the form of the body is understood as the fragmentation of the intentional arc. This has consequences both for the patient's relation to others and also to their experience of spatiality: 'This [fragmentation]', Fuchs writes, 'leads to a sense of artificiality and distance, both in the patient's experience of an emotion and in the expression visible to others. Even if the emotion is felt, its meaning remains obscure to the patient' (102). As with depersonalization, we find here a symptomatic rapport alongside a set of differences with schizophrenic in several important ways. Above all, the misattribution of agency found in the schizophrenic patient is generally not found in anxious subjects (cf. Gallagher 2004; Marks 1987). Whereas schizophrenia tends to involve a delusion of control, such that the source of action is ascribed to another person or thing, for the anxious or agoraphobic subject, the experience is not that another agent has taken control of a person's actions, but that the body, presented as an image of unification and coherence, has fragmented. Having fragmented, the body is thus experienced as dispossessed.

Alongside this difference, schizophrenia and anxiety join in their perception of the world as a 'phantom', hence 'the artificial, enigmatic, and uncanny alteration of the environment experienced especially in the early stages of [schizophrenia]' (Fuchs 2005, 102). Yet if the anxious and schizophrenic subject experience a series of gaps marking their relation with the world, then in the case of anxious subjects, this distance tends to appear only in the extreme paroxysm of anxiety rather than as a constant state. This has significant implications for the felt sense of being a self. If the anxious subject is able to return to a non-anxious state, as is broadly the case, then a distance is afforded, which allows the subject to gain a distance on their disordered relation to things. The consistency of the schizophrenic patient's relation to the world suggests a significantly more static body image than that of the anxious subject. Where the body image of the anxious self is marked by volatility between anxious and non-anxious states, in the case of the schizophrenic, the propensity is of a 'consistent disturbance' in body image (Priebe and Röhricht 2001). Fuchs offers an incisive summary:

> Schizophrenic patients often speak of a split between their mind and their body, of feeling detached from their lived performance like a machine or a robot. In particular, they may experience a disintegration of habits or automatic practices, a 'disautomation'. Instead of simply dressing, driving, walking, etc., they have to prepare and produce each single action deliberately, in a way that could be called a 'Cartesian' action of the mind on the body. (Fuchs 2009, 553)

On the theme of gaps in a subject's world, consider again Pascal's abyss. As we have seen, this episode concerns the case of a philosopher who experiences himself as being forever on the verge of falling. In the light of contemporary research, to what extent can this condition be understood as a disordering of image or schema? On the surface, the existence of an abyss in space seems tied up with the notion of a body image. Here, our focus would be on body as an object of intentional beliefs, one of these beliefs being that the body is shaped by a void. The image of the body as being shaped by a void is both a perceptual experience and an emotional attitude towards the body (Gallagher and Zahavi 2008, 146). The perception of an abyss creates a hollow in the side of the body, and consequently the perception of the body is of a body on the edge of a precipice, and at all times needing a prop to support it.

But this is only one side of the story. To give an explanatory account of the abyss in terms of a disturbed body image is to overlook the constriction in movement associated with the dysfunction of the body schema. In this respect, Pascal's abyss is exemplary. Here, we can ask a speculative question: without the chair to support himself, how does Pascal move in the world? It is worth noting that Pascal's abyss is one that pursues him. In a report from the time, we are told that 'afterwards [Pascal] used at times to see an imaginary precipice by his bedside, or at the foot of the chair on which he was sitting' (cited in Vidler 2000, 19). The fact that he relies intently on the chair not only to steady his body but also to steady his anxiety means that in the absence of this prop, movement would be at best stifled, at worst impossible. From where does this inhibition of movement derive? Notably, we are presented here not only with a disturbance of the body schema by the body image but also a disturbance of the body image by the body schema. The inability to walk from one corner of a room to another without the need of prop to support oneself suggests that disturbance comes about because of a malformed body image. But given that there is a certain degree of autonomy in the body schema, it may come as a surprise to Pascal that he is unable to move freely in the world without being accompanied by the anxiety of falling. Indeed, the sense of surprise that comes in the anxiety of falling testifies to a non-possessable and uncontrollable element of the body analogous to a nervous tic or even a phantom limb.

The recent research on body image and body schema allows us to understand the complex ways in which these two terms are both separate but also how they can become reversible. While central in helping us to understand the malleable nature of the body, the characterization of body image as being a perceptual representation of one's body leaves to one side the function of the image as the site of an identification with a form exterior to oneself. Moreover, what remains to be said is to what extent the identification with an image outside of oneself comes with the paradoxical consequence of being alienated from oneself. We wish in the remaining part of the chapter to build upon the phenomenological understanding of the body image by connecting it with a psychoanalytical account. In turn, this rapport between the disciplines will provide us with a far richer understanding of anxiety than were we to take these methodologies in isolation from one another.

FIGURE 5.3 *Le Maïdo, La Réunion.*

Beyond the mirror

You assume a role in life. Over time, the role hardens, in turn
becoming indistinguishable from your sense of self. From nowhere,
you will become a doctor, a lawyer, a father or a convict. Habits that
you formed early on life will follow you through the duration of
your existence, and in times of crisis, you will re-enact these rituals
so as to remind you of the place where you have emerged from.
You will form a social circle, where other like-minded people will
gravitate. In the gaze, movements, speech patterns and inflexions
of your allies, you will reaffirm a knowledge of yourself that is
already familiar. The social world opens itself up to you from the
zero point of your own consciousness, it is singled out as a stage
upon which other people, objects, and the entire cosmos appears as
a spectacle to behold. A complex layer of culture covers the entire

world; it is thick and often impenetrable, but carries with it at all times an unrivalled sense of reality. Your reality is unquestioned; it is complete in itself.

At times, however, the thick patina of roles, intersubjective domains and regions of culture, each of which is given in their dominance, recede in their clarity. An anxiety, unwavering and brilliant, pierces through the atmosphere, drawing attention to a dark undercurrent sketching out a place in your existence. Before you, another existence took place. In its reappearance, it confronts you with the limits of an illusion: that self you attach yourself to is conceived through an unassailable anxiety. You are a placeholder for the roles you assume, and each of the roles is ultimately anterior to your existence, either inherited from the past or disposed towards the future. Before and after you, variants of a self you have cultivated existed or will otherwise come into existence. There is a dream of being a self, through which an unfillable gap remains vacant. In it, your dream collides with a wakefulness that occupies the same body, a black hole where selfhood comes into being.

* * *

'The illusion of unity', so Lacan writes, 'in which a human being is always looking forward to self-mastery, entails a constant danger of sliding back again into the chaos from which he started; it hangs over the abyss of a dizzy Ascent in which one can perhaps see the very essence of Anxiety' (Lacan 1953, 15). Lacan situates us at the midst of anxiety, at the very point where the self is no longer able to fend off its own fragmentation through a series of elaborate rituals, props and conjurations. We have arrived on the other side of this *dupery* (to invoke a Levinasian term), now faced with the vast space between the sense of being a self and the unrecoverable gap that undermines this self-presence. But how did we get to this edge, to this dissolution of form? To answer this, we will need to retrace our steps. We will need to circle Lacan in sketching the genesis of a self, from its premature beginnings to its ever-present danger before anxiety.

Lacan's thoughts are worth pursuing for at least two reasons. One, he draws our attention to the relation between the emergence of anxiety and the effacement of one's sense of self. In doing so, he renders anxiety a constitutional facet in the structure of the subject, rather than a fault in an otherwise stable self. Two, he formulates anxiety as the presence of pure alterity, which at no point can be employed to disclose a specious 'wisdom'. His analysis of anxiety thus stands in contrast to the traditional (especially Heideggerian) approach to anxiety, which would treat the mood as an opportunity for the realization of the subject. At the same time, his emphasis on alterity and the partial collapse in identity converges with our own phenomenological account of anxiety, which accents the partial formlessness and impersonalization of the body. Our foray into Lacan is not an exposition of his overall thoughts on anxiety, the complexity of which exceed our present aims. Rather, we wish to a certain extent to instrumentalize Lacan (quite against his own intentions, of course) in order to forward our own cause. To narrow this aim down, our concern falls to what is left outside of the mirror image, and to what end this 'remainder' contributes to the production of anxiety. It is on this hinge between the specular image and its remainder that phenomenology aligns with psychoanalysis. We will begin with Lacan's account of the mirror stage. Our engagement with this well-known lecture is driven by a desire to understand how a body image is not only a perception we have of our own corporeality, but how this relation also marks a movement of identification with an unified form exterior to oneself.

At the outset, Lacan's account of the body image differs from the contemporary understanding in suggesting that the image functions to both unify and alienate the subject. This joint function is not circumscribed to early life alone before being integrated into adult life, but instead remains active as a structure of subjectivity itself. It is important to explicitly note that the subject one finds in Lacan is constitutionally and not contingently alienated. Despite Lacan's non-developmental reading of the mirror stage, we begin with childhood. Childhood is the site of a genesis of the mirror image, but one that is carried with us throughout life. An infant enters the world as a set of uncoordinated motor mechanisms, each of which fails to integrate into a whole. This is what Lacan terms 'the prematurity of birth': a birth that arrives on the scene too soon, and long before the organism is equipped to negotiate with the world and survive alone. But then something happens in this movement: the child identifies with a visual image of him or herself. Lacan reports that when a child assumes a body image in the face of a mirror, the response is one of jubilation (Lacan 2006, 76). What is unveiled before the mirror is an identification with a specular image, an image that transforms the baby who is 'still trapped in his motor impotence and nursling dependence' to a primordial *I* (76). Lacan elaborates on the significance of this moment:

> But the important point is that this form situates the agency known as the ego, prior to its social determination, in a fictional direction that will remain irreducible for any single individual or, rather, that will only asymptotically approach the subject's becoming, no matter how successful the dialectical synthesis by which he must resolve, as *I*, his discordance with reality. (76)

To look ahead, already in this passage we have the basis for Lacan's revision of anxiety. As with Heidegger, Lacan phrases anxiety as a privileged affect, one that is not simply concerned with a localized experience of the world, but instead with the very structure of the subject. Here, we must make a distinction between what Lacan terms 'the ego' and the subject. The subject for Lacan is not that of the Freudian ego, much less the phenomenological 'I', as it would be understood in Husserlian terms. For Lacan, the ego is a product of the imaginary order, an order in which I experience myself, by way of an optical illusion, as a discrete self. Lacanian psychoanalysis, as a method of interrogating a human being, is thus not primarily concerned with the egocentric self, except as a way of delineating its imaginary structure. For him, the ego is a necessary fiction we must tell ourselves, and to this extent is described by Lacan as a 'symptom'. 'The ego', he writes, 'is structured exactly like a symptom. At the heart of the subject, it is only a privileged symptom, the human symptom par excellence, the mental illness of man' (Lacan 1991a, 16). The subject, on the other hand, does not belong to the imaginary order in the way that the ego does. When he speaks of the subject, Lacan is not referring to a Cartesian subject as a substance. If the ego can manipulate its own image, then the subject for Lacan operates at another level. Indeed, his conception of the subject is distinct from how the term is commonly employed in a philosophical sense. The subject is largely unconscious, and while appearing through the ego (and by consequence, the body), it is nevertheless different from it.

The formation of the ego from the subject occurs as a 'mirage' (Lacan 2006, 76). This mirage is predicated on a *méconnaissance* – a misrecognition – in which the child recognizes himself or herself as the image presented in the mirror. Of course, we need not understand mirror in a strictly literal sense, but can also grasp how intersubjective relations also function to either reinforce or collapse the production of a sense of self. Indeed, Lacan will go to great lengths to explain how the irreducible unknowability of what the Other wants from me leads to profound anxiety, such that I am unable to place the image I have of myself within relation to their gaze. This structure is predicated on the function of what Lacan terms the *imago* – the illusion that both alienates and unites the ego, and which is compelled at all times by a 'discordance with reality', never left behind, but instead which remains 'irreducible for any single individual' (76). As structured by a 'certain dehiscence at the very heart of the organism, a primordial Discord', Lacan's concept of the ego as a work of fiction thus stands in contrast to any philosophy of the self that presents the self as already given to consciousness. This opposition includes the 'contemporary philosophy of being and nothingness [which] grasps negativity only within the limits of a self-sufficiency of consciousness' (80). Lacan's indictment against Sartre (and, by dint of consequence, Merleau-Ponty), frames the phenomenological account of negativity as being situated within an already established order of consciousness, framed from the outset by 'the illusion of autonomy' (80). What follows is a narrative of seduction and alienation.

Through being 'caught up in the lure of spatial identification', the individual undergoes a jubilant transformation from a 'fragmented image of the body to what I will call an "orthopedic" form of its totality' (78). Throughout this process, the fragmentation of the body persists in its irreducible materiality, thus forging a split between the image of unity and the persistence of disunity experienced in the body. This makeshift unity comes with a price, however: in the process of reforming the body as a whole, a 'donned armour of alienating identity' is produced, which carries with it a movement of self-alienation (78). In not only accepting but also jubilantly identifying with the specular image as oneself, the individual is alienated by way of this *méconnaissance* of what one actually is. In turn the image itself takes place of the self. There is, then, a fundamental gap in the infant, and from this gap, the question of what am I *beyond the body image* exacts a haunting presence in the life of the individual.

To speak in terms of an alienated identity begs the question of what the self is alienated from? Such a question is to misconstrue the place of alienation within Lacan. Once again, it is necessary to note that the mirror stage is ultimately irreducible to a linear procession of movements. There is not, to put it in terms other than Lacan's, the experience of a fragmented body prior to its identification with the specular image. Nor is there an eventual reintegration of the body as fragmented through the image. It is only in a retroactive way that we regain and recognize (if we do so at all) the 'primordial Discord' that preceded identification – that is, when the discord manifests itself symptomatically, not least as anxiety. Understood in this way, the self-alienation evident in Lacan is not an alienation from one's lived experience, as such (although, of course, this may well exist, too). Rather, the alienation is a constitutive alienation formed by the gap between what one actually is and what one sees in the mirror.

What one sees in mirror need not, of course, refer in concrete terms to visual mirror. More than this, the mirror is any reflective surface – above all, a human face – that either reinforces the image I identify as being me, or otherwise contests it, thus revealing the gap between ego and the subject. This understanding of the body image is manifestly at odds with an analysis of the image as deriving from an already established set of conscious beliefs and attitudes on our body. For the most part, human existence is characterized by a sense of ownership of one's bodily existence. The body as it is lived is that which reinforces my sense of who I am in the world, and this is informed by the sense of the body image as a Gestalt. As Lacan sees it, far from a conscious set of beliefs and representations about one's lived body, the body image is precisely that which unifies selfhood through a process of alienating identification with a fictional image.

The 'lure' of this movement is tied up, then, with the prematurity of birth. The contrast between the reflection of oneself as united and the perception of one's body, by contrast, as fragmented serves only to reinforce a dependency on the image as an (illusory) means of unification. For this reason, the image can never repair or conjoin the fragmented body with the self, but only conceal the body that will appear in dreams 'in the form of disconnected limbs or organs exoscopically represented' (78). Yet in other expressions, the body

FIGURE 5.4 *Anse des Cascades, La Réunion.*

appears in 'bits and pieces' (*imago du corps morcel*é) and elsewhere in 'images of castration, emasculation, mutilation, dismemberment, dislocation, evisceration, devouring, bursting open of the body' (Lacan 1953, 13; Lacan 2006, 85). Deprived of its overall lucidity, a series of uncanny images is unveiled, 'trunks cut up in slices and stuffed with the most unlikely fillings, strange appendages in eccentric positions' (Lacan 1953, 13).

The spectre of anxiety

With his mention of 'strange appendages in eccentric positions', we are returned to the 'dizzy Ascent in which one can perhaps see the very essence of Anxiety' (15). The ego that emerges from the mirror stage does so out of necessity. To function coherently, it becomes necessary to bring order to chaos, to reduce the irreducible to the image of having a form. Given its mandatory role in rendering oneself coherent, the ego assumes a stubborn place within the self, framed by an 'element of inertia' (12). Yet at certain times, and especially in moments of anxiety, the obstinacy of the human ego is exposed to the possibility of regressing back to the disintegrated and fragmented body from where it derives. Indeed, what is anxiety-inducing concerns what cannot be captured in the specular image, and is marked out in Lacan as an 'un-imaged residue of the body', which anxiety exposes us to (Lacan 2014, 46).

In *Seminar II*, Lacan gives us a striking account of this irreconcilability between anxiety and the ego. The context for this description is that of a patient of Freud's called Irma. On the night 23 July 1895, Freud has a dream about Irma. She is unwell, with something lodged in her throat. When Freud looks in her throat, he finds evidence of 'extensive whitish grey scabs upon some remarkable curly structures which were evidently modelled on the turbinal bones of the nose' (Freud 2010, 132). As it turns out, Irma had been administrated an injection with a sullied syringe. Lacan presents to us his reflections on this encounter.

> There is a horrendous discovery here, that of the flesh one never sees, the foundation of things, the other side of the head, of the face, the secretory glands *par excellence*, the flesh from which everything exudes, at the very heart of the mystery, the flesh in as much as it is suffering, is formless, in as much as form in itself is something which provokes anxiety. Spectre of anxiety, identification of anxiety, the final revelation of *you are this* – *You are this, which is so far from you, this which is the ultimate formlessness.* (Lacan 1991b, 154–155)

Lacan draws us close to the essence of uncanny anxiety. Something returns from what is ostensibly the most familiar of things: the face. Far from revealing itself in its totality, the surface of the face conceals its mysterious interior. 'The other side of the head' is marked in its uncanniness as the space we live alongside yet forever remain oblivious to. Upon contact with it, the threat of dissolution is made real. Formlessness is not the destruction of matter, but the confrontation with matter deprived of its image. Always out-of-view, yet always present, Lacan never strays too far from the Freudian link between anxiety and the uncanny: *You are this, which is so far from you, this which is the ultimate formlessness.* Lacan locates with some specificity the spectral domain of anxiety. Anxiety is there, anonymous and without form. At the same time, it remains irrecoverable and inaccessible, for as soon as it appears, it is reconstituted as an image, destined to the placelessness 'one never sees'.

This reversal of anxiety generates a different account of its origin. Lacan's anxiety is not a humanized anxiety that takes place at the level of an intra-psychic conflict within different aspects of the ego. Instead, anxiety is situated at the very grounds from where the ego appears. Indeed, the birth of the ego is a necessity in order for anxiety to be contained, and without this stabilizing illusion, a dissolution – even a death – of self would be the outcome. Strictly speaking, therefore, it makes questionable sense to speak of anxiety in terms of its various sub-divisions (generalized anxiety disorder, phobic anxiety, obsessive anxiety and so forth). While these categories delineate the specific *expression* of anxiety, for Lacan, there can only be one anxiety: an anxiety that precedes the self, and which constitutes selfhood without ever being reducible to selfhood. Anxiety emerges here not as a rupture within an already defined self, but as a 'primordial Discord', which is never experienced on its own terms. Given the primacy of anxiety in Lacan, subjectivity is always endangered by the possibility of falling back into a dizzying abyss from where it emerges.

Despite Lacan's tendency to underplay the body, in his account of the relation between the genesis of self and the primordiality of anxiety, we find a series of parallels with our own analysis. As we have phrased it, anxiety is framed as an encounter with the impersonal level of existence. The impersonal level is given as a constant underside of existence, as that of Lacan's dizzying precipice, on top of which the narrative of selfhood is constructed. In each case, anxiety is registered on the border where selfhood risks becoming effaced by its own constitution. For this reason, our alignment with Lacan is not only phrased as an anxiety concerned with the loss of self; it is also structured as a dissolution that comes *from within* rather than from beyond. Just as Lacan phrases anxiety's dizzying movement as entailing a confrontation with the 'primordial Discord ... at the very heart of the organism', so we have sought to show from a phenomenological perspective how anxiety is structured as an indirect encounter with the body's irreducible anteriority, grasped affectively as a sense of slimy uncanniness.

Given the parallels between Lacan's account of anxiety and our own, we can see now how the work of re-personalization is ultimately consistent with the formation of ego. As with Lacan, even when the mirror affords the infant a space of identification with an exterior, there is no actual transformation of the body: it remains fragmented. The same is true of the impersonal body: it remains impersonal throughout its 'conversion' to becoming one's own. In this respect, the function of identification dovetails with the work of re-personalization: both operations seek to conceal a gap in the structure of selfhood. For Lacan, the gap is between the fragmented and unified image of oneself; whereas for us, the gap concerns the space between personal and impersonal dimensions of bodily existence. In each case, there is a leftover or remainder that cannot fit into the image of oneself, and which is marked as an object of anxiety.

Throughout this border affair, phenomenology presents us with the appearance of anxiety in a clothed form while recognizing how anxiety necessarily exceeds phenomenality, operating at a level that is only semi-accessible through the lens of the specular image. It is for these reasons, that anxiety's locus is not, as Heidegger and Freud suggest, with the potential of absence, but instead, as Lacan sees it, with presence, albeit a presence registered as the 'flesh one never sees', to repeat again his formulation. If we were to formulate this invisible flesh in existentialist terms, then we could phrase it as a *nothingness*. Only the nothingness at stake would not be the indefinite void found in Heidegger and Sartre. Rather, the nothingness of anxiety, as we see it, is a dynamic force, plentiful and expressive in material form.

Of this distinction, Lacan writes, 'I have opposed the psychologizing tradition that distinguishes fear from anxiety by virtue of its correlates in reality. In this I have changed things, maintaining of anxiety – *it is not without an object*' (Lacan 1987, 82). Lacan is referring here to the concept of *objet petit a* (always in the French). An elaboration of the concept would lead us beyond our concerns, not least because his formulation undergoes a series of revisions, which do not justify pursuing presently. The fundamental idea is that for Lacan, the *objet petit a* is the leftover that is marked as the 'Other's otherness' (Lacan 2014, 27). The object becomes bound with desire, insofar as Lacan understands desire not only as a concern with what is missing in the subject, but also with anxiety insofar as he understands anxiety as the return of that which cannot be integrated into the specular image. Notwithstanding the technicalities of the *objet petit a*, the formulation of anxiety as not without an object is worth stating. In fact, this formulation appears time and again in his seminar on anxiety.

At first, he declares that 'this object is not properly speaking the object of anxiety', in that the object is not a direct correlative with anxiety (Lacan 2014, 89). At the same time, to posit the existence of an object of anxiety is not to suggest that this object appears in a clear and distinct way: 'This relation of being not without having doesn't mean that one knows which object is involved. When I say, *He isn't without resources, He isn't without cunning*, that means, at least for me, that his resources are obscure, his cunning isn't run of the mill' (89). The obscurity confuses the presence of the object, positioning it in a non-place, which precludes it from being readily available before our eyes as a discernible phenomenon, much less to be analysed scientifically. Indeed, to approach the object of anxiety from the perspective of 'scientific discourse … would be yet another way of getting rid of anxiety' (131). To eliminate anxiety would mean superimposing a stationary image upon it, or otherwise to reduce it to a set of predetermined characteristics. As we know, however, this domestication falls short of its aims, and in the gaps where the superimposition of form comes undone, anxiety reappears in another guise.

Nowhere is this return of anxiety clearer than in the encounter with voids puncturing the reflective surface of the mirror, be it an actual mirror or another person. When we return to the mirror, then we do so with caution, knowing that the specular image is impregnated with a double, which will appear from time-to-time as that imageless body that articulates itself as anxiety. At times, the void in the mirror becomes visible. A stranger turns to us, their face unreadable, with a gaze full of questions. When confronted with their face, the look demands something of us that is nowhere to be found. As a result, misrecognition ensues. One of Stanley Hall's patients '[w]as long frightened at the eyes of a picture hung on the wall, which followed her to every corner till fright yielded to anger' (Hall 1897, 211). Another 'had long played with a dog till one day he gazed into its eye and caught a panic, which made him shun it for weeks' (211). Illustrations such as this underscore the agency of the reflective surface. The eye not only glares out from the face, it also registers what it sees thanks to its expressive power. Under such circumstances, the specular image also becomes a spectral image, a 'mirage' that recedes the more we enclose upon it (Lacan 2006, 76). In Merleau-Ponty's own reading of the mirror stage, this rapport between the specular image and that of a phantom occupying that image is reinforced (Merleau-Ponty 1964b, 128). The uncanniness of the mirror image derives from the fact that the ego occupies two places at the same time, without those two places (and egos) being strictly identifiable with one another. Rather, they come into contact with one another 'in a bizarre way', as in the case of 'certain hypnotic states, and in drowning people', where we assume the body image of the drowning or dying person is reconstituted (129). Merleau-Ponty singles out a certain strangeness located in the mirror image. If the mirror image is like me, then there is something nevertheless omitted in this image, around which I approach cautiously, never entirely confident that what appears for me does so as a reflection or a gesture of repulsion.

With this strangeness, Merleau-Ponty invites us to consider the significance attached to images: 'In a singular way the image incarnates and makes appear the person represented in it, as spirits are made to appear at a séance. Even an adult will hesitate to step on an image or photograph; if he does, it will be with aggressive intent' (132). There is something in the image that cannot be tied down to appearances, a hidden – indeed, imageless – dimension that obligates us to step with hesitation in the face of a shadow that vision alone cannot frame. Even as adults, Merleau-Ponty reminds us, when the prematurity of our birth has been rationalized to a discrete episode in our narrative, this spectre still haunts us. The image seen in the mirror retains its uncanny ability to spook us, retaining a presence in our dreams long after we have stepped away from the mirror.

What haunts us is not simply the doubt and uncertainty that lurks within the mirror, but the anxious prospect that the mirror will dissolve the image constructed of ourselves, as Merleau-Ponty writes, 'we never completely eliminate the corporeal condition that gives us, in the presence of a mirror, the impression of finding in it something of ourselves...this magic belief...never truly disappears' (138). As with Lacan, Merleau-Ponty suggests that the self-alienation structuring subjectivity is neither contingent nor resolved into maturity. A dimension of ourselves remains outside cognition: 'If the comprehension of the specular image were solely a matter of cognition, then once the phenomenon was understood its past would be completely reassimilated' (138). Of course, this reassimilation never occurs, and despite an abstract apprehension that the mirror image is only an approximation of reality, the mirror stage continues to exist on the 'threshold of the visible world' (Lacan 2006, 77).

To think of this threshold in specific terms, turn towards the gaze that can never be captured by the specular image.

Even in the experience of the mirror, a moment can come about when the image we believe we abide by undergoes modification. If this specular image we have facing us, which is our stature, our face, our two eyes, allows the dimension of our gaze to emerge, the value of the image starts to change – above all if there's a moment when this gaze that appears in the mirror starts not to look at us any more. There's an *initium*, an aura, a dawning sense of uncanniness which leaves the door open to anxiety. (88)

We have arrived at the kernel of anxiety, at the point in which the mirror betrays us. A gap appears, small enough to go unnoticed, but visible enough to force a collapse in the structure of self-identification. What escapes us is the irreducible remainder, that which exceeds both the frame of the mirror and the materiality of the body as a visible thing. For Lacan, it is the gaze that is always present but never fully visible to experience, and thus incarnates the object of anxiety. Before the mirror, the gaze makes itself available to scrutiny. But to *see* it as we would an object means freezing it. What then emerges is something inhuman if not monstrous, a gaze that is dislocated from its body now reduced to the status of being a still-life: 'The gaze, my gaze, is insufficient when it comes to capturing everything that stands to be absorbed from the outside' (189). The gaze remains as an impossible object, a literal blind spot, which we can never apprehend or reduce to perception, but which has a life of its own, outside of us.

'My body', so Merleau-Ponty writes in concordance with Lacan, 'escapes observation and presents itself as a simulacrum of my tactile body' (Merleau-Ponty 1964a, 94). Against this evasion, anxiety appears in the place where the mirror should fill the frame. What is reflected back is not the gaze of another subjectivity, but instead the absolute presence of impersonal existence. The crack in reality is potent enough to 'leave the door open to anxiety', and to fill this void left open an attempt is made to restore the mirror image back to the illusion of being unified and plentiful. One need only think of the fragmented identity of Roquentin and his attempt to frame anxiety by fixing his eyes upon things, given that 'as long as I could stare at things nothing would happen' (Sartre 1964, 78). Let us also think of the incidents we have encountered throughout our study: namely, the premature experience of waking up in one's home and catching sight of the other side of the intimacy and dwelling as fundamentally alien; the anxiety that leads us to experience our limbs as foreign vessels, both a part of us and also remote from us; the experience of other people as anonymous and beyond comprehension; the sense of being lost, both specifically and ontologically; and, finally, the experience of one's sense of self undergoing a radical dissolution, such that what remains intact is the minimal sense that it is *I* who am undergoing these experiences, while the *I* that is the origin of memories, desire, values, beliefs, proceeds to disband. In each of these cases, personal existence – what Lacan calls the ego and what is otherwise termed 'the narrative self' – is betrayed by what lies beyond the mirror: that which is formless and abyssal, outside of reach, and yet at all times the nearest thing to us. To turn away from the mirror only to re-turn towards it is to reattempt a restoration of the mirror's broken surface. But all along, the attempt at re-personalizing things only reinforces the fundamental incompletion that belongs to the mirror, not as an accident in perception, but as an inscribable structure of its very existence. That which escapes the mirror is what also escapes our sense of self; namely that blind spot, taken up in the invisible gaze of the body, which can never catch sight of itself as a whole, given that there was never a unified whole to begin with.

CONCLUSION

The Index of an Enigma

There is a perpetual uneasiness in the state of being conscious.

(MERLEAU-PONTY, *SENSE AND NONSENSE*)

The Musée d'Orsay

The roof of the Musée d'Orsay arches elaborately from one wall of the museum to another. It is a massive space, punctuated by huge windows, through which shafts of light flood in from above. Down below – on the museum floor – crowds of people line the main space before trailing off into the countless rooms and different levels structuring the place. Within this cavernous domain, you have sought sanctuary behind Jean-Baptiste Carpeaux's immense monument, 'Les Quatre Parties du Monde Soutenant la Sphère Celeste [The Four Parts of the World Holding the Celestial Sphere]'. The size of the monument mirrors the scale of the museum. Upon its great black base – already the size of an adult human – four figures, each representing different continents, are dancing in a circular motion, while holding a globe above their hands. The figures tower over you, and when you look upwards, the circumference of the globe appears as a colossal earth, unable to be supported by the hands of the figures below. The monument is shielding you from the gaze of the space and the people who occupy it. When you peer out from the sculpture, the space in front of you – known as l'allée centrale des sculptures – appears to be infinite. Yet you know in abstract that the space is finite, and that in order to leave the Musée d'Orsay it will become necessary for you to traverse the world in between the 'Les Quatre Parties du Monde Soutenant la Sphère Celeste' and the exit.

Your first movement beyond the sculpture is cautious. The movements you make are full of reservation, and only with greatest reluctance do you free the hand that is rigidly attached to the black base of the monument. Once your hands are free, your body moves with uncertainty, weaving erratically between the columns of people that stand before you and the outside world. As the crowds of people thicken in your midst, so your orientation becomes increasingly distorted. The colossal monument that had previously guided you in the Musée d'Orsay now becomes smothered in the dense crowds moving in and around the museum. Only the tip of the globe is visible, but in your disorientation, it is no longer possible for you to return to that place of sanctuary. You are unable to proceed. Frozen in your tracks, in this nowhere between the sculpture and the exit, you lose sight of yourself and begin to drift elsewhere.

The dream takes place in the daylight. You are aware of yourself as a discrete body standing in the hallway of sculptures, but despite this identification of your body as your own, you are nevertheless unable to move. Frozen in the gap between places, your body loses its unassailable presence as being *here*. As you attempt to move one foot in front of the other, you experience the moving foot as leaving a trail behind itself, as though it took a second or two for the materiality of the limb to catch up with its own motion. Likewise, when you turn your head rapidly from one corner of the hallway to another corner, your head continues to move even when it comes to a complete standstill. This fragmentation of bodily form is mirrored in the lack of distinction between the sculptures and the people that occupy the vast hallway. As these figures pass you by, your body jolts violently, as though your limbs were tethered between your own body and the bodies of others.

The field of vision that ordinarily guides you in the world is now marked with tiny specks of light, each of which is falling in a diagonal direction. This gentle movement generates the sense of both falling into and drifting away from space, a free-flowing motion that induces both anxiety and pleasure at once. In response to this uneasy mixture of joy and anguish, you raise the palm of your hand to your face in order to verify that it still occupies space and time. The face remains there, but does nothing to reconstitute your sense of self. As you close your eyes to regain your composure, a series of images floods your vision. At one moment, you are stuck in an airport unable to find your luggage; at another point, you are in an apartment and hear the sounds of a woman but cannot identify what room the sound is coming from; yet with another image, you are attempting to escape from a corridor, but must cross barbed wire in order to do so. You are brought back to the present when you feel the floor beneath you contort itself, as happens when you lie horizontally and suddenly feel the ground beneath you undulate. As this motion unfolds, paintings from corridors and rooms outside of your reach extend themselves from their confided space and seep through the hallway. The gaunt stare of Léon Spilliaert, captured in one of his self-portraits from 1903, meets your gaze. The painter's sullen cheeks and pallid skin break away from the canvas, now occupying the same space as that of your own face. Every painting that is visible to you exacerbates and amplifies your sense of dread. In the depth of the dark reds and violent motions depicted on distant and near canvases, you are nauseated. These dynamic contours serve only to confuse the boundary line between where you begin and where the paintings end. Falling deeper and deeper into a state that is not you, you continue nevertheless to witness your own self as wedged in the Musée d'Orsay while all around you existence in its stubborn normality continues unabated.

'As in a dream'

An abiding sense of strangeness haunts the topophobic experience of the world. In the face of empty plazas, constricted hallways and open fields, the phobic subject comes to a standstill, paralysed by a danger that is invisible to those around him, but is entirely real within his own anxiety. He himself is unable to explain the occurrence of these anomalies within experience, except to regard them as gaps in what is otherwise a 'normal' existence. Both in the midst of and in the aftermath of these episodes, the subject of anxiety is never fully present to himself, but instead situated in a

divergent relation to the experiences he is undergoing. Our usage of
the second-person narrative has intended to accentuate this rapport
between my own experience of anxiety and an anxiety that evades
that experience. To be either fully present or absent is impossible,
and to speak accurately of the experience of being anxious, it is
necessary to speak of a 'you' that addresses an 'I'.

This disjunction between the intimacy of the I and the foreignness
of the you underscores the strangeness peculiar to anxiety. It is a
structure that is situated between conscious and unconscious levels
of experience, at once neither present nor absent entirely, but instead
operating in an interstitial space that collapses all fixed dichotomies.
This dissolution of form during the experience of phobic anxiety is
relayed in historic accounts, especially in the case of agoraphobia.
We are already familiar with the motifs that mark the agoraphobe's
experience of space. The experience is one of alienation ('he does
not know why he is different from other people'); of derealization
('he began to feel strange all at once, almost like a "hangover"'); of
rationalization ('he likes to believe he is normal'); of irrationality
('he is absolutely unable to offer a specific reason for his feeling
of anxiety; it is just there despite all reasoning'); and above all, of
strangeness ('he feels as in a dream') (Knapp 1988, 62, 63, 67, 70).

As in a dream. Time and again, it is this oneiric realm that
anxiety leads us towards. It is a world where things become
bathed with an aura of weirdness. Materiality persists in and
through this strangeness, but only now is divested of its quality
as being irreducibly real. Prior to Westphal's patients, a case from
1847 attests to this anxious dreamscape. The patient 'claimed to
feel as if she were not dead or alive, as if living in a continuous
dream…objects [in her environment] looked as if surrounded by
a cloud; people seemed to move like shadows, and words seemed
to come from a far away world' (cited in Sierra 2012, 8). Should
we take the admission of dreaming as a mere rhetorical device,
employed to describe what cannot be articulated in conventional
terms? Or is there more to this expression than metaphor? Is there,
in fact, something peculiar to the experience of anxiety that aligns
it with the structure of dreaming? Our response to this question
will depend in large on how we frame the subjectivity of dreaming.
Whether or not dreaming is a departure or continuation from
waking life has significant implications for our understanding of
anxiety. By way of a conclusion to this book, we wish, so far as

phenomenology will enable us to get close to the phenomena, to describe this strange dream that accompanies the experience of anxiety.

The verge of dreaming

In our experience of waking from a dream, there exist those brief moments, termed the 'hypnagogic state', when the world has yet to be reconstituted in the image we conferred upon it prior to falling asleep. Within this brief interval, all too readily covered up, we become lost. In the same fashion of being lost in the forest, the lack of orientation is ontological and concerns the very grounds of our being, for it is a loss that impinges upon the fabric of identity. For Edgar Allan Poe, hypnagogic images present themselves as a

> class of fancies, of exquisite delicacy, which are thoughts: they seem to me psychal rather than intellectual. They arise in the soul … only its epochs of most intense tranquility – and at those mere points in time where the confines of the waking world blend with those of the world of dreams. I am aware of these 'fancies' only when I am on the very brink of sleep, with the consciousness that I am so. (cited in Mavromatis 1983, 13)

A number of points come to the surface. First, the hypnagogic state is a liminal state, and it occurs in between dreaming and waking, such that there is an overlap between the two spheres. Alongside this delicate, unstable oscillation between dreaming and waking, Poe's 'fancies' gravitate towards the threshold of sleep and dream without ever falling into dreaming itself. The movement is delicate precisely because of its instability. At any point, but especially upon deliberate self-reflection, the dreamer can break the spell of the hypnagogic state, returning him to the wakeful realm from where he began his journey. 'To tell the truth', so Sartre writes, 'a certain indulgence is necessary on my part. It remains in my power to shake this enchantment, to knock down these cardboard walls and to return to the wakeful world. This is why the transitory, unstable hypnagogic state is, in a sense, an artificial state' (Sartre 2004, 44). Through the artificial episode, consciousness remains intact, and is not extinguished by the onset of hypnagogia. Indeed, consciousness is not only operational but also silently self-aware of its own augmentation, as Sartre puts it: 'Consciousness would be a modifying capacity, endowed with a certain efficacy, which withdraws from the game and lets the phenomena unroll in blind succession, in the case of half-sleep' (43). What is displaced from the scene, then, is not reality as understood in an objective sense, but rather the centrality of the ego. If we take the intellectual aspect of consciousness that Poe mentions to refer to the self-identifying ego, which identifies consciousness with the sense of being 'me', then hypnagogia provides us with evidence of a consciousness that exists independently of this ego.

Hypnagogia thus takes its point of departure the notion of the ego as a construct employed to discriminate and forge boundaries between self and other. These boundaries entail a series of restrictions, not only between the ego and its environment, but also between 'wanted' and 'unwanted' information (Mavromatis 1983, 464). One source of such unwanted information is an 'intolerance of ambiguity' (464). When the boundaries of the ego are loosened, either through deep relaxation or through disorders of the self, perceptual and conceptual boundaries are partly dissolved, in turn, 'objects merge into one another and their meanings change, concepts lose their sharpness and expand to include other concepts remotely related to them or become identified with apparently entirely unrelated concepts' (465).

To pass from hypnagogia to dreaming is to recuperate a referential world, in which I myself am situated and to some extent distanced from the theatre of images that unfolds before me. As Evan Thompson argues, whereas the hypnagogic state is characterized by the presentation of visual patterns that absorb us, in dreaming, we ourselves are at the centre of the dream world (Thompson 2015, 127). It is true that the subject who appears in a dream is a distorted, strange and often uncanny version of the self we identify with in waking life. But even within this haze, what is intact in dreaming is the totality of a world, in which I become immersed (127). In contrast to the dream, the manifestation of the hypnagogic image does not emerge for me from a fixed position, whereby I still retain a contemplative distance. Rather, consciousness becomes absorbed with it, tied up in it, and thereby enchanted by its sheer presence. What is preserved through the dream, beyond the augmentations of one's mirror image and even when perceiving oneself in the third person, is the felt sense of mineness. It is I who am affected by the contents of the dream, whether it be horrifying or pleasurable, and when I awake from the dream, then it is I who am reflecting upon an experience that I have just undergone.

'Where am I?'

Ostensibly, hypnagogia states are thought of as being restorative if not relaxing (Mavromatis 1983, 106). From Poe to Proust, the experience of hypnagogia is imbued with a felicitous orientation, providing a source of inspiration for the literary imagination. Indeed, the experience of toppling between wakefulness and sleep is one of pleasure, a movement of freedom and spontaneity, in which the semi-dreamer enters a state of deep relaxation while displacing the residual sense of self that ordinarily accompanies us. Inversely, a heightening of anxiety tends to inhibit the production of hypnagogia, given that hypnagogic images are predicated on the capacity to enter a 'receptive mode' of consciousness freed from a concern with futural action, which tends to be prevalent in anxiety (106). Where, then, does the anxiety of dreaming (and the dream of anxiety) fit into this peaceful realm? The point of departure for the anxious subject's relation to hypnagogia begins not with an affirmation of the fluidity of the self but with a self that is fortified against ambiguity and otherness. As we have seen, the anxious self is a fragmented self. Divided into parts, each fails to form an intelligible unity, but instead fragments the self into contradictory and opposing aspects. For this reason, the anxious self is *either* a self *or* a no-self, and there is no space for ambiguity therein. One of the striking dimensions of hypnagogia in this respect is that it reveals a certain divergence between the ego and consciousness, and thus raises the question of who the actual subject of perception is. For the anxious subject, the unbound consciousness, now freed of its domesticity to the self, is experienced as a deviant consciousness, a consciousness that betrays the sense of self as having one story, and one story alone. For this reason, the hypnagogic consciousness is registered as an invasive and unsettling presence. In a report from 1879, the American psychologist G. Stanley Hall provides us with evidence of this disturbing presence.

Children's dreams of place are very vivid and melt like dissolving views into the waking sense of the real environment. 'Where am I?' is often the first problem of the morning consciousness, and there are often as strange ossifications and mosaics of two states, as in hypnagogic phenomena. Everything in the room is a lighthouse or buoy to aid them into safe harbour from the far dream voyages, and so cannot be moved without confusion. (Hall 1897, 161)

We have a precise account of the anxiety tied up with sleeping. The gap between sleepfulness and wakefulness is framed as a moment of vulnerability, in which the semi-dreamer no longer knows where he is and also what he is. In order to find his way back to the world, beacons of stability must survive the night, so that they can form a sense of temporal continuity. Hall's reference to objects in the room being lighthouses is an exemplary way to phrase this relation. As with the lighthouse, the familiar object in the room radiates its presence through the fog of sleep, dispatching a homely signal long before the dreamer has returned to the homeworld. For this reason, another patient 'can never have furniture moved in her bedroom, because the feeling of being turned around gives her a terrible panic' (160). To conceal this object or to position it elsewhere would be to dissolve the integrity of the room as a whole. It is thus not a question of the object as a localized entity; rather, the object acts as a waypoint, around which the patient orients himself or herself both when sleeping and when waking. As this orientation is collapsed, the residue of dreaming creeps into waking life, unnerving the distinctions between form and formlessness, self and non-self. Finding ourselves in a waking dream is to be confronted with the strange texture of dreaming transplanted into everyday life. The relational nexus between things is dissolved, causing a collapse in both spatial and temporal orderings. Characteristically, the dream of anxiety (and the anxiety of dreaming) is a dream of immobility, of being present but unable to act in the face of impending threat. This stasis is predicated on a dispossession of space and time, each of which is seized from our control. As a result, we remain passive in the face of a world that takes place irrespective of our attitude towards it.

Clinical reports verify that the experience of waking up and falling to sleep is a crystallization of the anxiety tied up with the loss of selfhood. Thus we read of a patient who 'often woke up in terror and cried loudly because she could not think where she was, even whether in bed or not' (Halls 1879, 160). Another who 'sweats, feels faint and nauseated if she cannot instantly locate every door and window on waking nights' (160). Yet another who 'is speechless and motionless with dread if she wakes up crossways or diagonally in bed, often thinking she has been carried elsewhere' (160). To not know where one is; to be unable to locate the means of escape; and to wake in a position different to how one went to sleep: with each of these cases, waking (and thus sleeping) elucidates with peculiar clarity the gap between the image imposed upon the world and the opaque, anonymous and constitutionally unfamiliar zone of existence that underpins that image. Sartre himself reinforces this anxiety in his discussion of hypnagogia, writing how, '[o]ne feels one's body very confusedly, even more vaguely the contact with the sheets and the mattress. The spatial position of the body is very poorly defined. The orientation is prone to blatant disorders. The perception of time is uncertain' (Sartre 2004, 40). The confused and anxious quality of hypnagogia finds root in these distortions of boundaries. The question of where I am is thus also a temporal question concerning at which point I cease to be 'me'.

The continuation of dreaming into waking life, no matter how brief, suggests an indivision between dreaming and non-dreaming. Merleau-Ponty reminds us that what preserves the liaison between these dimensions is the primordiality of the body (Merleau-Ponty 2012, 297). Just as the body haunts us in our dreams, so it remains with us in waking consciousness, providing us with a link to that other world, of which we only ever gain a momentary glimpse. To ask, in this light, whether dream and sleep move us away from waking life is also to ask where the strangeness inherent in anxiety leads us. Once again, we return to the tension between first and second-person experience: where am *I* when anxious? It is true; I am here situated in place. But the lack of self-coherence undermines the sense of being present to myself. As a result, I look upon myself, as though I were an object in a distant landscape. This sense of being pacified by anxiety draws us close to the quality of being in a dream. Of course, in the case of agoraphobic anxiety, we could search for an explanation for the dreamlike quality in positivistic terms. We could, for example, suggest that through being overly sensitized to his or her bodily experience of lived space, the subject of anxiety experiences a momentary loss of orientation in their proprioceptive awareness, with the resultant state 'resembling' that of being in a dream. But such an explanation would delineate in advance a place for dreaming that is sealed off from waking life, and thus reduce the experience to an 'error' in perception. 'Every sensation', so Merleau-Ponty writes, 'includes a seed of dream or depersonalization, as we experience through this sort of stupor into which it puts us when we truly live at the level of sensation' (223). This placement of dreaming at the heart of sensation runs counter to the positivistic analysis of dreaming as belonging to a nonsensical side of existence. Rather, what Merleau-Ponty finds in dreaming is evidence of the primordial and anonymous existence that structures waking life without ever being reducible to that life. Alongside Merleau-Ponty, we do not take dreaming as a departure from waking life, but instead see it as an amplification of the impersonal and anonymous sphere that constitutes everyday existence, rendering life possible while at the same time marking a space of anxiety.

The gaps in the wall

Faced with a gap in our understanding of the world, such as the agoraphobe experiences when crossing a plaza, our compulsion is to search for an explanation in order to fill it. Left unexplained, the gap presents itself as an anomaly, both physically and psychically. As it draws attention to itself, so the fissure marks itself out as an inscription of absence within an otherwise plentiful existence, gnawing at both our waking and sleeping lives. In the case of dreaming, the elusiveness of the 'phantom zone' between sleeping and waking, between the foreignness of the dreamscape and the nativity of the homeworld is soon reduced to the semblance of stable existence, thanks to the power of memory and habit. But as is evident from experience, archiving the dream to the realm of unconsciousness does not, as it were, put the dream to sleep. Rather, the murky sense of the dream stays with us, drawing attention to the gaps and points of uncertainties in our supposed mastery of selfhood.

In the birth of psychoanalysis, it was Freud who, with his intolerance of the 'defects' in the 'data of consciousness', sought to fill the gaps of understanding with recourse to the unconscious (Freud 1991, 110). For Freud, the very existence of the unconscious is legitimated not as a discovery but as an 'assumption', which retroactively furnishes an explanatory account of symptoms, obsessions, and, above all, dreams (110). In 'the mind of the hysterical patient', bizarre symptoms can be traced back to 'active unconscious ideas', which are revealed through the course of psychoanalysis to varying levels of success (35). This 'gain in meaning and connection', which the unconscious provides, carries psychoanalysis 'beyond the limitations of direct experience' and allows Freud to position himself as an archaeologist in search of a lost origin, existing both beneath and behind the surface of consciousness, and waiting patiently to be recovered. In an image that he will return to time and again, he asks that we envision the following scenario.

> Imagine that an explorer arrives in a little-known region where his interest is aroused by an expanse of ruins, with remains of walls, fragments of columns, and tablets with half-effaced and unreadable inscriptions…He may have brought picks, shovels and spades with him, and he may set the inhabitants to work with these implements. Together with them he may start upon the ruins, clear away the rubbish, and, beginning from the visible remains, uncover what is buried. If his work is crowned with success, the discoveries are self-explanatory; the ruined walls are part of the ramparts of a palace or a treasure house; the fragments of columns can be filled out into a temple; the numerous inscriptions, which, by good luck, may be bilingual, reveal an alphabet and a language, and, when they have been deciphered and translated, yield undreamed-of information about the events of the remote past, to commemorate which the monuments were built. (Freud 2001a, 192)

Freud's delight in the image of the analyst as explorer is evidently both theoretical and personal. What archaeology brings to Freudian analysis is evidence of the indestructibility of the past, an indestructibility that serves as a foundation for what Freud sees as the eventual fruition of psychoanalysis. In *Civilization and its Discontents*, Freud consolidates these themes of archaeology and psychoanalysis by inviting us to the 'Eternal City of Rome' (Freud 2001b, 69). 'In mental life', so he writes, 'nothing which has once been formed can perish – that everything is somehow preserved and that in suitable circumstances…it can once more be brought to light' (69). In order to demonstrate this point, Freud asks us to consider the walls and ruins marking Rome's history (69).

> Except for a few gaps, he will see the wall of Aurelian almost unchanged. In some places he will be able to find sections of the Servian Wall where they have been excavated and brought to light…Of the buildings which once occupied this ancient area he will find nothing, or only scanty remains, for they no longer exist…Their place is now taken by ruins, but not by ruins of themselves but of later restorations made after fires or destruction. There is certainly not a little that is ancient still buried in the soil of the city or beneath its modern buildings. This is the manner in which the past is preserved in historical sites like Rome. (69–70)

Inspired by his flair for archaeological description, Freud pushes the analogy a step further asking that we consider Rome as a 'psychical entity', with a long past and where the earlier phases of development continue to live alongside the present ones (70).

FIGURE C.1 *Rue Beautreillis, Paris.*

The result of this spatial–temporal anarchism is that the ruins, castles and palaces of Rome now occupy the same spot instead of being preserved individually. Thus where 'the Coliseum now stands we could at the same time admire Nero's vanished Golden House', leading Freud to 'things that are unimaginable and even absurd' (70). The problem, such as it is, concerns the impossibility of two or more different pasts occupying the same space simultaneously. The existence of this impossible city – perhaps even a dream city – forces Freud to draw his metaphor to an abrupt close: 'A city is thus *a priori* unsuited for a comparison of this sort with a mental organism' (71).

'The stone that one drags up'

Freud's account of archaeology draws us to the missing gap in our own phenomenology; namely, the unconscious. If the unconscious has been missing, then in a parallel sense, it has been there all along, unarticulated but nevertheless present. Already we have touched upon an entire set of gaps and limits in our phenomenological analysis of anxiety. Indeed, the very materialization of anxiety through the human body gives shape to this field of voids. As we have seen, in the midst of everyday life, events such as being unable to leave one's home or cross a bridge leave our understanding of the world and of ourselves in a state of disarray. At first, the gaps in experience lend themselves to be contained and avoided. A series of strategies are employed to house and place anxiety. Thanks to this cautious stance, life persists, albeit in a constricted fashion. Before long, however, the anxiety previously conscribed to the corner resurfaces in another form, reinforcing its presence as an invariant facet of subjectivity rather than an incidental component.

The topographical structure of our journey testifies to the constant resurfacing of anxiety in its manifold forms. We began in the home, safeguarding ourselves from the instability of the outside world. Within the nooks and corners of the home, anxiety has no place. But this shelter is both precarious and porous, and even within the home we find ourselves in a world of contingency, surrounded on all sides by the brute possibility that our bodies will betray us. Just as the inescapable body possesses, so it resists being possessed itself, a dimension that is given voice in our intersubjective relations. Other people enter the horizon of experience, not as additional aspects of an otherwise solitary adventure, but as constituents of the structure of perception. Throughout this narrative, anxiety is never abated nor buried, but instead transferred from object to object. This process of transference is finite, and ultimately anxiety exceeds the constraints placed upon it, effectively disarming the image superimposed upon it. Perhaps it will be in the experience of being in a small room or perhaps it will be in the experience of flying, but one way or another, the props and rituals constructed and enacted to keep anxiety at the door will reveal themselves for what they are: mechanisms of personalization. In its return to the surface of appearances, anxiety asks to what extent we can endure the gap between who we take ourselves to be and what we actually are. More than this, anxiety forces us to ask whether or not we can tolerate the uncertainty of being a self, unknown and unknowable. Far from suggesting a resolution to these questions, the undeceivable dimension of anxiety repels any attempt at humanization. To 'explain' anxiety by way of befriending or personalizing it as a source of wisdom or rendering it an ally is only to defer if not reinforce its fundamental alterity.

Throughout this analysis, the temptation might have been to employ the unconscious as an explanatory device for experiences, which are otherwise inexplicable. To follow the Freudian model, we would be led to fill the gaps in consciousness through summoning the indestructible content that belongs to unconsciousness. This restoration of lost experience looks *prima facie* to be especially pertinent to phobic anxiety. Why does a human being come to a standstill in the face of a situation where danger is objectively speaking not present? Phenomenology comes to these experiences with a view of describing the affective and relational dimension of anxiety. Here, phenomenology retains its legitimacy as a method concerned with elaborating and rediscovering what is already close to us in experience, but often overlooked or obscured. A phenomenology of anxiety, as a study of thematic content, is a necessary but limited analysis. It is necessary, because without this analysis, the lived experience of anxiety – or any other mood – would be unvoiced. Yet the specificity of anxiety, both structurally and thematically, is that it calls into question the very place of the subject, such that a complete analysis of anxiety would presuppose the very dissolution of selfhood. There is thus a hither side of anxiety, which does not lend itself to conscious experience, but instead must be considered from the perspective of what is not conscious to experience. To this end, it becomes necessary to speak of anxiety in both phenomenological and non-phenomenological terms. On the one hand, anxiety appears for the subject as belonging to the realm of corporeal experience. In this context, the complexity of the lifeworld is mediated through the body's perception of things. The emergence of anxiety for a subject – we need to think only of the crystalline simplicity of a person unable to leave his or her home – does so in the form of rupture. Anxiety breaks the spell with the world, such that the world protrudes, obtrudes and intrudes upon experience, alienating the subject from himself, others and the world more broadly. Just as the body is revealed in its otherness, so too is the world, which can never again be trusted as it did prior to anxiety. Beyond this phenomenological lens, however, anxiety alludes to that which lies beyond conscious experience.

The implicit status of the unconscious in our preceding explorations is evident in that Freud's own formulation of the unconscious as being hidden and active mirrors Merleau-Ponty's analysis of the body as operating on different levels. Just as the body is identifiable with subjectivity, so it also evades subjectivity, unveiling an impersonal level of existence, which can never be appropriated as my own. From the inception of his thought to its eventual conclusion, Merleau-Ponty approaches phenomenology's relationship to consciousness from multiple angles. Already in the notion of phenomenological intentionality, with which Merleau-Ponty begins his thinking, we are faced with a consciousness that exceeds its own margins, thus denying phenomenology of the possibility of a 'complete reduction', to use his emblematic formulation (Merleau-Ponty 2012, lxxvii). That phenomenology is unable to achieve a complete reduction only reinforces the importance of Merleau-Ponty's reconceptualization of the body as a layered body, operating within unreflected zones of experience, each of which structures intentionality itself. It is thanks to the multidimensional aspect of the body that lived experience gains its unifying quality through the primordial relation between body and world, a relation that is structured in a meaningful and dynamic fashion. Against this backdrop, symptoms do not have a meaning when considered in isolation, but instead take shape when situated in a broader context.

Merleau-Ponty's Freudianism only becomes more pronounced as his thinking proceeds. In 'Man and World', Merleau-Ponty praises Freud for developing a 'new idea of the body', which refuses the 'dichotomy of soul and body', and which is guided by a 'hidden or latent logic' (Merleau-Ponty 1964b, 227–229). 'Freud's great discovery', so Merleau-Ponty continues on this tone of veneration, consists of locating the 'osmosis between the body's anonymous life and the person's official life', which was 'Freud's unconscious' (229). To the end, Merleau-Ponty retains the archaeological current of Freud's unconscious, rejecting its static foundationalism, and instead accenting its quality as a 'paradox', paradoxical insofar as it marries the phenomenological with the non-phenomenological, the conscious and unconscious, and the immemorial and the contemporary without conflating them (Merleau-Ponty 1993, 70–71). This set of pairings is not a series of divisions etched in stone, but rather the space in which an impossible unconsciousness is located. Merleau-Ponty writes in the following terms:

> Since our philosophy has given us no better way to express that *intemporal*, that *indestructible* element in us which, says Freud, is the unconscious itself, perhaps we should continue calling it the unconscious – so long as we do not forget that the word is the *index of an enigma* – because the term retains, like the algae or the stone that one drags up, something of the sea from which it was taken. (71. Emphasis added)

Merleau-Ponty's terminology is telling. In the first instance, the unconscious is not an object to be approached discreetly, nor is it a sedimented layer of content, much less where that content is tied up with a pathology. Merleau-Ponty's sense of the unconscious as an element moves us beyond the orthodox account of unconscious as becoming visible only in the case of a symptomatic appearance. Rather, the unconscious is an 'enigma' and an 'element', that which is 'in us' without ever being identifiable with us. For these reasons, the unconscious is coexistent with life and thus with phenomenology, as he writes in *The Visible and the Invisible*: 'This unconscious is to be sought not at the bottom of ourselves, behind the back of our "consciousness", but in front of us, as articulations of our field' (Merleau-Ponty 1968, 180). By way of bridging the rapport between the personal and the impersonal, the unconscious serves as a non-thematic structural role, marking the strange adhesion between things without becoming an object in and of itself. It is the unconscious that serves to bridge the realm between the phenomenological and the non-phenomenological, between the immemorial and the contemporary. As silent, invisible and beyond thematization, the unconscious is the means by which the world is given its structure outside of the phenomena presented to us. The unconscious is that which is taken up in the *atmosphere* as a surrounding influence that accompanies our existence. As in front of us, the unconscious transcends the thematic dimensions that constitute our experiences, providing therein a rich undercurrent that both belongs to us while also evading us. Before our waking eyes, the unconscious thus spreads itself over consciousness, exceeding the gaps previously constructed to put it in its place, and marking its placelessness as one of uncanniness. In the image of a stone one drags up, carrying with it an oceanic life, we encounter a remainder that embodies this terrain, belonging to both the sea and the earth at once, to dream and wakefulness, without any rigid distinction separating them.

'The oneirism of wakefulness'

From the index of an enigma to dreaming, we are led at all times by an experience of anxiety that reveals to us a series of gaps that cannot be filled with recourse to a topographical model of unconsciousness. Phenomenology alone confirms this. We take the haziness that surrounds anxiety – its quality as being dreamlike – seriously. The haziness is available to us in experience, and the dream that accompanies anxiety is far from a whimsical retreat into a Bachelardian state of reverie. When located on the verge of a perilous drop, trapped beneath the ground or lost at sea, anxiety takes root as a bodily experience. But this bodily anguish is also an experience of one's sense of self falling apart. We have seen throughout this book, both in case studies and in first-person experience, that those who are subject to anxiety are especially vulnerable to the ontological disorientation that comes with this haziness. At the heart of this disorientation is the brief encounter with the impersonal infrastructure of existence, and it is a level of experience that is interwoven in our bodies, in our relation with others, and in our rapport with the home.

As these clear and distinct sensations unfold for us, a joint sense of not being present to oneself emerges. We treat this experience as having both a phenomenological and non-phenomenological dimension, having both a translucent and opaque side. We find, moreover, that the strangeness accompanying anxiety not only resembles the state of hypnagogic dreaming, but in fact is structurally parallel in a quite specific sense to the brief moments we wake from sleeping. There is an inherent haziness to be found in anxiety, whereupon the hypnagogic structure of the experience spills over the supposed gap between reality and appearance, and between dream and wakefulness. The subject of dreaming and anxiety is pacified and instituted at once, and what is carried through in the dream is not an invasion from the outside, but an intensification of what was already there. 'At that moment', so we read in a case study from 1887, 'it seems to us that all of a sudden the surroundings become hazy, as something quite remote and of no concern at all…The impressions from the surroundings do not convey the familiar picture of everyday reality, instead they become dream-like or shadowy…as if seen through a veil' (cited in Sierra 2012, 12). This osmotic haze is the space where dreaming and reality collapse into the same space, an impossible space previously denied by Freud in his quest for a sequential archaeology, and made flesh in the experience of anxiety.

Anxiety and dreaming are bound, then, in that both mark a 'lowering of the barrier of the official personality' (Merleau-Ponty 2010, 149). To embark on dreaming is not to be negated by the impersonality of the body, nor is it to be destroyed by anxiety. Rather, it is to be carried into the 'oneirism of wakefulness' that haunts both dreaming and anxiety at once (152). 'Our waking relations with things', so Merleau-Ponty writes, 'and, above all, with others, have in principle an oneiric character: others are present to us as dreams, as myths, and that is enough to contest the cleavage between the real and the imaginary' (206). The oneiric quality of existence accompanies us in waking life and need not announce itself in the form of anxiety. Throughout, there is an interweaving of distinctions; a life that is always exposed to the outside, a dream that infringes upon wakefulness, and a wakefulness that finds itself on the inside of a dream. If this ambiguity between states involves a certain pleasure, then it is a pleasure always rooted in anxiety. Thus, the 'lowering of the barrier of the official personality' finds root in both dreaming and anxiety. Where dreaming is concerned, we are carried off into a world that is both close and distant to us at once. It is a world that remains on the periphery of our waking life, folding over into that life, while at times betraying the image we adhere to in non-dreaming existence. Anxiety, on the other hand, follows the logic of hypnagogic dreaming in its partial effacement of the personalized self, revealing therein another layer of existence that both constitutes and denies identity in the same turn. The specificity of anxiety in contrast to hypnagogia is that it takes as its point of departure a subject unable to endure ambiguity and uncertainty. To depart, as the anxious subject must do, from himself is, indeed, to occupy a dreamscape. For it is a realm in which the personal I – the official self – is no longer sovereign, but instead caught up in a semi-formless haze.

Let us pause at the intersection between dreaming and anxiety to ask what happens when we are awoken with a start. To be awoken is to be faced with something that contests our identity, a thing that is ordinarily masked in our self-mastery. Dreaming and anxiety merge, and consequently we return to life in order to salvage what risks being destroyed in the dream. But the terrors of the night are not those that are left behind, but instead become imprinted into our waking consciousness. In the gradual relief of the official personality, the 'orthopaedic' (to use Lacan's terms) brace that holds the fragmented body together in an image of being a coherent whole is weakened. Consequently, the story told to oneself of who one is loses its conviction. What is provoked when the control of this desire is 'overly manifested' is, in Merleau-Ponty's own words, '*anxiety and reawakening*' (149. Emphasis added). As the dream begins, be it in a nocturnal context or in a daydream, the distinctions that keep the self at the door to the home are unclothed. Through this metamorphosis, the oneiric haze deforming boundaries is enacted as the primary mode of perception.

Against the breach in a person's official life, Merleau-Ponty is led to ask the same question we ask of the subject of anxiety, namely, 'Where is the dream for the dreamer?' (150). Of course, the dream is 'there' for the subject undergoing the dream. But as soon as the person enters the scene of the dream, so the dream dissolves. The same is true of the experience of anxiety. The subject is there,

FIGURE C.2 *Piton de la Fournaise, La Réunion.*

in the midst of anxiety, but at the same time, he himself as a centre of personalized existence is partly suspended. It is for this reason necessary to return to the scene of anxiety (even if that only means turning one's head towards the place one has just left) in order to grasp what took place. And what took place did so on the edge between personal and impersonal existence, between dreaming and wakefulness. In hypnagogic dreaming, we open ourselves more fully to the level of impersonal existence that is for the most part masked by the primacy of the ego. The eclipse of the ego through the awakening of the impersonal side of existence forces us to live at the level of pure sensation, oneiric and unarticulated, silent and obscure, yet experienced from the perspective of the still functioning self. If dreaming affords us a dizzying fusion of pleasure and strangeness, then where anxiety alone is concerned, the lowering of the ego coexists with an impending sense of collapse. Here, any such pleasure in the adventure of (un)consciousness is augmented with a sense of being too close to the unfillable gap, which threatens to annihilate the sense of self, and thus underscores the realization that *I am not me.*

In this respect, both hypnagogia and anxiety mark a partial return to a body that is in some sense pre-human, emerging before the subject has crystallized as a person. If perception renews this pre-history as unfolding into the present, then there is also 'that *intemporal*, that *indestructible* element in us' which is not reducible to humanity and is conceivable only in terms of a 'return to the unarticulated, the withdrawal to a global or pre-personal relation to the world' (Merleau-Ponty 1994, 71; Merleau-Ponty 2010, 206). In a final note from *The Visible and the Invisible*, Merleau-Ponty reinstates the point that the subject of dreaming is not strictly me, insomuch as I take partial leave of myself upon dreaming: 'The "subject" of dreaming (and of anguish, and of all life) is the *one*' (Merleau-Ponty 1968, 263). The *one* is that level of existence we have been tracing, pursuing and haunting throughout our foray into the phenomenology of anxiety. On a phenomenological level, the *one* appears through its indirection as the body that dissents from my possession. It is the body that marks the point where the I comes into contact with its own otherness. The *one* is that which cannot be integrated into my image of myself as a self. It is the excess of the impersonal organism rendering itself visible in the gaps between what I am and what I take myself to be.

In the vivid moments prior to sleep and upon awakening, we experience that anxious space where the I catches sight of the anonymous *one* both appearing and receding into the twilight. For a brief second, the body becomes imageless, illuminating the brute and impersonal substructure that renders our world visible. To dream, to be anxious, we leave behind that part of ourselves that strives towards self-mastery and self-possession, finding within each mode of being a world that exceeds our grasp while also being the very ground from where we evolve. Insofar as anxiety gnaws at our lives without ever becoming a discrete object of perception, and that it constitutes our subjectivity without ever revealing itself directly in the flesh, then for all its corporeal weight, anxiety stands at the threshold of dreaming and waking, revealing a glimmer of the fundamental otherness that lies in the midst of being *you.*

WORKS CITED

Abramowitz, Jonathan. (2005). *Understanding and Treating Obsessive-compulsive Disorder: A Cognitive Behavioural Approach*. New York: Routledge.

Bachelard, Gaston. (1994). *The Poetics of Space*. Trans. Maria Jolas. Boston: Beacon Press.

Bachelard, Gaston. (2011). *Earth and Reveries of Repose: An Essay on Images of Interiority*. Trans. Mary McAllester Jones. Texas: The Dallas Institute Publication.

Ballard, J. G. (1991). *Crash*. New York: Farrar, Straus and Giroux.

Ballard, J. G. (2002). *The Complete Short Stories*. New York: Harper Collins.

Barlow, David. (2004). *Anxiety and Its Disorders: The Nature and Treatment of Anxiety*. New York: The Guilford Press.

Baudelaire, Charles. (2008). *The Flowers of Evil*. Trans. James McGowan. Oxford: Oxford World's Classics.

Burwood, Stephen. (2008). 'The Apparent Truth of Dualism and the Uncanny Body', in *Phenomenology and the Cognitive Sciences* 7: 263–278.

Callard, Felicity. (2006). '"The Sensation of Infinite Vastness": Or, the Emergence of Agoraphobia in the Late 19th Century', in *Environment and Planning D: Society and Space* 24: 873–889.

Capps, Lisa & Ochs, Elinor. (1995). *Constructing Panic: The Discourse of Agoraphobia*. Cambridge and London: Harvard University Press.

Carel, Havi. (2013). 'Bodily Doubt', in *Journal of Consciousness Studies* 20: 178–197.

Carter, Paul. (2002). *Repressed Space: The Poetics of Agoraphobia*. London: Reaktion Books.

Casey, Edward. (1993). *Getting Back into Place: Toward a Renewed Understanding of the Place World*. Bloomington: Indiana University Press.

Chambless, Dianne & Goldstein, Alan. (1982). *Agoraphobia: Multiple Perspectives on Theory and Treatment*. Chichester: Wiley and Sons.

Collins, Christiane Crasemann. (2006). *Camillo Sitte: The Birth of Modern City Planning*. New York: Dover.

Davidson, Joyce. (2003). *Phobic Geographies: The Phenomenology of Spatial Identity*. London: Ashgate Press.

Decker, Hannah. (2013). *The Making of DSM-III*. Oxford: Oxford University Press.

Dillon, M. C. (1997). *Merleau-Ponty's Ontology*. Evanston: Northwestern University Press.

Dufrenne, Mikel. (1989). *The Phenomenology of Aesthetic Experience*. Trans. Edward S. Casey. Evanston: Northwestern University Press.

Foucault, Michel. (1986). 'Of Other Spaces', in *Diacritics* 16: 22–27. Trans. Jay Miskowiec.

Freud, Sigmund. (1991). *General Psychological Theory: Papers on Metapsychology*. New York: Simon & Schuster.

Freud, Sigmund. (2001a). *The Standard Edition of the Complete Works of Sigmund Freud, Volume III*. Trans. James Starchey. New York: Vintage.

Freud, Sigmund. (2001b). *The Standard Edition of the Complete Works of Sigmund Freud, Volume XXI*. Trans. James Starchey. New York: Vintage.

Freud, Sigmund. (2003). *The Uncanny*. Trans. David McLintock. Harmondsorth: Penguin.

Freud, Sigmund. (2010). *The Interpretation of Dreams*. Trans. James Starchey. New York: Basic Books.

Fuchs, Thomas. (2005). 'Corporealized and Disembodied Minds. A Phenomenological View of the Body in Melancholia and Schizophrenia', in *Philosophy, Psychiatry, and Psychology* 12: 95–107.

Fuchs, Thomas. (2009). 'Phenomenology and Psychopathology', in *Handbook of Phenomenology and Cognitive Science*. Eds, Shaun Gallagher & Daniel Schmicking. 546–573. New York: Springer.

Gallagher, Shaun. (1986). 'Lived Body and Environment', in *Research in Phenomenology* 16: 139–170.

Gallagher, Shaun. (2004). 'Agency, Ownership, and Alien Control in Schizophrenia', in *The Structure and Development of Self-consciousness: Interdisciplinary Perspectives*. Ed. Dan Zahavi *et al*. 89–104. Amsterdam: John Benjamins Publishers.

Gallagher, Shaun. (2005). *How the Body Shapes the Mind*. Oxford: Oxford University Press.

Gallagher, Shaun. (2012). *Phenomenology*. New York: Palgrave.

Gallagher, Shaun & Zahavi, Dan. (2008). *The Phenomenological Mind*. London: Routledge.

Goldstein, Kurt. (1966). *Human Nature in Light of Psychopathology*. New York: Schocken Books.

Hall, Stanley. (1897). 'A Study of Fears', in *The American Journal of Psychology* 8: 147–249.

Hazell, Jane & Wilkins, Arnold. (1990). 'A Contribution of Fluorescent Lighting to Agoraphobia', in *Psychological Medicine* 20: 591–596.

Heidegger, Martin. (1977). *Basic Writings*. Trans. Albert Hofstadter. New York: Harper & Row.

Heidegger, Martin. (1996). *Being and Time*. Trans. Joan Stambaugh. New York: SUNY Press.

Horwitz, Allan. (2013). *Anxiety: A Short History*. Baltimore: John Hopkins University Press.

Hunter, E. C. *et al.* (2004). 'The Epidemiology of Depersonalisation and Derealisation. A Systematic Review', in *Social Psychiatry and Psychiatric Epidemiology* 39: 9–18.

Husserl, Edmund. (1970). *The Crisis of European Sciences and Transcendental Phenomenology*. Trans. David Carr. Evanston: Northwestern University Press.

Husserl, Edmund. (1977). *Cartesian Mediations: An Introduction to Phenomenology*. Trans. Dorion Cairns. Boston: Martinus Nijhoff Publishers.

Jacobson, Kirsten. (2009). 'A Developed Nature: A Phenomenological Account of the Experience of Home', in *Continental Philosophy Review* 42: 355–373.

Jacobson, Kirsten. (2011).'Embodied Domestics, Embodied Politics: Women, Home, and Agoraphobia', in *Human Studies* 34: 1–21.

James, William. (1950). *The Principles of Psychology, Vol. 2*. New York: Dover Publications.

Jaspers, Karl. (1997). *General Psychopathology*. Trans. J. Hoenig. Baltimore: John Hopkins University Press.

Johnson, Galen. (1993). *The Merleau-Ponty Aesthetics Reader: Philosophy and Painting*. Evanston: Northwestern University Press.

Jones, Ernst. (1974). *Life and Work of Sigmund Freud*. New York: Basic Books.

Kamboj, S.K. *et al.* (2015). 'Bowel and Bladder-control Anxiety: A Preliminary Description of a Viscerally-centred Phobic Syndrome', in *Behavioural and Cognitive psychotherapy* 43: 142–157.

Kierkegaard, Søren. (1981). *The Concept of Anxiety: A Simple Psychologically Orienting Deliberation on the Dogmatic Issue of Hereditary Sin*. Trans. Reidar Thomte. New Jersey: Princeton University Press.

Knapp, Terry. (1988). *Westphal's 'Die Agoraphobie' with Commentary: The Beginnings of Agoraphobia*.Trans. Michael T. Schumacher. Lanham: University Press of America.

Lacan, Jacques. (1953). 'Some Reflections on the Ego', in *International Journal of Psychoanalysis* 34: 11–17.

Lacan, Jacques. (1987). 'Introduction to the Name-of-the-Father-Seminar', in *October* 40: 81–95.

Lacan, Jacques. (1991a). *The Seminar of Jacques Lacan: Book I, Freud's Papers on Technique, 1953–1954*. Trans. John Forrester. New York: Norton.

Lacan, Jacques. (1991b). *The Seminar of Jacques Lacan: Book II, The Ego in Freud's Theory and in the Technique of Psychoanalysis, 1954–1955*. Trans. Sylvana Tomaselli. New York: Norton.

Lacan, Jacques. (2006). *Ecrits: The Complete Edition in English*. Trans. Bruce Fink. New York: Norton.

Lacan, Jacques. (2014). *Anxiety: The Seminar of Jacques Lacan, Book X*. Trans. Adrian Price. London: Polity Press.

Laing, R. D. (1990). *The Divided Self: An Existential Study of Sanity and Madness*. Harmondsworth: Penguin.

Leder, Drew. (1990). *The Absent Body*. Chicago and London: University of Chicago Press.

Legrand du Saulle, Henri. (1878). *Étude clinique sur la peur des espaces*. Extract translated by Audrey Petit-Trigg. Paris: V. Adrien Dalahaye.

Levinas, Emmanuel. (1969). *Totality and Infinity: An Essay on Exteriority*. Trans. Alphonso Lingis. Pittsburgh: Duquesne University Press.

Levinas, Emmanuel. (1985). *Ethics and Infinity*. Trans. Richard Cohen. Pittsburgh: Duquesne University Press.

Levinas, Emmanuel. (2001). *Existence and Existents*. Trans. Alphonso Lingis. Pittsburgh: Duquesne University Press.

Levinas, Emmanuel. (2005). *Time and the Other*. Trans. Richard Cohen. Pittsburgh: Duquesne University Press.

Lyotard, Jean-François. (1992). *The Inhuman: Reflections on Time*. Trans. Geoffrey Bennington. California: Stanford University Press.

Marks, Isaac. (1987). *Fears, Phobias, and Rituals: Panic, Anxiety, and Their Disorders*. Oxford: Oxford University Press.

Mavromatis, Andreas. (1983). *Hypnagogia: The Nature and Function of the Hypnagogic State*. PhD Thesis, Brunel University.

May, Rollo. (1977). *The Meaning of Anxiety*. New York: Norton.

Merleau-Ponty, Maurice. (1964a). *The Primacy of Perception*. Trans. William Cobb. Evanston: Northwestern University Press.

Merleau-Ponty, Maurice. (1964b). *Signs*. Trans. Richard McCleary. Evanston: Northwestern University Press.

Merleau-Ponty, Maurice. (1968). *The Visible and the Invisible*. Trans. Alphonso Lingis. Evanston: Northwestern University Press.

Merleau-Ponty, Maurice. (1993). 'Preface to Hesnard's L'Oeuvre de Freud', in *Merleau-Ponty and Psychology*. Trans. Alden L. Fisher. 67–72. New Jersey: Humanities Press.

Merleau-Ponty, Maurice. (2010). *Institution and Passivity: Course Notes from the Collège de France (1954–1955)*. Trans. Leonard Lawlor & Heath Massey. Evanston: Northwestern University Press.

Merleau-Ponty, Maurice. (2012). *Phenomenology of Perception*. Trans. Donald Landes. London: Routledge.

Nancy, Jean-Luc. (2000). 'L'Intrus', Trans. Susan Hanson, in *CR: The New Centennial Review* 2.3: 1–14.

Neale, J. H. (1898). 'Agoraphobia', in *Lancet* 152.3925: 1322–1323.

Parnas, Josef & Gallagher, Shaun. (2015). 'Phenomenology and the Interpretation of Pathological Experience', in *Re-Visioning Psychiatry*. Ed. Laurence Kirmayer. Cambridge: Cambridge University Press.

Phillips, James & Paris, Joel. (2013). *Making the DSM-5: Concepts and Controversies*. New York: Springer.

Priebe, S. & Röhricht, F. (2001). 'Specific Body Image Pathology in Acute Schizophrenia', in *Psychiatry Research* 101: 289–301.

Quinodoz, Danielle. (1997). *Emotional Vertigo: Between Anxiety and Pleasure*. Trans. Arnold Pomerans. London and New York: Routledge.

Ratcliffe, Matthew. (2015). *Experiences of Depression: A Study in Phenomenology*. Oxford: Oxford University Press.

Rilke, Rainer Maria. (2009). *Duino Elegies and the Sonnets to Orpheus*. Trans. Stephen Mitchell. New York: Vintage.

Roth, Martin. (1959). 'The Phobic Anxiety-Depersonalization Syndrome', in *Proceedings of the Royal Society of Medicine* 52: 587–595.

Sadowsky, Stewart. (1997). 'Agoraphobia, Erwin Straus and Phenomenological Psychopathology', in *The Humanistic Psychologist* 25: 30–44.

Sartre, Jean-Paul. (1964). *Nausea*. Trans. Lloyd Alexander. New York: New Directions.

Sartre, Jean-Paul. (1998). *Being and Nothingness*. Trans. Hazel E. Barnes. London: Routledge.

Sartre, Jean-Paul. (2004). *The Imaginary: A Phenomenological Psychology of the Imagination*. Trans. Jonathan Webber. London: Routledge.

Saul, Jennifer. (2001). *Phobias: Fighting the Fear*. New York: Harper Collins.

Shawn, Allen. (2007). *Wish I Could Be There: Notes from a Phobic Life*. New York: Viking Press.

Sierra, M., Medford, N., Wyatt, G. & David, A. (2012). 'Depersonalization Disorder and Anxiety: A Special Relationship?' in *Psychiatry Research* 197: 123–127.

Sierra, Mauricio. (2012). *Depersonalization: A New Look at a Neglected Syndrome*. Cambridge: Cambridge University Press.

Steinbock, Anthony. (2010). 'Temporality, Transcendence, and Being Bound to Others in Trust', in *Trust, Sociality, Selfhood*. Eds, A. Grøn & C. Welz. 83–102. Tübingen: Mohr Siebeck.

Svenaeus, Fredrik. (2000). 'The Body Uncanny: Further Steps Toward a Phenomenology of Illness', in *Medicine, Health Care and Philosophy* 3: 125–137.

Thompson, Evan. (2015). *Waking, Dreaming, Being: Self and Consciousness in Neuroscience, Mediation, and Philosophy*. New York: Columbia University Press.

Trigg, Dylan. (2006). *The Aesthetics of Decay: Nothingness, Nostalgia, and the Absence of Reason*. New York: Peter Lang.

Trigg, Dylan. (2012). *The Memory of Place: A Phenomenology of the Uncanny*. Athens: Ohio University Press.

Trigg, Dylan. (2013a). *Body Parts*. Paris and Edinburgh: 3:AM Press.

Trigg, Dylan. (2013b). 'Bodily Moods and Unhomely Environments: The Hermeneutics of Agoraphobia and the Spirit of Place', in *Interpreting Nature: The Emerging Field of Environmental Hermeneutics*. Ed. Forrest Clingerman *et al*. 160–177. New York: Fordham University Press.

Trigg, Dylan. (2014a). 'The Role of the Earth in Merleau-Ponty's Archaeological Phenomenology', in *Chiasmi International* 16: 255–273.

Trigg, Dylan. (2014b). *The Thing: A Phenomenology of Horror*. Winchester: Zero Books.

Trotter, David. (2004). 'The Invention of Agoraphobia', in *Victorian Literature and Culture* 32: 463–474.

Tuan, Yi-Fu. (1979). *Landscapes of Fear*. Minneapolis: University of Minnesota Press.

Van den Berg, J. H. (2001). *Different Existence: Principles of Phenomenological Psychopathology*. Pittsburgh: Duquesne University Press.

Vidler, Anthony. (2000). *Warped Space: Art Architecture, and Anxiety in Modern Culture*. Cambridge, MA: MIT Press.

Vincent. (1919). 'Confessions of an Agoraphobic Victim', in *The American Journal of Psychology* 30.3: 295–299.

Watts, Fraser. & Wilkins, Arnold. (1989). 'The Role of Provocative Visual Stimuli in Agoraphobia', in *Psychological Medicine* 19: 875–885.

Weiss, Gail. (1999). 'Body Image Intercourse: A Corporeal Dialogue between Merleau-Ponty and Schilder', in *Merleau-Ponty: Interiority and Exteriority, Psychic Life and the World*. Ed. James Morley *et al*. 121–143. Albany, NY: SUNY Press.

White, Prosser. (1884). 'Agoraphobia', in *The Lancet* 124: 1140–1141.

Zaner, Richard. (1981). *Contexts of Self: Phenomenological Inquiry*. Athens: Ohio University Press.

INDEX

INDEX **211**

and the body 51, 56, 65–6, 70, 88, 120
unconsciousness 93, 182, 188
  and the cellar 127–8
  in Freud 189
  in Merleau-Ponty 191, 194
  and phenomenology 192–3, 195
unfamiliarity 78, 93–5, 99, 118, 120
  of the home 3, 20, 31, 39, 136–8
  and travel 68
  and the uncanny 62
  of the world 140–1, 187

unreality 7–8. *See also* reality
  and the home 133, 140–1

van den Berg, J.H. 130, 132–3
vertigo 56, 70–1, 143, 147–51, 153, 159

Westphal, Carl 7, 75, 121, 134, 150, 182
windows 76, 92, 107, 132, 144, 179, 187
  and Bachelard 16
  of the home 2, 16

Zaner, Richard 58–60